Copyright © 1979 by
SAGE Publications Ltd

All rights reserved. No part of this book may be reproduced or utilized in any form or by any means, electronic or mechanical, including photocopying, recording, or by any information storage and retrieval system, without permission in writing from the Publisher.

For information address

SAGE Publications Ltd
28 Banner Street
London EC1Y 8QE

SAGE Publications Inc
275 South Beverly Drive
Beverly Hills, California 90212

British Library Cataloguing in Publication Data

Power, capabilities, interdependence.
(Sage modern politics series; vol. 3).
1. International relations
I. Goldmann, Kjell   II. Sjostedt, Gunnar
III. European Consortium for Political Research
327   JX1391   77-084076

ISBN 0-8039-9884-8
ISBN 0-8039-9885-6 Pbk

First Printing

POWER, CAPABILITIES, INTERDEPENDENCE
PROBLEMS IN THE STUDY OF INTERNATIONAL INFLUENCE

Editors
**Kjell Goldmann
Gunnar Sjöstedt**

SAGE Modern Politics Series   Volume 3
sponsored by the European Consortium for Political Research/ECPR

SAGE Publications · London and Beverly Hills

SAGE Modern Politics Series

Editorial Board

Arend Lijphart (Chairman) *University of Leiden, Holland*
Jean Blondel *University of Essex, UK*
Monica and Jean Charlot, European Journal of Political Research, *University of Sorbonne, Paris*
Hans Daalder *European University Institute, Florence*
Serge Hurtig *National Foundation of Political Sciences, Paris*
Stein Rokkan *University of Bergen, Norway*
Klaus von Beyme *University of Heidelberg, Germany*
John H Whyte *Queen's University, Belfast*

Contents

Introduction
Kjell Goldmann   1

I
THE BASES OF POWER

1. The International Power Structure:
Traditional Theory and New Reality
Kjell Goldmann   7

2. Power Base:
The Long Road from Definition to Measurement
Gunnar Sjöstedt   37

3. The Paradoxes of Superpower:
Omnipotence or Impotence?
Christer Jönsson   63

4. Capabilities, Issue-Areas, and Inter-State Power
Olav Knudsen   85

5. Tension Between the Strong, and the Power of the Weak:
Is the Relation Positive or Negative?
Kjell Goldmann   115

II
INTERDEPENDENCE AND POWER

6. The Concept of Interdependence:
Its Uses and Misuses
Philip A. Reynolds and **Robert D. McKinlay**   141

7. National Power in an Economically Interdependent World
Klaus Knorr   167

8. Autonomy:
What Do We Mean, and What Do We Know?
Bertil Dunér   193

9. Multinational Corporations and the Small
Industrialized State:
Some Aspects of Dependency and Potential Power
Olav Knudsen   209

10 International Power and Foreign Policy Behavior:
The Formulation of Danish Security Policy
in the 1870-1914 Period
Nikolaj Petersen 235

Concluding Remarks
Gunnar Sjöstedt 271

Notes on Contributors 299

Acknowledgements

Most of this book is based on papers presented at a planning session about 'Power and Influence in International Politics' taking place during the ECPR Joint Sessions of Workshops in Louvain-la-neuve, Belgium, in 1976, and in a workshop on the same theme during the Joint Sessions in West Berlin in 1977. A grant from the Nordic Cooperation Committee for International Politics made it possible for all but two of the contributors to meet in Stockholm in March 1978 to engage in what was in effect collective editing of major parts of the book. We have accumulated debts of gratitude, both individually to colleagues in our respective academic environments in Aarhus, Lancaster, Lund, Oslo, Princeton, and Stockholm, and collectively to the ECPR and to SAGE. We are also indebted to one another for penetrating criticism and constructive comments.

Introduction
Kjell Goldmann
University of Stockholm

The classical image of the international system is one of a military hierarchy of states. It is common to point out that this image has become obsolete. Military capability used to be decisive, but nowadays, in a different kind of international system, economic structures determine the distribution of power; governments used to be the only international actors, but in today's world non-state actors are equally significant; power used to be a matter of bilateral confrontation but is increasingly a question of multilateral interaction; and so on. The traditional concern with the 'balance of power' between the 'Great Powers' has less and less relevance for international realities, some analysts argue.

The problem, however, is less with the questions to be asked about international politics than with the answers traditionally given to the questions. To use a concept like 'Great Power', or to make the 'balance of power' into one's object of study may seem old-fashioned to some, but the current preoccupation with phenomena like 'imperialism' and 'transnational relations' reflects an interest in what is in many ways the same thing. Power in the sense of who controls whom remains at the core of the study of politics, including international politics. What is at stake is not whether it is fruitful to enquire into the nature of international power but whether the classical *theory* of international power is tenable. The solution to our difficulty in understanding international power is not to stop asking the questions but to try and improve the answers.

The present book is a modest attempt to move in that direction. Its point of departure was two meetings organized by the European Consortium for Political Research, one in Louvain-la-neuve in 1976 and the other in West Berlin in 1977. The topic of both meetings was 'Power and Influence in International Politics', a broad formulation generating multifarious papers. Some of them had in common their relevance for the question of the tension between traditional theory and current reality. To edit a book based on them seemed to offer the possibility of contributing constructively to the re-examination of what may be called the traditional paradigm about international politics. Since so-called economic interdependence is at the core of what is supposedly 'new' in international relations, and since none of the Louvain and Berlin papers dealt thoroughly with the question of how economic interdependence affects power, we asked Klaus Knorr, with whom I had previously been in contact about these matters, to contribute. Apart from his chapter the book consists in its entirety of revised ECPR papers.

The book is divided into two parts, reflecting not a sharp difference in focus but a clear difference in emphasis. We call Part One 'The Bases of Power' and Part Two 'Interdependence and Power'. Part One is primarily about the extent to which traditional notions about resources and capabilities remain tenable. Part Two is primarily concerned with the implications of those systematic changes which are commonly summarized as an increase in international interdependence. Both Part One and Part Two contain a mixture of conceptual analysis, attempts at theory construction, the application of empirical materials to old and new hypotheses about international power, and suggestions for future research.

Admittedly, the structure of the book does not follow a strict plan. The contributions have been typologized *ex post facto* by the editors rather than commissioned by them on the basis of a clear notion of what the book should ideally be like. We regard this as a natural reflection of the anarchic-tentative-pluralistic state of the debate about the classical paradigm. Even more striking a reflection of this state of affairs is the fact that no common terminology is consistently adhered to in these essays. Experience shows how difficult it is to obtain agreement among political scientists about the meaning of 'power' and power-related terms. The concept of power is not only complex but value-loaded, a fact that may help explain the firmness of the convictions many people have about what power 'really' is. Since these convictions are not compatible, terminological consensus cannot be expected. Even if agreement on terms would have been desirable among the contributors to this book — and we are not convinced that it would — such agreement

Introduction

would not have been easy to attain. This is the case, it should be noted, not merely with the term 'power', which some of us use in different ways (contrast for example Goldmann in Chapter 1 with Knudsen in Chapter 4) but also with 'interdependence', about which there is rather sharp disagreement (cf. in particular Reynolds and McKinlay in Chapter 6 with Knorr in Chapter 7).

The book begins with an attempt to specify the problem of the incompatibility between traditional theory and current reality by identifying the essentials of the traditional paradigm and the objections against it, and taking this as the point of departure for proposing an agenda for research about international power. 'Power base' is the chief concept in Chapter 1; the traditional paradigm is largely interpreted as a theory about power bases, and the research agenda largely consists in proposals for research about who has what kind of power base. In Chapter 2 Gunnar Sjöstedt penetrates deeper into the problem by discussing how to aggregate into a whole all the elements which together make up an actor's power base and how to compare power bases in time and space. That such aggregation and comparison is possible is assumed in the theoretical tradition, otherwise the traditionalist's unidimensional hierarchy of nations would be impossible. What Sjöstedt shows is how simplistic an assumption this may be.

The remaining chapters in Part One continue the examination of the tenability of the traditional theory of international power. In post-1945 applications of the traditional paradigm it has come to be assumed that the possession of overwhelming nuclear capability is what makes a superpower a superpower; this notion is analyzed by Christer Jönsson in Chapter 3. Another key assumption in the classical paradigm, strongly linked to the belief that the elements of a power base can be meaningfully aggregated into a whole, is that measures of the overall capability of a state, such as measures of its general military or economic strength, are valid indicators of its actual influence; in Chapter 4 Olav Knudsen puts this assumption into question by examining empirically the predictive power of general power indicators within a specific issue area, namely, international shipping. A further complication in the traditional paradigm is taken up in Chapter 5: classical thinking on international power includes the notion that power of a Great Power is a function not merely of its own capability but also of its relations with other Great Powers, and Chapter 5 explores the possibility of going from this triviality to more precise hypotheses about the way in which changing Great Power relations may affect the position of smaller states.

In Part Two the very usefulness of its core concept 'interdependence' is first questioned by Philip Reynolds and Robert McKinlay (Chapter 6). Their conclusion is that the broadness of the concept makes it unsuitable as an analytical tool. Klaus Knorr thinks differently: to him 'interdependence' signifies in a meaningful way an important trend in international economic relations, a change that is bound to affect national power. He discusses in Chapter 7 how increasing economic interdependence may affect the military as well as the economic power of states.

Knorr's perspective remains the one which is typical for analyses of international power. The question commonly asked is: what factors determine the power of an actor X over others? This question can be rephrased and thereby acquire a different meaning: what factors determine the power of others over X? Such a shift in perspective is visible in more than one of the contributions to this book and is the essence of Chapter 8, in which Bertil Dunér discusses the autonomy problem of states in an international system characterized by increasing interdependence. The multinational corporation is sometimes regarded as an incarnation of the modern threat to the autonomy of states; important aspects of the question of whether such fears are well-founded are taken up in Olav Knudsen's second contribution (Chapter 9). Nikolaj Petersen also tends to approach the problem of power from the point of view of the influencee rather than the influencer; in Chapter 10 he sees the foreign policy of a nation — Denmark is his empirical example — as a function not only of its 'influence capability' but also of its 'stress sensitivity'.

For the most part — but there are exceptions — the contributions to the book represent mere preparations for systematic research designed to provide us with improved, data-based theory about international power. Given the current state of the debate it could hardly be otherwise. It should come as no surprise that the book ends, not with a synthesis of substantive findings, but with a framework for further research: in his concluding remarks Sjöstedt suggests that the study of the actual exercise of power, particularly

Introduction

non-coercive and multilateral power, is one way, and in his opinion the best way, to improve our ability to grasp the international power structure.

One substantive conclusion can undoubtedly be drawn, however: international power is an immensely more complex phenomenon than is assumed in the traditional paradigm. Chapter 1 ends with the suggestion that there may in fact not be anything that deserves to be called the power structure of the international system. Chapter 2 puts into question whether it is at all meaningful to ascribe a single entity called the power base to an international actor. Similar viewpoints can be found in other chapters, on or between the lines. These may be exaggerations. At any rate they do not imply that the concept of power is useless in the study of international politics. What they do imply is that power in the sense of control over others may be more uncommon, more fluid, and distributed in a more complex way than has usually been assumed. This insight does not represent conceptual failure but theoretical progress.

1 The Bases of Power

1 The International Power Structure: Traditional Theory and New Reality

Kjell Goldmann
University of Stockholm

INTRODUCTION

In the theoretical discussion about the international system, at least three different images of the system's power structure can be discerned. 'Military capability' is the key concept in the traditional image. Against this image is set one based on the concept of 'economic dependence' and another in which the notion of 'complex interdependence' is the essence.

For the analyst working within the framework of the traditional paradigm the most fundamental fact about the power structure of the international system is the existence of two military superpowers, the United States and the Soviet Union. There are other Great Powers — China, France, West Germany, Britain — but the US-USSR bipolarity is assumed to be the system's most significant characteristic. The economic dependence approach emphasizes instead the power position of the OECD countries and the exposed situation of the developing countries, the 'underdogs', the objects of 'imperialism'. Its main thesis is that international relations are dominated from Washington and Brussels, but not so much from Moscow. The complex interdependence approach stresses the extent to which the strong are dependent on the weak. One of its implications is that in the age of international interdependence not even the United States is as powerful as most of us have been assuming.

This discussion does not always appear fruitful. A confrontation of contending approaches is frequently constructive, but a precondition is that it is clear in what ways the approaches are contending, i.e. what kind of information which, if available, would determine the points at issue. The object of this essay is to help improve the situation in three ways.

First, in the next section definitions are proposed of some key terms, including 'power structure'; this is done in the hope of getting rid of those aspects of the problem that are trivial in the sense of being semantic. The third section then attempts to identify the core of the traditional paradigm with regard to the international system, and also the main objections that may be levelled against it. Against this background the fourth section suggests an agenda for research aimed at improving our understanding of the way in which the traditional paradigm has become invalid and the extent to which it remains capable of providing insights into the nature of the international power structure.

'POWER' AND 'POWER BASE': DEFINITIONS

Terminological diversity increases the probability that time will be wasted on pseudo-problems. Whether the European Community is 'a superpower in the making' (Galtung, 1973) is in part a matter of definition. Those who mean by 'superpower' a unit of great *consequence* to others will arrive at one conclusion; those who consider a superpower to be a unit with an unusual ability to get what it *wants* and who believe that the ability of the EC to behave as a single actor with a common set of preferences is small, will arrive at another. The two schools of thought may agree on the actual situation; the disagreement may be semantic. Similarly, the controversy about whether 'power' is inherently coercive or not is trivial. Whether a political actor exercises power when succeeding to convince others by rational argument to do what he wants is a terminological question. It is interesting to discuss the conditions for an actor getting what he wants by rational argument; it is less interesting to argue about whether this is 'power'. The following terminological suggestions are intended to minimize the likelihood of pseudo-controversy.

In what follows 'power base' is the key concept. It will be suggested that many issues in the analysis of international power are usefully formulated as questions about elements in the power bases of international actors. However, in order to define power base we first have to define what we mean by the 'possession' of power. This presupposes in turn a definition of the less abstract notion of the 'exercise' of power.[1]

The exercise of power

What do we mean when we say that an actor A 'exercises power' over another actor B? 'My intuitive idea of power,' Dahl writes in a frequently quoted passage, 'is something like this: A has power over B to the extent that he can get B to do something that B would not otherwise do' (Dahl, 1957:202 – 3). Simon suggests that what we want to observe is 'how a change in the behaviour of one (the influencer) alters the behaviour of the other (the influencee)' (Simon, 1953:516). In the words of a psychologist, power is 'the ability or capacity of O to produce...intended effects on the behaviour or emotions of another person P' (Winter 1973:5). These authors have a similar notion of power. The following definition, which will be our point of departure, falls within the same tradition:

(D1) A exercises power over B: A causes B to behave in the way A wants.

There are many problems with this definition. Some of them are classics in the power literature, such as the relation between power and causality (e.g. Riker, 1964, and Nagel, 1975) and the usefulness of the concept of intention (e.g. Allison, 1974). From the point of view of the present study two other features of the definition are more significant, however. They concern the verbs 'cause' and 'behave'.

Cause is deliberately ambiguous. The above definition is intended to be completely open with regard to the question of *how* A causes B to behave in the desired way. This terminology is different from the one chosen by several other authors. It is common to distinguish between 'power', 'influence', 'authority' and the like precisely in terms of *why* B behaves in the way A wants and to associate 'power' with the use or threat of negative sanctions, with coercion (e.g. Lasswell and Kaplan, 1950:71, 75, 133; Bachrach and Baratz, 1963). Other authors regard positive sanctions as equally relevant to the exercise of power (e.g. Baldwin, 1971; Knorr, 1975:7 – 8).[2] My concept of power is even more extensive, however. It is easy to imagine cases in which A's behaviour is a prerequisite for B's behaving in the way A wants in spite of the fact that A's behaviour has nothing to do with sanctions. One strategy A may use is to give B information B would otherwise lack. Another is to provide B with those material resources B must have in order to be able to do what A wants. And in international relations an important power mechanism consists in manipulating the political process within the other party, influencing not the considerations of decision-makers but the composition of the group making the decisions. Further possibilities exist; the point is their multiplicity. If we are concerned with the ability of an actor to control the behaviour of other actors, and not merely with control by some particular method, it must be advantageous to start out with a concept of power wide enough not to exclude by definition part of what we want to study. Such a wide concept of power may be at variance with common language but is not unusual among social scientists (examples are Nagel, 1975, and Winter, 1973).

The dependent variable in definition D1 is B's behaviour. The main objection against such definitions of power is that they 'focus excessively on interpersonal power and neglect power over systems' (Nagel, 1975:13). The objection is common among international relationists. One author emphasizes the need to 'distinguish power over others from power over outcomes or over the system as a whole' and the importance of not ignoring the latter (Nye, 1976:145). Others, concerned with phenomena like dominance and imperialism, stress that the crucial aspect of the relation between A and B may be A's control over B's internal structure rather than of somebody's behaviour. 'For many purposes, the systemic outcome... would be a better dependent variable than the behaviour of any transient intermediary' (Nagel, 1975:13). Perhaps we should follow Nagel's example and define power as a relation 'between the preferences of an actor regarding an outcome and the outcome itself' (Nagel, 1975:29).

I am inclined to take the view that this is less of a problem than it may appear to be. Nagel illustrates his point with an example: 'an economic elite might maintain control over national tax rates by influencing, at one time or another, a variety of individuals — presidents, key congressmen, judges, bureaucrats, lawyers, economists', but, he argues, it is the systemic outcome, the tax rates, that is significant, not the existence of these intermediaries (Nagel, 1975:13). However, to define the exercise of power in such a way that there must be behaviour by some actor B between A's preferences and the systemic outcome does not compel us to examine in empirical investigations the behaviour of specific intermediaries, or even to identify them. Nor does it prevent us from examining A's control of the outcome. True, with behaviour as the dependent variable in our definition of power we may run some risk of fragmentizing the analysis to such an extent that we overlook the main feature of the situation, that the elite controls the tax rates. However, with outcome as the dependent variable there is another risk, the one that disregard of the fact that the outcome is produced by the manipulation of people causes us to misunderstand the nature of the elite's power. Both risks seem to be small. This is largely one of the pseudo-problems obscuring the analysis of power.

But not entirely. On one point there is consensus among social scientists writing about power: as social scientists we are not concerned with power over nature, only with 'social' power (e.g. Winter, 1973:4; Nagel, 1975:14). We are, in other words, not concerned with goal-attainment in general, only with goal-attainment that is 'social' in the sense of being related to other people. Now there is a grey area between social power and other power. It is possible to bring about outcomes affecting other human beings without causing anybody to behave in some particular way. For example, I can change the value-distribution of a social system by simply giving away what I have or taking what I want. It is important for our analysis whether we regard this as social power or not. I have chosen the narrower kind of power definition; the reason is that the distinction between power and goal-attainment seems difficult to maintain, if power is defined as control over outcomes rather than behaviour (for an example of the broader approach see Chapter 4 in this volume).

The possession of power

Those who conceive of the exercise of power as A's behaviour affecting or determining that of B usually define the possession of power as A's *ability* to cause B to behave in the desired way. But what, more precisely, does this mean?

One answer is: the ability to exercise power is inferred from the actual exercise of power. If in a number of instances A has caused B to behave in the desired way, this implies that A has possessed power over B. If we have identified all likely future interactions between A and B and concluded that A will probably cause B to behave in the way A wants in most or all of these cases, this conclusion can be expressed as A having power over B. The possession of power presupposes the exercise of power. Statements about the possession of power are descriptive generalizations about the exercise of power.

The obvious argument against such a concept of power is made over and over again in the literature. If power presupposes the actual exercise of power, we rule out the possibility of control by anticipation. If we are concerned with the ability of actors to control the behaviour of others, we should guard against overlooking those cases where A is so much more powerful than B that he gets what he wants without exercising power. More generally, the relation between the amount of power an actor has and the amount of power he exercises should be kept an open empirical question and not made into a question that is answered by definition. We cannot always learn enough about an iceberg by examining its top.

An alternative is to conceive of the 'possession of power' as a dispositional concept (cf. Wagner, 1969:11, and Nagel, 1975:30-31). The common example of a dispositional concept is 'brittleness'. Such a concept refers to a tendency of some object to react or behave in a certain way in certain circumstances. The statement 'A has power over B' now in effect becomes a theory or a hypothesis about the relation between A's preferences and B's behaviour. Let x denote what A wants B to do; 'A has power over B'means that whatever x is, *if A should want B to do x, and if B would do non-x if A did not do something about it, then A would cause B to do x.* Actual instances of A's exercising power over B may serve as evidence supporting the hypothesis that A actually has power over *B* but — and this is the crucial point — *A* may have power over *B* without ever exercising power over *B*, and even without having any particular preferences regarding *B*'s behaviour. The logical relation between the possession and the exercise of power becomes similar to that between a theory and empirical evidence supporting the theory. Or, expressed in terms of the so-called covering law theory, the assertion *A* has power over *B* is a law-like statement, a universal hypothesis, which can serve as one of the premises in explanations and predictions of *B*'s behaviour (Hempel, 1965, chs. 9, 10).

How should a dispositional definition of possession of power be worded? If we want to know whether *A* has power over *B*, we want to know how *B* will behave in cases when *A* has a preference concerning *B*'s behaviour. There are three possibilities in each such case: (1) *B* behaves in the way *A* wants, but *B*'s behaviour can be fully explained without reference to *A*'s behaviour. (2) *B* behaves in the way *A* wants as a consequence of *A* exercising power over *B*. (3) *B* behaves in a different way from what *A* wants. The consequence of *A* possessing power over *B* is that if *A* wants *B* to behave in a certain way, *B* *always* behaves in the way *A* wants, whatever *A* wants, either because of *A* exercising power over *B*, or for some other reason. The essence of the idea that *A* has power over *B* is precisely that if *A* wants something, he gets it, *so oder so*. If *A* has power over *B* and wants *B* to behave in a certain way, and if *A*'s will is known to us, we can predict *B*'s behaviour. The assertion that *A* has power over *B* implies that *A* will cause *B* to behave in the way *A* wants, *if the need were ever to arise*.

This notion of power as a disposition is hopefully conveyed by the following definition:

(D2) *A* has power over *B*: If *A* wants *B* to do x, B will do x.

Note that x represents *whatever A* may want *B* to do and that definition D2 thus means that *B* will do *whatever A* may want *B* to do, if *A* has power over *B*.

For the sake of clarity definition D2 is formulated in absolute terms: the possession of power is defined as an all-or-nothing phenomenon. To introduce some nuances and complexities in the definition is easy. One such refinement is to regard the two basic variables in the definition, *A*'s preference and *B*'s behaviour, as continuous rather than dichotomous; A's power over B may be a matter of degree, and the amount of power A has over B may be defined as a function of the extent to which B behaves in the way A wants. Another refinement is to make distinctions in terms of issue areas and situational conditions; A may have power over B with regard to some issues but not others, and under some circumstances but not others. Moreover, we may take the step from the dyad to the n-ad and regard A's power as a matter of his ability to control more than one influencee: not just B but also $C, D, E \ldots, N$, or even the larger system in which A is one of several components. These elaborations of definition D2 correspond to a standard element in the literature on the concept of power: the notion that power may vary with regard to degree, domain, and scope.

A less common distinction, which however may be fruitful for the purpose of this book, is the one between 'offensive' and 'defensive' power. Offensive power is what is defined in definition D2. Defensive power is the kind of power B possesses if B will do x regardless of A's preferences. Put differently, B has defensive power in relation to A to the extent that A is unable to control B's behaviour. A's offensive power over B and B's defensive power over A are thus by definition the same phenomenon seen in different perspectives. The expression 'the power of an actor' may refer both to the ability of the actor to control others (i.e. his role as A) and to his ability to avoid being controlled by others (i.e. his role as B).

Power in the dispositional sense can be thought of as a quality that is distributed in some fashion among the components of a social system. This distribution is what I have in mind when using the term 'power structure' in the present essay. By the power structure of the international system I thus simply mean the distribution of power among the system's components. With this terminology, to characterize the power structure of a system is nothing more and nothing less than to describe the distribution of power within it.

Every power distribution should not be regarded as a power structure, however. It may be reasonable to define this term in such a way that certain minimum conditions must be fulfilled regarding 'significance', 'duration', and 'simplicity' in order for a structure to exist at all.

By 'significance' I mean the extent to which occurrences in the system depend on the distribution of power. Much of what happens in the system may be beyond the control of any actor. Power may be rare. If it is, it may be misleading to say that the system has a power structure.

That a power structure must be relatively enduring seems implied in the very concept of structure. A constantly changing distribution of power is hardly a 'structure'. The more important shifting situational circumstances are in determining whether B behaves in the way A wants, the more questionable it may be to talk of a power structure.

'Simplicity' refers to issue areas. If the power distribution varies from issue area to issue area, if in other words there are literally dozens of different power distributions, then it seems questionable to ascribe a power structure to the system.

It is sometimes taken for granted that since there is necessarily a distribution of values in a social system, there is also necessarily a distribution of power. As is often the case, this idea becomes more interesting if it is not true by definition but an open empirical question. An important possibility is that the distribution of international power is increasingly insignificant, variable, and complex to the point of making the concept of an international power structure misleading. More about this below.

The power base

How do we identify the distribution of power in a given system? The standard operationalization, at least so far as international relations are concerned, is to examine 'resources', 'capabilities', 'potential power', i.e. those phenomena that may be exploited by actors for the purpose of causing others to behave in the way they want. What are those phenomena?

Essentially the same question can be formulated in the following way: *Why* does A have power over B? The resources or capabilities can be seen as preconditions for the possession of power. If we are interested in predicting the power structure of a system we must be able to predict resources, capabilities. If we are dissatisfied with the power structure, it is the distribution of resources, of capabilities we should modify. But what is a resource? What should be analysed if we want to predict the distribution of power? What should be manipulated if we want to change the power structure?

When trying to answer such questions it may be important to avoid being constrained by conventional terminology. There is no a priori reason to limit one's search for power-determining factors to the study of what is traditionally called resources or capabilities. Not merely A's military or economic strength but also B's economic dependence on A or B's obligation to obey A may give A power over B. In order to emphasize that phenomena quite different from resources in a narrow sense may be functional equivalents of resources, I prefer to use the term 'power base', defined as follows:

(D3) A's power base in relation to B: Those characteristics of A, of the relation between A and B, and of the system in which A and B are components, which lead to A's possessing power over B.

The power base of an actor can be said to consist of a number of 'power base elements' (PBEs).

According to definition D3, the power base of an actor may contain three different kinds of PBEs. These distinctions may be ambiguous; it may not always be clear whether a certain phenomenon is a characteristic of an actor, a relation, or a system. In the present context it is however less important to be able to distinguish between them than to realize their fundamental similarity: all of them give A power over B. A distinction may be made between the 'resource structure', the 'dependence structure', and the 'authority structure' of a social system; all of them are relevant to the power bases of the system's members. Military capabilities and economic dependencies are obvious examples of the two first-mentioned types of PBEs. The 'authority structure' exemplifies the possibility that a characteristic of the whole system may also be a PBE of its members. I have in mind the possibility that there exists in a system a set of norms specifying who should, and who need not, obey whom. Such norms may give some actors offensive or defensive power in relation to other actors.

Hence, the statement 'x is a PBE' is short for a theory to the effect that if x is present, other actors will tend to behave in the way one particular actor, A, wishes. Such a theory can be called a *power base theory*. If x is used as an indicator of power, the truth of a power base theory is assumed, that is, a theory according to which x is a PBE.

Definition D3 makes power base a broad concept indeed. Its broadness is intended to minimize the risk of arriving at erroneous conclusions about power structures, for example by overemphasizing resource structures to the neglect of dependence and authority structures. The other side of the coin is the difficulty of distinguishing between PBEs and other determinants of an actor's power. Definition D3 is vague in at least two respects.

First, a PBE is, according to the definition, a 'characteristic' of an actor, a relation, or a system; very transient conditions cannot be regarded as characteristics, but it is unclear where to draw the line between characteristics and conditions. For example, it seems meaningful to regard the Cold War as part of the power base of the Swedish military so far as Sweden's security policy in the 1950s and early 1960s was concerned; it is more questionable whether a briefer European crisis like the one following the Soviet invasion of Czechoslovakia in 1968 can also be seen as one of their PBEs.

Secondly, according to the definition a phenomenon is a PBE if it 'leads' to A's possessing power over B; it has not been my intention to suggest that very indirect determinants of A's power should be seen as PBEs, but in this case too it is unclear where to draw the line. For example, it makes sense to regard Alva Myrdal's personality as a Swedish PBE in disarmament matters over a number of years; it is open to question to what extent factors shaping and maintaining this personality can also be seen as Swedish PBEs.

The fact that definition D3 is ambiguous in these respects does not imply that the concept of power base is unlikely to be fruitful. It does imply that it will have to be further developed. This is in fact done in some of the chapters of this book, especially in Chapter 2.

The chief deficiency in our ability to understand international power can now be expressed as *the primitivity of our power base theories*, and the chief concern underlying this book can be thought of as a desire to *improve our knowledge of international power bases*. Improvement is necessary in several respects.

(a) *Data-based theory should be substituted for armchair speculation*. One problem with our current knowledge of international power is its low quality. Speculation is the rule; precise conceptual analysis in combination with systematic data analysis is the exception. The beliefs people have about the usefulness or uselessness of military capability belong to the former category, as do most contributions to the debate about the so-called structural power of the European Community and other presumed economic power-holders. Systematic research about PBEs is necessary.

(b) *Our power base theories should take into account the full range of phenomena that may provide actors with power over one another.* The offensive and defensive power of an international actor is unlikely to be based solely on its military capability or its position in the international economic structure; it is more likely composed of a complex set of interacting factors of a highly diverse kind. Less simplistic theories about power bases are needed.

(c) *More precise knowledge of power bases should be sought.* It was pointed out in the foregoing section that the possession of power may be a matter of degree, and that the power an actor has in relation to another actor may vary with issue-area and situational conditions as well as with the influencee. By the same token a phenomenon may be a PBE to a varying extent, in some issue areas but not in others, under some circumstances but not under others, vis-à-vis some actors but not others. Take for example the idea that if the United States withdraws from Europe, West Europe will become 'finlandized' due to Soviet military superiority. Or take the notion that the European Community is developing into a superpower dominating the Third World. Both statements are so imprecise that they are little more than vague clichés. There is a need for power analysis, and hence for power base theories, specifying (1) to what extent a certain PBE gives A power; (2) in which issue areas this is the case; (3) which are the situational conditions for this PBE's giving A power, and (4) over whom A gets power due to this particular PBE. If the chief theoretical problem in the analysis of international power concerns power bases, then an increase in the precision of our power base theories is our most pressing need; we have to get away from sweeping statements about finlandization and imperialism.

THE TRADITIONAL PARADIGM AND ITS LIMITATIONS

Underlying much of this volume is the notion that our ability to understand international power is in crisis. The traditional paradigm is under attack from many directions. But, more precisely, what does the traditional paradigm say about international power, and which are its chief limitations? Three ideas may be said to dominate the traditional paradigm.

(1) *The characteristics of the international system are significant determinants of international politics.* International occurrences cannot be accounted for merely in terms of the characteristics of individual actors and relations. Much as crime is in large measure societally determined and not a consequence only of the attributes of the criminal or the nature of the relation between him and his victim, a phenomenon like war is largely a result of the structure of the international system and cannot be fully understood by reference to the personalities of decision-makers or the objectives of governments, or to events, structures, processes within single actors or relations.

(2) *The most important characteristic of the international system is that it is composed of sovereign states and lacks a central authority.* Within each state there exist a government, courts, police; in every state there is a central authority with a monopoly on the legitimate use of force. In the system of sovereign states there is anarchy. Self-help is necessary. Power reigns, not justice. The system is doomed to instability; anarchy causes security to be the chief concern of every state but makes security unattainable for most states during most of the time. The best we can hope for are periods of peaceful coexistence based on a balance of power.

(3) *In such a system the power of an actor is a function of its ability to inflict damage on others, primarily with military means.* Anarchy implies that there is little or no authoritative value-allocation at the systemic level. Values are allocated instead by direct interaction between those concerned. Anarchy implies, moreover, that the outcome of such interaction is likely to be determined by the ability of the parties to credibly threaten negative sanctions. Since the use of military force can rarely be ruled out,

value-allocation is bound to reflect the distribution of military capabilities.

Whether these points succeed in capturing the essence of what may reasonably be called a theoretical tradition or traditional paradigm may be debatable. Others have however described what they regard as the traditional paradigm in a similar way (Lijphart, 1974). Moreover, content analyses of scholarly journals (Handelman et al., 1973) and of textbooks (Rosenau et al., 1977) suggest that ideas like the above dominate the field. The three basic ideas may have been formulated above in a too extreme way; traditionally-minded authors like Aron and Morgenthau are aware of the fact that there is more to international power than merely the ability to threaten war. However, they do seem to share the opinion that because of international anarchy, military capability is the decisive PBE.[3]

It may be possible to go a step further in interpreting the traditional power base theory. Tegenbos has examined twenty-five theoretical works in which international power is discussed, and sixteen empirical studies in which the quantitative measurement of power is attempted (Tegenbos, 1974). He finds it possible to place virtually all PBEs mentioned in the theoretical works in one of five categories: natural resources, economy, technology, political cohesion, and military strength. Almost all of the twenty-five authors regard natural resources, the economy, and military strength as PBEs, but more than half of them also mention technology and political cohesion. Among the empirical, quantitative studies economic indicators are used in thirteen out of sixteen cases (usually one or several of GNP or GDP, energy production and consumption, and iron and steel production). In nine studies measures of military capability are used (predominantly military expenditures, men in arms, and nuclear weapons). Nine studies are also measuring natural resources (in most cases this means that population size and area are interpreted as power indicators). Indicators of technological level and of political cohesion are uncommon.

The question now is how those non-military PBEs which are common in both theoretical and empirical studies are believed to be related to the military ones. It is my impression that the theoretical tradition can be ascribed a power base theory of the kind illustrated in Figure 1. In this figure the continuous lines represent the main causal linkages, whereas the broken lines indicate linkages that, although worthy of consideration, are of secondary importance. In this interpretation the traditional power base theory maintains not only that military capability directly affects a nation's power but also that other factors provide an actor with power primarily by influencing his military capability. At least natural resources and economic strength may affect the power of states in other ways as well, but this is their less important function, according to this interpretation of the traditional theory.

Whether the interpretation is valid is difficult to determine conclusively: the power base theories of theoretical authors tend to be ambiguous, and those of quantitative investigators tend to be implicit. It is however not difficult to find authors who express themselves along the lines of the figure. For example, Morgenthau finds it obvious, too obvious to require elaboration, that a nation's power is a function of its military capability; 'what gives the factors of geography, natural resources, and industrial capacity their actual importance for the power of a nation is military preparedness' (Morgenthau, 1967:114). In his study *The Power Capabilities of Nation-States* Ferris starts out by maintaining that the power capabilities of states are 'composed of those factors that enable one state to threaten sanctions vis-à-vis another'; he then goes on to measure power primarily with data on armed forces personnel, defence expenditures, government revenue, population, trade value, and area; and he justifies this choice of indicators by suggesting that all of them are related to military capability, directly or indirectly (Ferris, 1973:33 – 36). And in *Long Term Projections of Power* Morgenstern, Knorr, and Heiss stress that although quantitative power measurements may be misleading, there is one 'material resource which decisively influences the economic and military power of any one nation or region', and that is energy; this is so because the amount of energy consumption determines and reflects technological capacity, which in turn determines not only economic but also military capability (Morgenstern et al., 1973: 103, 188, and chs. 5 – 6, passim).

A power base theory like the one in Figure 1 makes it natural to conclude that the distribution of power in the international system is extremely unequal. In particular, a small group of states stands

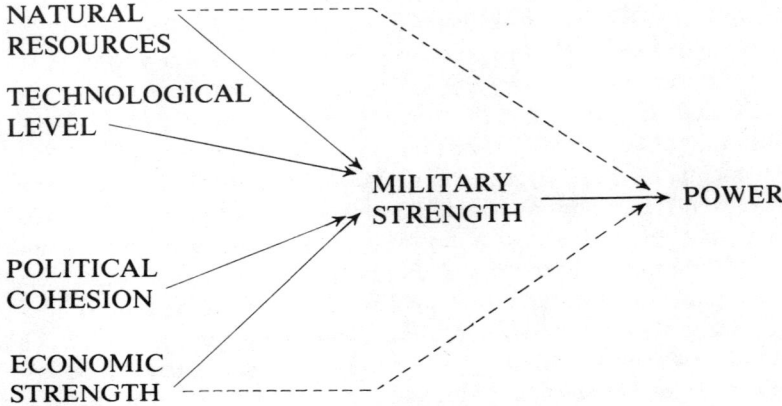

Figure 1. An interpretation of the traditional power base theory.

out as very much more powerful than the others. Most of what happens in the system depends on these 'Great Powers'. The chief task of the analyst attempting to map the essentials of the international system is to identify the Great Powers, the pattern of relations between them, and the spheres of interest around them. Is the European Community a 'superpower in the making'? Will world politics continue to be dominated by Sino-Soviet conflict in combination with East – West détente? What kind of realignments are likely to occur among smaller states? Such questions are characteristic of international power analysis within the framework of the traditional paradigm.

So much for the tradition. We now turn to its critics. Some of the objections that have been made, or can be made, against the traditional paradigm may be summarized as follows.

(1) *The main sources of foreign policy are domestic.* Only in an imprecise and superficial way can international politics be accounted for in terms of the characteristics of the international system. Much of what goes on in the system is better understood as the output of big organizations functioning in accordance with standard operating procedures, or as the outcome of domestic politics, rather than as the result of the rational adaption of unitary actors to their systemic environment (Allison, 1971). Parties and pressure groups, doctrines and personalities are key factors, not the international system.

(2) *The division into sovereign states is less important a characteristic of the international system than it used to be.* There is increasing international interdependence. The ties between nations are getting more numerous and more complex. International relations are becoming transnational and transgovernmental (Keohane and Nye, 1977). Governments are no longer the only significant international actors, and the sovereignty of the states is increasingly undermined. Interdependence and transnationalization do not necessarily imply peace, but they do imply that the image of an anarchic system of sovereign states is becoming obsolete.

(3) *Military capability is not the only significant PBE and may in fact not be very significant at all.* The traditional power base theory is misleading in several ways. It is too state-centred, it underestimates or overlooks non-military PBEs, it has a too one-dimensional view of international power. Excessive preoccupation

with international anarchy has led the traditionalist to a simplistic view of the international power structure.

The controversy between adherents and critics of the traditional paradigm is not wholly a matter of conflicting perceptions of reality. To some extent the controversy reflects the fact that traditionalists and non-traditionalists are concerned with different problems. The subtitle of Keohane's and Nye's *Power and Interdependence* is *World Politics in Transition* (1977), but in fact the book focuses on a limited aspect of 'world politics': regime changes with regard to oceans and money on the one hand, and US-Canadian and US-Australian relations on the other. The traditional paradigm is more relevant for 'high politics' than 'low politics', more concerned with essentially conflictful relations than with essentially co-operative ones. It is not peculiar that a theory about security policy is unsatisfactory as a theory about economic policy. Put differently, Keohane and Nye are trying to answer questions that are in part different from those asked in the theoretical tradition; it is more unclear to what extent they provide new answers to the old questions.

To the extent that the two schools of thought are in fact concerned with the same issues, the controversy between them is in large measure primitive. The questions are often too imprecise and the answers too loosely founded. It cannot be fruitful to argue in a general way about whether military PBEs are significant or not; it cannot be satisfactory to support one's position in such an argument with mere speculation about the kind of calculations a rational actor would make under given circumstances or with references to empirical cases of unknown representativity.

What we do know is that the traditional power base theory is unacceptable even as a rough approximation. This insight is important enough. It implies that a chief task of international politics scholars is to improve our knowledge of international power. In the next section some suggestions are made about research likely to help us attain this objective.

TOPICS FOR RESEARCH

Actors

Is the international system's power structure a matter of the distribution of power merely among states, or should other actors such as international organizations and multinational corporations also be taken into account? This question is an empirical one, but in order to answer it the concept 'international actor' needs to be defined. The debate about the significance of non-state actors suggests that in order to be an 'international actor', a unit must have a minimum of 'actor capability', autonomy, and power.

The term actor capability was coined by Gunnar Sjöstedt in the context of a study of political integration in the European Community (Sjöstedt, 1977). Sjöstedt's point of departure was the assumption that the Community could be regarded as a Great Power comparable to the United States and the Soviet Union only if it were capable of unitary external behaviour to the same extent as a state. He formulated his research problem as the question of whether the EC possessed the quality of actor capability.

In order to answer it he examined, on the one hand, whether in the past the Community had proven capable of carrying out actor behaviour and, on the other hand, whether the Community possessed that kind of structure which must be required of an international actor; the structural characteristics Sjöstedt had in mind included for example systems for the making of common decisions and for the common mobilization of resources necessary to carry out these decisions.

Sjöstedt's analysis is useful in specifying the main problem regarding an international organization as an international actor. A group of states is an actor only to the extent that it is permanently capable of behaving as a unit vis-à-vis its environment. States, corporations, and of course individuals are actors in this sense, but with regard to international organizations the matter is less obvious. Actor capability is the chief issue so far as some non-state international actors are concerned. The actor capability of international organizations, coalitions, alliances is an important topic for research.

With regard to the multinationals, the main problem is autonomy rather than actor capability. The notion that the multinationals are as significant international actors as many states does not only imply the obvious — that some such corporations are big and that their boards make decisions of great international consequence — but also what is less self-evident: that these decisions are made in an autonomous fashion and are unrelated to the preferences of governments. ITT, GM, IBM are perhaps better seen as US agents, bridgeheads, PBEs than as autonomous actors. Or maybe it is the other way around, maybe governments are agents of corporations; if yes, this does not make the corporations 'international actors' unless we are willing to regard every subnational actor with an impact on foreign policy, every party or pressure group, as an international actor. The autonomy of multinational corporations and other would-be international actors deserves further study.

Actor capability and autonomy are insufficient criteria for status as an international actor, however. Particularly in the era of transnational relations it is important to specify that in order to be an actor in the international system, a unit must also possess a minimum amount of power. Otherwise the question of the existence of non-state actors may degenerate into a dispute about trivialities. When critics of the traditional paradigm maintain that there are non-state international actors, they must be assumed to have in mind actors that are significant, actors comparable to states in terms of their power in international matters. The extent to which non-state actors fulfil this criterion is a third problem for research. This topic is more difficult to investigate than the ones about actor capability and autonomy; that empirical power research is complex is argued in the next section.

PBEs

Our problem when setting out to improve the traditional power base theory does not lie in the difficulty of discovering additional PBEs. Quite the contrary: anybody can easily draw up a long list of possible PBEs overlooked in the theoretical tradition. Rather, what we are unable to do is be specific about issue areas, situational conditions, and influencees, and we are for the most part unable to distinguish other than intuitively and imprecisely between what is important and what is not. This is why the discussion about international power often fails to advance beyond the stage of clichés about the 'structural power' of the European Community or the 'finlandization' of West Europe.

For those who want to do better than that, the checklist in Table 1 may be useful. The rows represent six types of PBEs which will be commented upon shortly. The columns are intended to keep us aware of the fact that the problem is not merely whether a phenomenon provides somebody with power but to arrive at specifics with regard to issue areas, situational conditions, and influencees, and to do what can be done to answer the question about the amount of power provided by a given PBE in various issue areas, under various conditions, and over various other actors. It goes without saying that neither rows nor columns are exhaustive; nor are they fully mutually exclusive.

TABLE 1
Checklist for the analysis of PBEs

	Issue areas	Situational conditions	Influencees	Significance
Military resources				
Non-military resources				
Mobilization and application capability				
Dependence				
Norms				
Coalitions				

Military resources. One of our immediate tasks is to substitute knowledge for speculation with regard to military PBEs. If it is simplistic to suggest, without further ado, that military capability is decisive, it is no more sophisticated to point out, without making distinctions in terms of issue areas, situations, influencees, that the balance of terror, the destructiveness of modern weapons, the communications revolution or some other factor has made the use of military force ineffective and hence made military capability insignificant as a PBE. In particular, it should not be taken for granted that the only way in which military superiority gives A power over B is by influencing B's decisional calculus. A distinction may be useful between the specific and the diffuse role of military capability. The former functions by the influencee taking into account the likely outcome of a military confrontation. The latter is exemplified by the trade negotiation the outcome of which is affected by the respective military capabilities in spite of the fact that everybody concerned takes it for granted that war is out of the question. Diffuse military power seems to be more than a hypothetical possibility. The pheonomenon may be worth looking into more closely. More precise knowledge about the specific as well as the diffuse role of military capability is needed. The central power base hypothesis in the theoretical tradition should be neither accepted nor rejected but refined.

Non-military resources. If the traditional power base theory is imprecise with regard to military resources, this is even more true concerning non-military ones. There exists a large and comparatively sophisticated literature on the usefulness of nuclear weapons; less effort has been devoted to inquiry into the way in which non-military resources may lead to power.[4] For example, little thought seems to have been devoted to the distinction between an actor's 'general strength' and his 'special assets' (see Chapter 2 of this book). The former is presumably the kind of PBE indicated by measures like gross national product or energy consumption; the latter may consist for example in the possession of raw materials like oil or bauxite, or in the availability of know-how in key areas like nuclear physics or computer technology. Moreover, as pointed out above, power need not necessarily be a matter of sanctions, threats, and occasionally promises. One way in which A may cause B to do what A wants is by giving B information which B would otherwise lack. Another is to intervene in the domestic politics of *B*. The former possibility emphasizes the relevance to power of knowledge and propaganda, the latter reminds us of the usefulness of being able to manipulate the internal power struggles of others. The topic of non-military resources is rich.

Mobilization and application capability. Resources do not provide their owner with power unless 'mobilized' and 'applied'; these terms, suggested by Gunnar Sjöstedt, are further discussed in Chapter 2 of this book. We need not only money but also the ability to use money in order to have economic power. The factors providing an actor with mobilization and application capability are vital to his power base. An improved power base theory would be more concerned with these factors than has traditionally been the case.

The mobilization and application capability seems to have at least three aspects, which we may tentatively call the practical, the political, and the diplomatic. The first-mentioned aspect has to do with the purely practical ability to exploit a resource: to have sufficient technical or economic competence, the necessary administrative efficiency, etc. The political aspect concerns the mobilization of political support for exploiting the resource in the desired way. The diplomatic aspect is related to the skill of the actor in using the resource against the influencee. All of this deserves closer study.

Another perspective on mobilization is that it takes time. The object of examining power bases is to be able to draw conclusions about who will get what he wants. The mobilization problem makes it necessary to decide on a time perspective. Some resources — the nuclear weapons of the United States, the oil of OPEC — can be mobilized almost immediately. Other resources — Pakistan's nuclear physicists, Zaire's minerals — may require years of effort before they become available as PBEs. It may be one of the more important weaknesses of previous power research that the time factor is overlooked; this is true also with regard to most of the present volume.

The link between mobilization and transnationalization is another topic for research. One way in which transnationalization may affect international power is by making it more difficult for some governments to mobilize their non-military resources. The result may be not so much a redistribution of power in the system as a net loss of power in the sense that international politics becomes less controllable. Transnationalization may however also imply that an increasing, and increasingly sophisticated, set of PBEs becomes available to governments once they have been mobilized. A third possibility is an increase in importance for those PBEs least vulnerable to transnationalization, i.e. the military ones. The power effects of transnationalization are likely to be complex.

Dependence. That asymmetrical dependence can be a PBE is obvious. But what is dependence? In one interpretation B is dependent on A if A possesses resources which are relevant to B; Sweden is dependent on the United States in the sense that the United States possesses a nuclear capability which can demolish Sweden altogether, and also in the sense that successful Swedish defence against an isolated Soviet attack may presuppose US military assistance. This concept of dependence is uninteresting in the sense of adding nothing to our previous discussion about resources; a power resource is a power resource precisely because its use or nonuse is of consequence to others. An alternative is available, however. Svante Iger has suggested a definition of economic dependence according to which B is dependent on A only if there is an *established economic relation* between them (Iger, 1974). The core of this more narrow concept of dependence is *adaptation*. The establishment of an economic relation between A and B may result in the emergence of an economic structure to which A and B adapt in the sense that it becomes costly for them to interrupt the relation. We may call this situation *structural dependence*. Here we find one more field of research which is underpopulated. What kind of structural dependence gives how much power over whom to whom, under what circumstances, and in what issue areas — the discussion about the 'structural power' of the European Community suggests how important it is to go from speculation to study.

Norms. It has already been suggested that a social system may contain not only a resource structure and a dependence structure but also an authority structure, i.e. a set of norms specifying who should obey whom. The international system's authority structure essentially implies that nobody should obey anybody; this is the essence of the norm about the sovereign equality of states. In other words: the inequality in resources and the asymmetries in dependence ought not to affect the power distribution. To some extent — how large an extent is unknown — this set of norms is likely to be a PBE for the weak, an equalizer among states.

We do not know nearly enough about this aspect of international power either. The traditional paradigm suggests that because of anarchy norms are ineffective. This issue has long been debated among international lawyers but is also relevant to the search of political scientists for improved power base theories. Of particular interest are those norms prohibiting a state from using what would otherwise be among its PBEs. There are of course legal rules limiting the use of military capabilities for political purposes; an interesting question is to what extent there have emerged more or less formalized and explicit norms about other kinds of PBEs, such as norms prohibiting states from exploiting politically a relation of economic dependence.

Coalitions. It is obvious that the formation of coalitions is of consequence for the distribution of power in a system; it is less obvious how to take this fact into account when analysing the system's *structure* of power rather than single instances of the *exercise* of power. Some coalitions may be ad hoc; they are not part of the system's structure. Other coalitions may be virtual international organizations; they may to some extent be seen as international actors in their own right. But there are intermediate cases, and they seem to pose intriguing theoretical and empirical problems. These problems are also among those which should be approached.

Dimensions

In the traditional paradigm power is a unidimensional phenomenon: it is possible to rank nations in terms of their power, to draw a line between Great Powers and others in an unambiguous way, etc. This may be an audacious assumption. In at least three respects there is reason to question the assumption of unidimensionality.

General versus specific power. On the whole indicators of military capability and of general economic and technological strength correlate highly, but some of the deviations from a perfect correlation are critical (Goldmann, 1977:11 – 14). In military terms the United States and the Soviet Union stand out as equals and as very much superior to everybody else; in economic terms the US is far superior to the USSR — in fact, a unified EC and not the USSR would be second to the US — and the gap between 'superpowers' and others is less pronounced. Moreover, in military terms the group of second-rate nations may be said to include China, West Germany, and France; but in economic respects Japan and also Canada must be added to this category. At a minimum a distinction must be made between military and economic power, between military Great Powers and economic Great Powers.

Even this moderate retreat from unidimensionality raises the fascinating theoretical problem of linkages between issue areas, between the international security policy system and the international economic-political system. But there may be reason to go a step further. A two-dimensionalization of the concept of international power may be insufficient. A truly fundamental challenge to the traditional paradigm lies in the possibility that in many issue areas other states than the Great Powers are among the most powerful. One of Olav Knudsen's contributions to this book (Chapter 4) consists in an empirical demonstration of this possibility: he shows that conventional indicators of the 'general strength' of nations are only partly successful as predictors of power in the area of international shipping. Keohane and Nye regard it as one of the critical changes in international politics that PBEs are becoming increasingly issue-specific; power is, as they put it, less and less fungible (Keohane and Nye, 1977: 30 – 32, 49 – 52).

The critical question is to what extent general power is a reality. Perhaps 'specific' power is the rule, i.e. power only in a certain issue area or under certain circumstances. Great Powers are in the traditional paradigm states that are exceptionally powerful in most cases, not just sometimes; the question is whether such Powers exist. Put differently: some PBEs provide actors with general power, other PBEs with specific power; the question is how common the latter is in relation to the former.

The possibility that the phenomenon demonstrated by Knudsen is common makes the issue of linkages between issue areas an even more significant task for future research. This in turn will require that more attention is devoted to the very concept of issue area.

Keohane and Nye should be praised for demonstrating the significance of issue-specific power and of linkages between issue areas; they should be criticized for not realizing that this whole approach to the analysis of international power is empty unless 'issue area' is made into a well-defined concept, theoretically and operationally.

Offensive versus defensive power. The distinction between offensive and defensive power was introduced earlier in this chapter. Offensive and defensive power need not covary. In particular, some of the leading states in terms of offensive power seem to be strikingly weak so far as defensive power is concerned. If we use trade relative to gross domestic product as a tentative indicator of defensive power, we find that the United States, the Soviet Union, and China remain at the top of the list with a percentage of six to eight, but for Japan the figure is 20 per cent, for France about 25 per cent, and for Great Britain and West Germany as high as 35 – 40 per cent; Germany ranks no. 5 in terms of an indicator of general strength like energy consumption but no. 60 in terms of trade/GDP.[5] Such figures do not prove much, of course, but they emphasize the necessity of examining not just offensive but also defensive international power.

Global versus regional power. What was generally interpreted as a dramatic growth in power on the part of Iran in the first half of the 1970s popularized the idea of Regional Great Powers or Regional Superpowers. Several other nations have been mentioned as candidates for such a status: Brazil, Nigeria, South Africa, Zaire, India and Vietnam. The concept of regional power is unclear in several respects. For example, how should the regions be delimited (is geography the only criterion)? How small may a region be (is Sweden a Regional Great Power in Scandinavia)? How many Great Powers may a region contain (can India, Iran, and Saudi Arabia be Regional Great Powers in the same region)? How small may a Regional Great Power be in global terms (is Cuba a Regional Great Power in the Caribbean)? There are many questions to answer. The concept of regional power seems potentially fruitful, however, so an effort to answer the questions may be worth while.

CONCLUSION

Research along the above lines may lead to the conclusion that the traditional image of the international system's power structure needs to be modified in some particular way, for example by taking into account new patterns of international interdependence. Or the conclusion may be that the traditional image should be replaced by a different one, for example one based on economic dependence rather than military capability. But one more possibility exists: that there is no international power structure at all. If a power structure is to fulfil certain minimum requirements in terms of significance, duration, and simplicity, then there is perhaps nothing that deserves to be called 'the power structure of the international system'. The very notion of an international power structure may be oversimplified enough to be more misleading than helpful. The situation may be too random, too fluid, too complex to warrant the designation 'power structure'. Only systematic research can make it possible to determine the extent to which this is actually the case.

NOTES

1. For a more detailed discussion of these and related concepts see Goldmann (1977).
2. Baldwin (1971:21 − 23) maintains that Lasswell and Kaplan, Bachrach and Baratz, and several other authors are in fact inconsistent on this point and sometimes, but not always, define power in terms not only of negative but also of positive sanctions. There can be no doubt, however, that they regard the former as vastly more central to the concept of power than the latter.
3. The contents of the traditional paradigm and the problem of determining whether the paradigm is 'traditional' are discussed in greater detail in Goldmann (1978).
4. For an exception see Knorr (1975).
5. The figures are from Petrén (1976:91 − 93, 118-120). They are based on yearly means for the period 1971 − 73.

REFERENCES

ALLISON, G. T. (1971) *Essence of Decision: Explaining the Cuban Missile Crisis.* Boston: Little, Brown.

ALLISON, L. (1974) 'The Nature of the Concept of Power', *European Journal of Political Research*, 2:131 – 142.

BACHRACH, P. and M. S. BARATZ (1963) 'Decisions and Non-Decisions: An Analytical Framework', *American Political Science Review*, 57:632 – 642.

BALDWIN, D. A. (1971) 'The Power of Positive Sanctions', *World Politics*, 24:19 – 38.

DAHL, R. A. (1957) 'The Concept of Power', *Behavioural Science*, 2:201 – 215.

FERRIS, W. H. (1973) *The Power Capabilities of Nation-States: International Conflict and War.* Lexington, Mass.: D. C. Heath.

GALTUNG, J. (1973) *The European Community: A Superpower in the Making.* Oslo: Universitetsforlaget.

GOLDMANN, K. (1977) 'Notes on the Power Structure of the International System', *Cooperation and Conflict*, 12:1 – 20.

—— (1978) *Det internationella systemet: en teori och dess begränsningar.* Stockholm: Aldus/Bonniers.

HANDELMAN, J. R., J. A. VASQUEZ, M. K. O'LEARY and W. D. COPLIN (1973) *Color it Morgenthau: A Data-Based Assessment of Quantitative International Relations Research.* New York: Syracuse University.

HEMPEL, C. G. (1965) *Aspects of Scientific Explanation, and Other Essays in the Philosophy of Science.* New York: The Free Press.

IGER, S. (1974) *Ekonomiskt beroende i ett maktperspektiv: en teoretisk diskussion och en operationalisering.* Stockholm: Swedish Institute of International Affairs.

KEOHANE, R. O. and J. S. NYE (1977) *Power and Interdependence: World Politics in Transition.* Boston: Little, Brown.

KNORR, K. (1975) *The Power of Nations: The Political Economy of International Relations.* New York: Basic Books.

LASSWELL, H. D. and A. KAPLAN (1950) *Power and Society: A Framework for Political Inquiry.* New Haven: Yale University Press.

LIJPHART, A. (1974) 'The Structure of the Theoretical Revolution in International Relations', *International Studies Quarterly*, 18:41 – 74.

MORGENSTERN, O., K. KNORR and L. P. HEISS (1973) *Long Term Projections of Power: Political, Economic, and Military Forecasting.* Cambridge, Mass.: Ballinger.

MORGENTHAU, H. J. (1967) *Politics among Nations: The Struggle for Power and Peace.* 4th edn. New York: Alfred A. Knopf.

NAGEL, J. H. (1975) *The Descriptive Analysis of Power.* New Haven: Yale University Press.

NYE, J. S. (1976) 'Independence and Interdependence', *Foreign Policy*, 22:130 – 161.

PETRÉN, K. (1976) *Maktstrukturens huvuddrag: en analys av 20 maktindikatorer.* Stockholm: Swedish Institute of International Affairs.

RIKER, W. H. (1964) 'Some Ambiguities in the Notion of Power', *American Political Science Review*, 58:341 – 349.
ROSENAU, J. N. et al. (1977) 'Of Syllabi, Texts, Students, and Scholarship in International Relations: Some Data and Interpretations on the State of a Burgeoning Field', *World Politics*, 29:263 – 341.
SIMON, H. A. (1953) 'Notes on the Observation and Measurement of Power', *Journal of Politics*, 15:500 – 516.
SJÖSTEDT, G. (1977) *The External Role of the European Community*. Farnborough, Hampshire: Teakfield.
TEGENBOS, G. (1974) 'De macht der staten: een inventarisatie van de alternatieven tot kwantificering', *Res Publica*, 16:133 – 159.
WAGNER, R. H. (1969) 'The Concept of Power and the Study of Politics', pp. 3 – 12 in R. Bell, D. V. Edwards and R. H. Wagner (eds.) *Political Power: A Reader in Theory and Research*. New York: The Free Press.
WINTER, D. G. (1973) *The Power Motive*. New York: The Free Press.

2 Power Base: The Long Road from Definition to Measurement

Gunnar Sjöstedt
The Swedish Institute of International Affairs

1. INTRODUCTION

At the present time many observers claim that a process of redistribution of power is going on in the international system. The superpowers are, for instance, according to some students of international relations, under way to lose their supremacy. The new pentagonial international system announced by president Nixon a few years back is one example of this view. The allegation has, however, been contested. Voices warning the world about the increasingly hegemonial behaviour of the Soviet Union and the United States have been heard from Peking for some time now.[1] It is not self-evident which of these two contradictory interpretations of world developments is most correct.[2]

The problem of assessing the power of nations is by no means restricted to the superpowers. Evaluations of the relative power of different international actors are notoriously difficult to carry out. There is a host of extremely important questions pertaining to international power relations to which no certain answers can be given. Is the power position of the Group of 77 improving or deteriorating? Is the European Community's large amount of external trade a sign of strength or of weakness? What is meant when Nigeria is referred to as a new sort of 'regional power?'

Any evaluation of power relations, it may concern one or many countries, must be based on an assessment of how powerful the individual nation is. For that reason it is not surprising that a large number of scholars have presented lists of indicators of the sources of national power. Measures frequently used are military forces, natural resources, industrial capabilities and the size of population. Sometimes geographical location and intangible phenomena like morale, ideology, and quality of leaders are added to the list.[3]

There seems to be a fairly great consensus about these indicators in the literature. This in turn gives the impression that the measurement of the power of nations is an uncontroversial issue among scholars and that satisfactory instruments of measurement exist. This impression is faulty. The measurement of power indeed involves great problems of a theoretical as well as of a practical nature, which have not been completely solved by any researcher so far. A closer look at the traditional indicators of power reveals that they deserve at least two sorts of critique.

First, it can be noted that although the indicators of power chosen by traditionalists may look reasonable from a common sense point of view, their validity is in principle dubious. Little systematically gathered data support the allegation that traditional indicators reflect the power of nations. These measures are quite general categories whose predictive capacity must be considered to be rather circumscribed even if it is accepted they must have something to do with the power of nations. So, the traditionalist indicators generally have to be regarded as operational concepts whose relation to the theoretical definition of power is not spelled out.

Second, most traditionalist scholars do not define power clearly. Most of them seem to mean that power is equal to the capacity of a nation to carry out coercive actions notably of a military nature, in order to make other nations behave in a certain way. The point to make here is that this conception is not spelled out explicitly and that this is not the only possible interpretation of what power is. The uncertainty as to what traditional indicators of power represent is therefore not only due to the unspecified relationship between theoretical and operational definitions; the lack of a precise theoretical definition of power is another and more fundamental cause to the ambiguity of the traditionalist indicators of power.

Traditionalist indicators are, thus, characterized by such shortcomings that they cannot uncritically be employed for the actual measurement of the power of nations. In spite of the large literature dealing with this question the conditions for the effective exercize of power in the international milieu still need clarification.

This is the general background of this chapter. Its aim is to try to clarify how a theoretically consistent definition of power can be expressed in operational terms and be employed for actual power measurements.
The structure of the chapter is as follows. First a general approach to the measurement of power will be indicated. The necessary theoretical concepts will then be introduced and an operational model of the power base of nations will be presented. Three theoretical problems connected with power measurements will be identified and illustrated with the help of this model. Finally a number of conclusions pertaining to future research about the power of nations will be drawn.

2. AN APPROACH TO THE MEASUREMENT OF POWER

When the power of a nation is measured this implies a comparison with other nations. The assertion that a given nation, say Nigeria, has a certain amount of power becomes meaningful only when this quantity is related to that of other nations. Then the quantification of Nigeria's power is an instrumental means to assess how much more or less powerful Nigeria is in relation to these other countries.

A comparative analysis of the power of two or more countries can take on different forms. But these various comparisons can seemingly be grouped into two main categories which may be referred to as *situationally conditioned* comparisons and *unconditional comparisons*. This distinction is important because these two types of comparison imply quite different requirements as to definition and indicators of the power of nations.

A situationally conditioned comparison pertains to a particular situation. In practice this can be expected to mean the study of the distribution of power within a certain delimited context. One example would be the power position of Nigeria in a certain geographical region, such as West Africa. Another example would be the evaluation of Nigeria's relative power within OPEC, where the situational context can be described as a certain organization or possibly a certain issue area.

The unconditional comparison of the power of nations is quite different in nature. Now the objective is to determine what the relative power of a given country is in a general sense, regardless of the situational context. Such measurements of power have at least two basic implications. The first is that when the power of the individual country is measured a comparison is made with *all* the other nations in the world simultaneously. A comparison relative to only a limited group of countries would in principle mean that a kind of situational context was defined. The second important implication is that the indicators of the power of nations can not pertain exclusively to a particular situation.

Neither situationally conditioned nor unconditional comparisons are problem-free. Both categories of power measurements involve considerable theoretical as well as other more practical difficulties to which no complete solutions have been found so far. In this chapter the interest will, however, be concentrated on the latter category, unconditional comparisons, which in several respects are especially tricky. They are also of crucial importance for the systematic gathering of knowledge concerning international power relations. This kind of comparative analysis is, thus, a prerequisite for any evaluation of the power of nations which purports to possess general validity. Any ranking of the nations of the world with respect to the amount of power they dispose of is, in principle, an unconditional comparison. Accordingly, all attempts to identify the power structure in the international system also presuppose that the theoretical and other difficulties characterizing unconditional comparisons have been eliminated.

The unconditional comparison of the power of nations presupposes some kind of objective measure. Such a measure, in turn, requires a basic definition of what international power is. The concept of *power base* defined by Kjell Goldmann in Chapter 1 is a solution. The power base is, generally speaking, a representation of the amount of power at the disposal of a nation. The greater the power base a country has the more powerful it is.

This proposition gives an idea of the general meaning of power base, but does not define it unambiguously. Such a clearcut definition requires more abstract formulations.

Goldmann's definition of power base is a composite of several theoretical propositions. The starting point is *the exercise of power*.

According to Goldmann, one nation, A, exercises power over another nation, B, when '...A causes B to behave in the way A wants.'

The next step is to define *'possession of power'*. 'A has power over B = If A wants B to do x B will do x.' This means that the possession of power can be described as a disposition to be powerful in relation to some other actor.

The definition of 'possession of power' begs, to speak with Goldmann, the question *why A* is able to have power over B. The explanation is *A's power base* in relation to B which is equal to '...(t)hose characteristics of A, of the relation between A and B, and of the system in which A and B are components which lead to A's possessing power over B.'

This definition implies that power may be exercized in different ways. The exercize of power does not necessarily pertain to a conflict situation. Nor does it stipulate that actions manifesting the exercize of power should take on the form of coercive activities. The definition includes the possibility that it may be meaningful to speak of the exercize of power even in such cases where the power holder, A, causes the target nation, B, to do something which is not really against B's interests.

Further, the present definition of power base stipulates that it is not only the properties of A itself that may give this actor power over other nations. A's relations with the external environment may also represent 'sources of power'. There is thus reason to believe that a great number of different phenomena may belong to the power base of a nation.

In order to use the above definition of power base for empirical research it has to be expressed in operational terms. For practical reasons it would be desirable to find a simple unidimensional representation of the power base. Proposals for this kind of indicator have in fact been offered in the literature. The Gross Domestic Product, GDP, is one such suggestion and the consumption of energy of a country is another.[4] The rationale for the choice of both these indicators is more or less the same. The underlying assumption is that these measures reflect the overall capabilities of a nation. A clear advantage is further that they are easy to express in quantitative terms permitting comparison between nations and over time and also that data are available for most countries. It can be argued that the consumption of energy is particularly suitable as an indicator of power as it can be measured in units of volume thereby avoiding all the pitfalls of monetary measures and also because it seems to co-vary strongly with most other likely indicators of power, including GDP (Petrén, 1976).

Unfortunately a simple indicator of the power base, like consumption of energy, cannot be considered to be a fully satisfactory representation of the power base of a nation. This kind of measure reflects a much more narrow conception of power than Goldmann's definition, which is leaned on here. It can thus hardly be asserted that consumption of energy — or e.g. GDP — takes the external relations of the country analysed into consideration.

In order to avoid this 'resource bias' a more complex model more in conformity with the theoretical definition of power base has to be constructed. The empirical evidence about power bases already available should naturally also be taken into consideration. But it has to be recalled that although a lot has been written about international power, systematic knowledge is scarce. There exists no pool of reliable information to draw from in order to present a detailed picture of what the power bases of nations consist of in real life. Therefore, it is only possible to present a tentative model of the power base here.[5] This model should, however, be sufficient for the present purposes. The aim is not to test the model or to draw substantive conclusions, e.g. about how powerful certain countries are. The purpose is only to sketch the general nature of the power base so that a number of fundamental theoretical problems pertaining to the use of this concept for empirical research can be discerned and discussed. My assessment is that the present model can be sufficiently defended with theoretical reasoning and with reference to the general knowledge we do after all possess about the power bases of nations to serve as such a means of illustration.

In line with the basic definition employed here the starting point for the identification of the elements of the power base is the exercize of power. It is assumed that power can be exercized in many different ways. Such actions can be grouped into a number of strategies which the power-holding nation, A, can use in order to exercize power over the target nation, B. In this case seven such strategies have been discerned. Four of these categories, types of the exercize of power, can be said to be of a coercive character. They are typically used when there is a conflict of interest between A and B or when a climate of hostility prevails between them for some other reason.

The non-coercive strategies do not necessarily presuppose conflict of interest or hostility between the two parties. Some of them may even be used when A and B are involved in a joint cooperative project. These strategies thus often have in common that they signify that A makes B do something which is not really against B's interests.

The coercive strategies can briefly be described as follows:

1. *Negative sanctions:* A uses, or threatens to use, punitive actions against B, in order to force B to do something desired by A.
2. *Deprivation:* A actually takes the object desired from B. One example of this contingency would be that A physically conquers a piece of territory from B, say an island of strategic value, which A needs for security reasons.
3. *Prevention:* A physically prevents B from doing something which A does not want B to do. One example would be that A blocks the transit over its territory of vehicles coming from B on their way to a third country which B wants to support.
4. *Rewards:* A offers or promises something to B which B needs as a compensation for doing something that A wants B to do. A, so to speak, 'bribes' B to behave in a certain way.

The non-coercive strategies are three in number:

5. *Support:* A gives B assistance to do something which B wants to do but cannot do unless help is provided from the exterior. A may, for example, provide certain sophisticated high technology components which make it possible for B to construct anti-aircraft missiles.
6. *Stimulation:* A demonstrates for B that a certain action is feasible to carry out at a certain point of time. This action is not against B's interests, but before A's intervention B has not been aware of this possibility. A variation of stimulation may be that A teaches B how a certain action, desired by both A and B, can be performed. Stimulation does thus not contain anything of persuasion on the part of A. A only 'triggers off' an action by B.
7. *Persuasion:* By means of rational argumentation A convinces B that the action that A wants B to undertake is preferable also for B.

In contrast to the other two non-coercive strategies persuasion presupposes an initial conflict between the two parties A and B. This conflict is, however, of such a character that neither A nor B considers the use of force to solve it. A rather takes advantage of a superior knowledge about the issue concerned. This makes it possible for A to define solutions to the conflict which are of such a character that it becomes hard for B to find alternatives for action, which B can convincingly demonstrate is superior to that proposed by A. Such an alternative solution may, for example, require that a number of 'objective' technical requirements are fulfilled, the attainment of which is outside the competence of B.

The fact that power can be exercized in so many different ways suggests a rather complex nature of the powerbase of nations. That conclusion can be drawn by means of sheer deduction. It is quite obvious that, for example, negative sanctions require a different set of conditions from successful persuasion. Sanctions, thus, have to do with relationships of dependence, whereas persuasion presupposes access to knowledge and skilful diplomats. In a similar way tentative conclusions about the necessary conditions for the effective exercize of power can be drawn from a study of all strategies for the exercize of power.

On the basis of such a deductive analysis a tentative model of the powerbase has been constructed. The basic feature of this model is that the power base consists of a number of elements, each of which is supposed to give support to one or more strategies of the exercize of power. Nine such elements of the powerbase have been included in the model.

The various elements of the power base will be described very briefly here, the purpose being only to give a rough idea of what they represent. The elements can be divided into three main groups. The first of these categories may be called *resource components*, which primarily have in common the fact they refer to properties of the acting nation itself. There are three elements of the powerbase which belong here:

1. *General strength* reflects a country's general and all-round capabilities to exert military as well as civilian power.
2. *Special assets* are resources, or other properties of a country, giving it influence over other actors in a well-defined and generally limited way. Typical 'special assets' are scarce raw

materials such as oil creating the conditions for strong market power.
3. *Creative capability* is the capacity of nations to produce knowledge, technology, and other innovations and also to adapt its socio-economic structures in the face of changing external and internal conditions.

The second category of elements of the power base may be referred to as *relational components*. These pertain to the external environment of the acting nation, A. Three such elements, relatively closely interrelated, may be discerned.

4. A's *control over the external environment* represents this country's capacity to monitor and control relationships of interdependence, flows of transactions, etc, in order to influence the behaviour of other actors.
5. *Position in the international system* is a function of those systemic properties, norms, 'rules of the game' etc, which work to A's advantage in a confrontation with other actors.
6. *Invulnerability* is equal to A's predisposition for evasion and counteraction in relation to attempts of other actors to control A's behaviour. Access to such a protective 'shield' against measures undertaken by other actors may be a condition for offensive actions by A.

The third and last category of the power base has been labelled *manipulation components*. They represent the capacity of actors to deliberately exploit their power base. There are two such elements, the *mobilization* and *application capabilities*. The first of these represent faculties which help the actor concerned to make the power base ready for employment whereas the other is equal to the capacity to actually use the power base to make an influence strategy effective (Sjöstedt, 1977).

3. THREE THEORETICAL PROBLEMS

When the model of the power base defined above, from now on

assumed to be valid, is employed for practical research purposes a host of difficulties arise. Some of these problems are of a practical character, such as lack of reliable data. These difficulties will be disregarded here. In the present context the attention is directed towards a number of more fundamental problems of a theoretical character, which can be expressed in the form of three questions:

— Firstly, which phenomena should be included in a model of the power base useful for practical research and at the same time possessing general validity? This is the *problem of delimitation*.
— Secondly, how should the relationships between the various components of the power base be conceived of? This may be described as the *problem of aggregation*.
— Thirdly, how should changes of the powerbase over time be defined? This is the *problem of temporal comparison*.

These three problems do not represent an exhaustive enumeration of all the difficulties involved in the measurement of power. But a discussion about them give some insights into the character of the obstacles which have to be surmounted before reliable unconditional comparisons of the power of nations can be accomplished. No definite solutions as to how the three problems can be solved will be suggested here. The purpose is simply to bring to the forefront a number of considerations which have to be made when research to elucidate the nature of power bases is initiated.

3.1 The problem of delimitation

According to the basic definition employed here the power base is supposed to be an expression of the general disposition of a country to be powerful in relation to other countries. This means that a number of phenomena which may be significant, even decisive, in the individual case of the exercize of power, have to be excluded from the power base. There are at least two categories of such phenomena which may give A power over B, but which in spite of this can not be included in a model of the powerbase claiming general validity. These phenomena may be referred to as 1) incidental factors or 2) idiosyncracies pertaining to the power-holding country or to a particular situation. These categories are somewhat overlapping, but they are sufficiently different to make it useful to distinguish between them.

1. *Incidental factors*. This category consists of actions undertaken by other actors than A and B, which help A exercize power over B. An example would be an intervention of a third party on the side of A in a conflict with B. Such incidents are unproblematic from a theoretical point of view as they are excluded from the power base already by the basic definition which stipulates that only *properties* of A or its external environment belong to the power base. This is no doubt a reasonable delimitation of the power base which it is no use to dispute.

2. *Idiosyncracies*. The model of power base is meant to serve as an instrument for unconditional comparisons. This means that the model should be such that it is possible in principle to apply it to any nation of the world in such a way that a comparison can be made with any other nation without reference to any particular context. This requirement obviously creates serious problems of delimitation. These difficulties are particularly noticable as regards the relational elements of the power base. This is easily discerned when the two elements here called 'control of the external environment' and 'invulnerability' are scrutinized a little.

Both these elements of the power base can be expected to be at least partially represented by relationships of dependence between the actor concerned, A, and its external environment. Take the case of invulnerability. A can be expected to be the less invulnerable the more A is dependent on the outside world. Indicators of this sort of dependence have been proposed in the literature. One measure commonly used is, for instance, A's external trade in relation to its GDP. The rationale behind the choice of this indicator is easily discernible. The more A has to rely on other countries for raw materials and other inputs to its industries and the more A's industries have to rely on foreign markets for its sales the more open for pressures and disturbances coming from the external environment must A presumably be.

This reasoning, although logical and in line with common sense, is open to certain objections. It is in fact not self-evident that in a given group of countries the nation with the greatest proportion of foreign trade in relation to its GDP is the most vulnerable. It could very well be the other way around. A great amount of foreign trade may also signify influence over other nations and should then accordingly be considered to be an indicator of 'control of the external environment' rather than of the degree of (in)vulnerability.

In order to determine if a given proportion of trade to GDP means that A is relatively vulnerable or influential it is necessary to specify a considerable number of circumstances. Factors of significance are, for example, the contents of the trade flows and the countries to which trade is concentrated.[6]

It is evidently helpful to know to how many products and to how many partners A's trade is concentrated in order to measure the degree of external control and invulnerability of this country. Conventional wisdom tells us that the higher the degree of concentration in these two respects the less invulnerable can A be expected to be. A common method to avoid becoming vulnerable is to diversify the external trade. But again this is not the only possible interpretation. If A's trade is dominated by a few products giving market power, say petroleum and gas, and A has a large proportion of its trade concentrated to a few much smaller nations this can also signify that A exerts influence over these trade partners. Or it may mean that A is invulnerable in relation to some of these partners but has control over others.

In order to determine which of these alternative interpretations is the most accurate it is necessary to know the identity of both A itself and of those trade partners to which A's trade is concentrated. This means that it is necessary to find out exactly over which particular countries A actually has control in order to assess A's general disposition to have control over other nations. This is not an unproblematic research procedure. One of the reasons why it is interesting to possess knowledge about the power base of A is that this is meant to predict the probability that A will be able to exercise power over other countries. But the measurement of the control of the external environment (as well as of invulnerability) has to be made with the help of indicators which represent A's actual control over certain countries. In other words, this is a case where the *explanandum* has to be explained in terms of the *explanans*. Control over the external environment can thus evidently be regarded as both a disposition to be powerful and as an expression of the exercise of power, and the line of delimitation between these two conceptions is not crystal clear.

Even if these particular problems of delimitation are disregarded other similar difficulties remain to be taken care of. Assume, for instance, that it has been established that A has trade relations with three neighbouring nations, X, Y, and W, which are of such a character that A can be said to have a disposition to exert control over them. What conclusions can be drawn from this observation as to A's general disposition to be powerful over other nations?

In order to investigate this it is useful to make a comparison with one of the resource elements of the power base, for instance general strength. One reasonably good indicator of general strength is the consumption of energy of the country concerned. The more energy consumed in a country the larger and the more developed can its economy be expected to be, which in turn means a correspondingly great amount of the general overall power capabilities of this nation. This is one of the reasons why this indicator can be said to possess general validity. A second reason is that it seems well-founded to assert, all other things being equal, that this indicator also can be expected to represent one nation's power over any other nation. This is, thus, a measure which should be suitable for unconditional comparison.

Now, returning to the discussion above about the external control of a country it can be noted that the indicators of this element of the power base of A are A's relationships (in this case limited to trade) with three other countries X, Y, and W. Using this indicator means that we measure the external control of A by means of an empirical investigation in which it is established that A has a potential control over these three nations. But at the same time we have also established that A *does not* have control over any other nations of the world. There is thus no ground for the claim that A has a general disposition to be powerful in relation to other countries irrespective of their identity. That disposition is limited to only X, Y, and W. This makes it difficult to compare the external control of A with that of other nations, such as B. It can be argued that the only meaningful comparison that can be made in this respect is in relation to X, Y, and W. It should be within reach to make an assessment if A or B has the greatest control over these three nations. But assume that B has no control over X, Y, and W but instead over three other nations K, L, and M. How should it then be determined if A or B has the greatest external control in an absolute sense? But the really crucial question is of course: What is the use of knowing that, say, A's control is greater than that of B when we also know that A actually only has control over Z, Y, and W.

In addition, other elements of the power base may be difficult to measure objectively. Take 'position in the international system'. This is an element which may prove to be of great significance in a confrontation between A and B. Established 'rules of the game' or norms in the international system may effectively prevent B from taking advantage of its superior resources. But how are factors like norms, 'rules of the game' and other systemic properties to be taken into consideration when an unconditional comparison of the power of A and B is undertaken. The same norms which help A work against B. 'Rules of the game' are often conditioned by a certain context, such as an international organization. So, it is obviously impossible to find generally valid indicators pertaining to most aspects of 'position in the international system' which permit the objective measurement of power.

There is thus a trade-off between explanatory capacity and comprehensiveness to take into consideration when indicators of the power base are looked for. This is a common problem which by no means is restricted to the measurement of power but which is particularly important to note in this case. Because if the conception of the power base as a country's disposition to be powerful in relation to other nations is to be upheld, the scope of the operational definition seemingly has to be severely limited. Many important phenomena have to be excluded because they cannot be generalized. Other components of the elements of the power base are of such a nature that they cannot be given sufficiently specific meaning without reference to some context or other.

There is thus a risk that it will not be possible to find operational representations which give justice to the theoretical definition of power base. It is indeed highly likely that the aspects of the power base which are possible to measure only represent a minor portion of the power base, as it is conceived of in the theoretical definition. This may represent a discrepancy between the theoretical and operational definitions which is intolerable. The choice is then to accept that or redefine power base in such a way that this concept becomes easier to express in operational terms.

3.2 The problem of aggregation

It may seem quite natural to think of the power base as a whole.[7] A closer look leads, however, to the conclusion that this conception of the power base is not easy to uphold in practise. It presupposes that relationships between the whole and the parts can be established: And this is not the case.

It should be recalled that the power base, according to the model employed here, is the common denomination for nine different categories of factors, which in different ways are supposed to give *A* power over *B*. It is far from clear how these *elements of the power base* are interrelated and how they can be aggregated so as to constitute the powerbase as a whole.

One possibility would be to look upon the power base as an additive index. This conception would mean that different elements simply are added together according to some formula determined by empirical and theoretical analysis. An additive relationship between the elements of the power base does not necessarily presuppose that these are all given an equal value when aggregated. One line of reasoning could for instance be that an element like general strength — representing the all-round capabilities of a nation — should be given a higher value than, say, special assets. The reason for this would be that economic strength can be expected to have a much greater impact in a greater number of situations, than special assets, or for that matter most of the other power base elements as well. Therefore, general strength can be said to give a greater contribution to the general disposition of a country to be powerful, thereby deserving to be given a greater value when the elements of the powerbase are aggregated. It is, however, obviously no easy task to evaluate the relative importance of different elements of the powerbase. Even if the logic behind the additive index is not complicated, this measure is hard to construct in practise: There is very little evidence as to how to weigh the various components of the power base.

The idea of the power base as an additive index can, however, easily be challenged. An illustrative example is the element here called invulnerability, and its relation to the rest of the power base. Invulnerability is, generally speaking, equal to the capacity of a nation, A, to resist pressures coming from the external milieu.[8] But invulnerability should not only be thought of as an instrument which can exclusively be used for strictly defensive purposes. This 'shield' is evidently in many cases a necessary prerequisite for the carrying out of at least some of the offensive influence strategies, particularly negative sanctions. Take for instance the case when A exerts pressure onto B by manipulating or exploiting a relationship of dependence between these two parties. Such measures are hardly practicable unless A has access to measures to protect itself from countermeasures undertaken by B. If, say, B is dependent on deliveries of oil by A this relationship hardly gives A leverage over B if A at the same time badly needs B's military umbrella to protect itself from a third party, C.

Invulnerability, thus, only gives A power over B in combination with other elements of the power base. This, in turn, indicates that there is a multiplicative rather than an additive relationship between, on the one hand, invulnerability and, on the other hand, at least some of the remaining power base elements. It should further be noted that the size of the interaction effect between invulnerability and other elements evidently varies from one case to another and is among other things dependent on what influence strategy A chooses to adopt.

Also the mobilization and application capabilities are probably tied to the rest of the power base by a multiplicative relationship. The protracted war between the United States and North Vietnam is a well-known case where the importance of the mobilization — and seemingly also the application — capability was clearly demonstrated. The resource elements of the American power base were strikingly superior to those of North Vietnam. But as the latter nation was able to mobilize its relatively modest resources, the actual effect of these power base elements was seemingly multiplied with a factor of a considerable size.

The probable existence of multiplicative relationships between elements of the power base obviously causes great problems when it comes to assessments of the total relative power of two or more nations. It is not sufficient to make a fair estimation of individual elements of the power base, a task which is difficult enough in itself. Unless 'multipliers' are identified and evaluated correctly the possible margins of error are so great that it can be questioned whether measurements are meaningful.

Take, for instance, a country, A, which scores high on several elements of the power base at Time 1, notably general strength and special assets (100), but whose capacity to take advantage of these 'resources' is severely hampered because the values for the capabilities of mobilization and application (manipulation) are very low (0.25); see Table 1. Country A should be compared to nation B which has 'normal' capabilities of mobilization and application (2,5) but whose other parts of the powerbase are considerably smaller than those of A (60). Table 1 illustrates what happens between Time 1 and Time 2, where only marginal increases occur in resource and relational elements of both A and B, but when at the same time A's mobilization/application capabilities grow to such an extent that they become comparable to those of B. The effect is that the power relationship between A and B is reversed: A was inferior at Time 1 but has turned out to be considerably stronger than B at Time 2.

TABLE 1.
Multiplicative Effects

	Nation A			Nation B		
	Mob/Appl	Re/Re	power base	Mob/Appl	Re/Re	power base
Time 1	0,25	100	25	2,5	60	150
Time 2	2,5	110	275	2,5	70	175

Mob/Appl = Mobilization and application capabilities
Re/Re   = Resource and relational components

3.3 The problem of temporal comparison

Mobilization of the power base may be regarded as a process and this in turn implies the passage of time. The duration of such a process can be expected to vary from one case to the next. It is fully conceivable that elements of the power base which in principle require mobilization before they can be employed still can be mobiliz-

assembles a number of tentative hypotheses about the mechanisms of change pertaining to the power base.

Expansion

The first mechanism to be mentioned may simply be labelled *growth*. The changes of the power base belonging to this category represent occurrences and developments completely outside the control of the agents of the powerholding nation A. One example of this kind of change would be the creation of a norm in the international system which is of such a nature that it gives A a certain advantage in a dispute — a power contest — with B. Another example would be multiplicative effects, due to the interaction of different elements of the power base.

A quite different mechanism of expansion of the power base is *build-up* which in principle is controlled by the decision-makers of A. The power base increases because the agents of A undertake deliberate actions to attain this effect. Examples of such measures would be a plan to make the diplomatic service of A more effective, measures to increase the birth rate, to accelerate technological development or transform oil into money and weapons. All such efforts to expand the power base of A by design may be described as expressions of a deliberate plan.

Diminution

Also the diminution of the power base may be deliberate. It is not inconceivable that decision-makers of a nation, A, may find it desirable to reallocate resources so that, for instance, the wealth of A will grow at the cost of a portion of the power base. In spite of the fact that national wealth and power in many ways can be expected to be cosely interrelated, a relationship of competitiveness can also be expected to exist between them. Some resources invested in the power base may be relatively unproductive as far as the creation of wealth is concerned. Therefore, the decision-makers may take deliberate actions to diminish the powerbase — to decrease it in terms of Figure 1 — in order to pursue some other national goal. An obvious example would be the reduction of military expenses so as to promote welfare.

Also 'automatic' diminution of the power base is conceivable. It cannot be excluded that processes completely outside the control of the agents of A can erode certain elements of the power base perhaps substantially. For example, norms which A can take advantage of may become diluted or even vanish completely.

Dynamic effects of the employment of the power base

The exercize of power may diminish the power base. The rationale behind this assertion is that the power base is thought of as something similar to a 'pool of resources' which will be tapped when power is exercized. If, for instance, A resorts to economic sanctions against B these measures will entail sacrifices for A, e.g. in the form of the loss of foreign markets on the part of A's industries. The more sanctions carried out by A, and the greater these are, the greater the sacrifices of the power base which are necessary for A to accept. Such *consumption* of the power base due to its activation can be expected to occur at least sometimes.

It is, however, not self-evident that the employment of the power base should always lead to its diminution. The exercize of power may also lead to the augmentation of the power base. This outcome may be brought about in at least two different ways:
1. The effect of power exertion — the results attained — may be that A, all things considered, gets a 'net profit' which contributes to the growth of its power base. An example would be that A conquers a mineral deposit from B, which eventually gives A resources to spend more money on technological development and its military forces thereby increasing the power base.
2. The exercize of power leads to the 'side effect' that the power base of A, the country exerting power, is built up. To speak in terms of Figure 1, there may be a *positive feed-back effect* emanating from the actions undertaken by the agents of A manifesting the exercize of power. One example would be the 'reputation' of A, considered to be an element of the power base of this country, whose significance at least to some extent can be ex-

pected to be a function of the number of times A exercizes power successfully, using its 'reputation' as a power base. The more often A demonstrates that it is powerful in relation to another country, B, the more powerful in the eyes of B can A be expected to become.

4. CONCLUDING REMARKS

A conceptual analysis of the kind undertaken above cannot in itself provide any factual evidence of what is the essence of the power of nations. But it has produced indications as to how the necessary empirical research to clarify the nature of power bases should be organized.

When the concept of power base is assessed it is vital to make a distinction between the various research aims that could possibly be attained if a better and more systematized knowledge about the power of nations were available. The elucidation of the concept of power base, of course, represents an important objective in its own right. But at the same time it looks well-founded to argue that the most important reason to search for reliable information about the nature of power bases is that researchers thereby are helped to answer questions and solve problems external to the concept of power base as such.

One important field of investigation which is dependent on accurate measurements of national power is the assessment of the would-be radical changes of the power structure of the international system. Knowledge of power bases could, however, also be used to attain a better understanding of individual cases of power exertion, or to predict the outcome thereof. Measurements of the power bases of nations could presumably be employed for other uses as well. But suffice it for the present purposes to limit the discussion to these two main alternatives; studies of power structures and of the exertion of power.

These two kinds of power research imply somewhat different qualities on the part of the instruments of analysis to be employed. This can be demonstrated by trying out how the model of the power base discussed above meets the requirements of, first, a study of the exercize of power and, second, of an analysis of the structure of power in the international system. In a study of the exercize of power the primary function of the power base is presumably to help predict outcomes. Assuming, for instance, that A wants B to do something that B does not want to do, 'perfect' knowledge of the power base of these two parties should considerably facilitate the task of foretelling how this confrontation will end. But the model of power base used here has to be regarded as a poor instrument of prediction. The combined effect of the three theoretical problems discussed above — the 'problem of delimitation', 'aggregation' and of 'temporal comparison' — is that it is very hard to reconcile the requirement of general validity with that of high predictive (or explanatory) capacity. In Chapter 4 Olav Knudsen convincingly argues that the most significant factors which help determine the relative power of an individual nation in a particular situation often are circumstances pertaining to that very situation. Unfortunately such phenomena are impossible to include in a model of the power base having general validity and applicability. The problems of aggregation and temporal comparison further mean that as long as these are not solved the margins of error may be intolerable when it comes to comparisons between nations. It has thus to be concluded that as far as the exercize of power is concerned the model of power base cannot be directly applied and employed for predictions. In order to attain such ambitious objectives a much more elaborate model than the one discussed here would have to be worked out. But as the discussion above has demonstrated considerable theoretical obstacles block the road for such an elaboration. It seems, in fact, improbable that it will prove possible to construct one single model of power base, which can help predict the outcome of an attempt to exercize power, regardless of the situation at hand.

The model of power base discussed here does not seem very useful for investigations of the structure of power in the international system either. A general feature of such analyses is the great number of observations which are necessary to make. Virtually all nations of the world have to be included, except perhaps a few mini-states. If the aim is to assess changes in the structure of power over time, measurements of the same nation at several points of time have to be made, which augments the number of observations still further. This sort of analysis requires a measure of the power base of nations which is easy to handle, and which permits the objective unconditional comparison of nations. The model of power base does not provide such measures.

The 'problem of delimitation' may be less of an obstacle for a structural analysis than for the study of individual cases of the exercize of power. This problem can to some extent be controlled if the requirement for a high degree of specification of the meaning of the various elements of the power base is compromised. There are probably ways to find indicators for most elements of the power base applicable to all nations if it is accepted that these are defined on a high level of generalization. An example would be 'trade in relation to GDP' as an indicator of the disposition of a country of being invulnerable. It should, however, be recalled from the discussion above that the 'problem of aggregation' — probably often in combination with the 'problem of temporal comparison' — leads to considerable risks for mistakes when the power base of a nation is assessed. How large these risks are we cannot know before these problems are eliminated. One of the causes of these margins of error is that we do not know the nature of the true relationship between different elements of the power base. It is not until these have been determined that it will become possible to know what the consequences are if, for example, linear additive relationships are incorrectly assumed to characterize the power base.

This means that as long as the 'problems of aggregation' and 'temporal comparison' remain unsolved objective quantitative measurement of the power base of nations should be regarded as in principle impossible. This includes the use of a unidimensional indicator like GDP or the consumption of energy. The theoretical problems discussed here are not eliminated only because a practical indicator easy to quantify is employed.

Research about the power base of nations is thus vital. The discussion pursued here indicates that this research has to be oriented in at least two different directions at the same time. There are strong indications that the ambition of constructing a generally valid model of the power base useful for the elucidation of how power is exercized has to be given up. So, some other approach has to be chosen.

One possibility would be to develop a number of partial models of the power base, which are specifically and systematically related either to various *types of situations*, such as, for example, open confrontation, bilateral or multilateral negotiation, or to various important *issue areas*.

Another possibility would perhaps be to abandon the idea of an independent model of the power base altogether and instead integrate elements of the existing knowledge of power and power bases into other theories and models pertaining to the exercize of power. Examples of such models which seem fruitful to expand in this way are theories of bargaining, negotiation and sanctions.

The results of these and other research efforts concerning the exercize of power can be expected to eventually become useful for the analysis of the structure of power in the international system. The more we know about the conditions for the effective exercize of power the better basis for an understanding of the anatomy of the power structure as well.

But such a generally improved understanding of the power base does not automatically create a measure — a model of the power base — which is satisfactorily specific and, at the same time, suitable for unconditional comparison. In order to attain that result special research efforts are needed. This is thus the second direction of research of the power base of nations to which research resources should be allocated.

NOTES

1. An expression of this Chinese anxiety is Chairman Mao's Theory of the Differentiation of the Three Worlds, *Peking Review*, 45, 4 November 1977.

2. The problems involved when it comes to specify the meaning of superpower is discussed by Christer Jönsson in Chapter 3 of this volume.

3. For an overview of the traditional indicators of power see for instance Coplin and Kegley (1971:106–107).

4. In Ferris (1973) and Petrén (1976) a more profound discussion is pursued about the usefulness of these indicators of the power of nations.

5. This tentative model has been described in more detail in Sjöstedt (1977). It has also been tried out for application on six countries: Brazil, the Federal Republic of Germany, India, Iran, Japan, and Nigeria. The purpose was to see to what extent the model could be used for empirical studies and to assess what conclusions could be drawn from such investigations if it is assumed that the model is valid. The result of this 'test' of the model will be reported in a forthcoming research report from the Swedish Institute of International Affairs.

6. Such a measure is Michaely's index of concentration which, with respect to trade partners, can be described as follows. I is the degree of concentration:

$$I = 100 \times \sqrt{(A \times B/A \times T)^2}$$

$A \times B = $ A's export to B

$A \times T = $ A's total export

7. This is in principle the kind of model of the power base employed here. The various elements of the power base represent a number of would-be aspects of the power base of nations.

8. The opposite to invulnerability is vulnerability, so that when the degree of invulnerability increases the degree of vulnerability decreases. The concept of invulnerability is used here because in contrast to vulnerability it can normally be expected to be a country's advantage. This term is therefore more logical to use as a designation of an element of the power base than vulnerability.

REFERENCES

COPLIN, W. and C. KEGLEY (1971) *A Multi-Method Introduction to International Politics*. Chicago: Markham Publishing Company.

FERRIS, W. H. (1973) *The Power Capabilities of Nation-States: International Conflict and War*. Lexington, Mass.: D. C. Heath.

NAGEL, J. H. (1975) *The Descriptive Analyses of Power*. New Haven: Yale University Press.

PEKING REVIEW (1977), 45, 4 November.

PETRÉN, K. (1976) *Maktstrukturens huvuddrag: en analys av 20 maktindikatorer*. Stockholm: The Swedish Institute of International Affairs.

SJÖSTEDT, G. (1977) 'The Exercise of International Civil Power: A Framework for Analysis' in *Cooperation and Conflict* XII: 21 – 39.

3 The Paradoxes of Superpower: Omnipotence or Impotence?

Christer Jönsson
University of Lund

'Two empires will then share all the advantages of civilisation, of the power of genius, of letters, of arts, of arms and industry: Russia on the eastern side and America... on the western side, and we other peoples of the nucleus will be too degraded, too debased, to know otherwise than by a vague and stupid tradition what we have been.'

(Baron Melchior von Grimm to Catherine II, 31 December 1790.)

'But the age of the superpowers is now drawing to an end.'

(Henry A. Kissinger, 1969.)

INTRODUCTION

'I know of nothing sublime' which is not some modification of power', said Edmund Burke. And while students of politics before and after him would generally agree that power is a pivotal concept, there is far less consensus concerning the meaning of the concept. In the vernacular of international politics the word 'power' is used in several different ways. A state is said to *possess* power; it may *exercise* power; and it may even *be* a power. To add to the confusion and ambiguity, our generation has introduced the concept of 'superpower' to denote the unprecedented amassment of power, however defined, in two states, the United States and the Soviet Union, in the contemporary international system.

Most definitions of superpower, whether explicit or implicit, are couched in terms of capabilities. Their second-strike nuclear-missile capability is the main factor distinguishing the American and Soviet superpowers from other states in the contemporary international system. The superpowers rank high on other capability indices as well, but only in the sphere of military force are their capabilities unrivalled. Already before the advent of the nuclear age, Fox (1944:21) defined superpower as 'great power plus great mobility of power'; and the development of nuclear weapons and intercontinental missiles signifies unprecedented geographical accessibility and global reach, extending superpower interests to encompass the entire globe. In the words of one caustic characterization, 'a super power is one able to wreck half the world, and committed upon conditions to do so' (Burns, 1971:xi).

Others maintain that the Soviet Union and the United States are superpowers rather by virtue of their combination of capabilities. However, they usually fail to address the aggregation problem (cf. Chapter 2 in this volume): how are we, for instance, to weigh economic capabilities vis-à-vis military capabilities? The question then also arises whether the superpower status of the Soviet Union is based on other than military capabilities; and the borderline between superpowers and other states becomes blurred. At a minimum, there seems to be a general consensus that nuclear capability (a) is a necessary, if not sufficient, criterion of superpower status, and (b) is a crucial factor making for the global extent of American and Soviet interests.

On the other hand, just as many analysts conceive of power in general as a relational concept, some authors have concluded that superpower also is a 'tacitly relational expression' (Burns, 1971: xii) which cannot be defined exclusively in terms of military capabilities. This recognition points to a redirection of the focus from the *bases* to the *exercise* of power (cf. Chapter 1 in this volume).

The purpose of this essay is to explore the relationship between *one* power base (nuclear weapons) and the actual exercise of power. This limited focus seems justified in light of the significance accrued to nuclear capabilities in conceptualizing 'superpower'. It must, of course, not be taken to imply any downgrading of the importance of other power bases. Rather, I propose that the paradoxes of superpower, understood in terms of nuclear capabilities, may help illuminate some problematic aspects of power in a more general sense. Specifically, I shall be arguing for the need to complement traditional power analysis with concepts and insights drawn from the literature on communication, bargaining, and cognitive processes.

In the political science literature power is commonly defined in terms of *compliance*. '*A* has power over *B* to the extent that he can get *B* to do something that *B* would not otherwise do', to quote Dahl's widely adopted definition (Dahl, 1957). This notion comes close to equating power with causality. The exercise of power on the part of *A* is seen as a necessary, if not sufficient, condition for *B*'s behavior.

Conceptualizing power in terms of compliance focuses on the *successful* exercise of power.

> Whether compliance occurs should be an empirical question, open to investigation, not an *a priori* assumption entailed by the concept power. Indeed, only when compliance is left out of the definition of power can one investigate adequately the conditions or calculations that determine whether compliance will in fact occur. Power defined in terms of outcomes (compliance) deflects our attention away from the processes by which these outcomes are generated (Bell, D.V.J., 1976: 8).

Thus, if we want to focus on the exercise of power without prejudging the question of its success or failure in terms of compliance or non-compliance, we need to conceptualize power in terms of the communication process involved in any influence attempt. Some kind of message has to be 'encoded' and transmitted by the influencer and received and 'decoded' by the influencee.

Different types of messages may be involved in the exercise of power. D.V.J. Bell (1975; 1976) has identified three basic 'linguistic paradigms' into which such messages can be translated.

(1) If you do X, I will do Y.
   The influencer makes his action Y contingent on the performance of action X by the influencee. X and Y may both be either positive or negative. The message conveys a *threat* in the

case that the influencee expects the outcome (X, Y) to be worse for himself than the outcome he would otherwise expect as a result of doing X; it conveys a promise if the influencee expects the outcome (X, Y) to be better for himself than the outcome he would otherwise expect as a result of doing X.

(2) If you do X, Y will happen.
This conditional message expresses a *warning* or an *encouragement*, when Y to the influencee is respectively undesirable or desirable. The difference between warnings and encouragements, on the one hand, and threats and promises, on the other hand, thus lies in the role played by their initiators in the causation of the predicted consequences.

(3) Do X.
This is a categorical rather than contingent statement. The effectiveness of such a command or *prescription* depends on the influencee's belief in the authority of the influencer.[1]

These paradigms may appear in different mixtures and combinations in actual messages. Threats and warnings are, for instance, often combined with promises and encouragements.

It should also be added that the communication involved in the exercise of power may be incomplete or indirect. Communication may in fact be tacit, involving nonverbal acts. The point is that the exercise of power entails the conveyance of a message through some kind of signal, often a combination of verbal statements and non-verbal acts.

To be effective, such a message must, first of all, be *perceived* by the influencee. It will be ineffective if the influencee is somehow unavailable for the message. For example, children are skilled at avoiding the receipt of a warning glance from a parent, knowing that if they perceive it the parent is obliged to punish noncompliance (cf. Schelling, 1963: 146 – 149).

If the message is perceived, the problem of *credibility* still remains. And whether or not the message will be believed by the influencee depends on a number of factors. The influencee's perception of the influencer's capabilities or *power bases* is, of course, one of these — but by no means the only one.

The influencer's message may convey varying degrees of *finality* (cf. for instance the conditional statement 'if you do X, I shall undoubtedly do Y' and 'if you do X, I might very well do Y') and *specificity* (cf. 'if you attack Berlin, I shall strike back at Moscow' and 'if you do something rash, I shall respond in kind'). As the latter examples show, both the conditions and the threatened or promised action can convey varying degrees of specificity. The point is that any loopholes the influencer leaves himself, if they are visible to the influencee, tend to reduce the credibility of the message.

Furthermore, the influencee may assess the message in terms of *continuity* (do the influencer's messages show some similarity over time?) and *consistency* (are all the influencer's messages compatible and not contradictory?). The influencee's assessment of the influencer's *reliability* based on his past experiences of the influencer's behavior (does he usually mean what he says or signals?) may also enter his credibility calculus. And the internal *cohesion* of the influencer is another factor of importance as a message apparently reflecting broad consensus within the influencer is deemed more credible than one about which there is visible internal disagreement. As these examples indicate, the influencee will, in Jervis's (1970) terminology, look beyond the manifest 'signals', which are readily subject to manipulation, for less easily manipulated 'indices' believed to be inextricably linked to the other actor's capabilities or intentions and untainted by deception.

In brief, as we redirect the focus from the static analysis of power bases to the dynamics of the exercise of power and accept a conceptualization of power which renders compliance problematic, we inevitably run into a number of complex subjective or psychological factors. This implies abandoning the simple stimulus-response thinking, common in power analysis (cf. Jervis, 1976: 343 – 355). 'Psycho-logic' is substituted for pure logic.

PARADOXES OF SUPERPOWER

In view of the crucial importance ascribed to nuclear weapons in defining the preponderant position of the United States and the

Soviet Union in the contemporary international hierarchy, a pertinent question seems to be how nuclear capabilities — the power base generally regarded to designate superpower — can be translated into power exercise. In terms of the approach outlined above, how can nuclear capabilities be utilized in transmitting power messages?

The general impact of nuclear weapons upon international politics has been, and remains, a subject of much speculation and controversy among policy-makers and scholars alike. While most observers agree that nuclear weapons have made for changes in international politics, there are clearly divergent views concerning the profundity and direction of the changes.

In May 1945 — that is, prior to the first successful detonation of an atomic bomb — US Secretary of War Stimson expressed the ambivalent expectations as to the impact of the new weapon. It might be 'a Frankenstein which would eat us up' or a project 'by which the peace of the world would be helped in becoming secure' (Sherwin, 1975: 205). Stimson's two-pronged image foreshadowed the divergencies between pessimistic and optimistic appraisals after the nuclear weapon became a reality.

Pessimists, of course, tend to emphasize the 'Frankenstein' characteristic of the new weapons. Even those who do not readily accept the doomsday prophecy of nuclear holocaust envisage profound negative transformations of the international system. For instance, Herz in an early, influential essay on the impact of nuclear weapons (Herz, 1959) posited that nuclear-missile technology has destroyed the 'impermeability' of the nation-state and foresaw the decline of the territorial state much in the same way as the 'gunpowder revolution' of the later Middle Ages in Europe rendered castles and walled cities obsolete as units of protection.

Optimists, on the other hand, see in nuclear weaponry a potential for reinforcing rather than destroying the international order. Witness, for example, Osgood's and Tucker's refutation of Herz's conclusions:

> Although the 'hard shell' or 'impermeability' that characterized the state in the past has vanished, in the case of nuclear states it has been succeeded by a new kind of shell, a new kind of impermeability. This new shell is no less 'real' than

the old simply because the old was rooted in the material quality of territoriality whereas the new is rooted in the psychological quality of deterrence. If 'reality' is but a synonym for effectiveness, we have reason to believe that the hard shell of deterrence is far more real than its predecessor (Osgood – Tucker, 1967: 326).

Perhaps the most eloquent optimist was Churchill who anticipated a 'process of sublime irony' whereby 'safety will be the sturdy child of terror, and survival the twin brother of annihiliation':

> When I was a schoolboy I was not good at arithmetic but I have since heard it said that certain mathematical quantities when they pass through infinity change their signs from plus to minus — or the other way round. It may be that this rule may have a novel application and that when the advance of destructive weapons enables everyone to kill everybody else nobody will want to kill anyone at all (quoted in Herz, 1959: 212).

In short, neither scholars nor policy-makers have been able to establish beyond doubt the impact and role of nuclear weapons. In the words of Kissinger (1969: 61), 'as power has grown more awesome, it has also turned abstract, intangible, elusive'. The elusiveness and ambiguity of nuclear capabilities are of course transferred to the superpowers. It is symptomatic that the Chinese have been pinning the dialectic epithet 'paper tiger' (something to be slighted strategically but taken seriously tactically) to nuclear weapons, the United States, and the Soviet Union, consecutively.

One prominent Cold War historian has entitled a chapter on US 'atomic diplomacy' in the immediate postwar era 'The Impotence of Omnipotence' (Gaddis, 1972). And Herz (1959: 41) argues that 'utmost strength now coincides with utmost vulnerability'. Such expressions epitomize the paradoxical nature of superpower. The apparent paradoxes of superpower may, furthermore, illustrate some underlying problems of power analysis, pertaining especially to the relationship between power bases and the psychological dimensions of power exercise alluded to above. Let us thus turn now from this brief discussion of the general impact of nuclear weapons to an attempt at sketching more specifically some paradoxical aspects of superpower efforts to translate this power base into power exercise in different regions of the world.

Vis-à-vis one another

The term 'deterrence' embodies the superpowers' notion of how nuclear capabilities can be translated into influence in their mutual relations.[2] Deterrence is based on a *threat* of violence contingent upon certain undesired behavior by the opponent. As such, the idea of deterrence is an old one.

> What is novel and oppressive about the peace of deterrence is not that it rests upon the threat of violence but that it rests upon a threat of violence which, if ever carried out, might make a future peace impossible. What is novel and oppressive about the order of deterrence is not that it rests upon the threat of disorder but that it rests upon a threat of disorder which, if ever carried out, might make the building of a new order impossible (Osgood – Tucker, 1967: 353).

The threat must, in other words, be absolutely effective, since the threatened action is not designed for repeated performance. The deterrence idea is appealingly simple, but a situation of *mutual deterrence* entails certain paradoxes.

The basic paradox of mutual deterrence by two superpowers possessing second-strike capabilities pertains to the credibility problem discussed above. If state A threatens nuclear war, it does so with the awareness that B can be expected to react with nuclear retaliation against any nuclear action by A. This means that A either does not really mean it (i.e. the threat is a bluff) or is actually prepared to inflict nuclear devastation even at the risk of being so devastated itself. But in the latter case A denies, at least for its own part, the deterring force of the nuclear threat. Why then should A assume that B will be deterred? (cf. Herz, 1959: 189–190). As Schelling bluntly puts it, 'there is no cheap, safe way of using nuclears that scares the wits out of the Russians without scaring us too' (Schelling, 1966: 114). Mutual deterrence, in brief, implies an element of 'self-deterrence'.

> Thus we have the paradox that the effectiveness of deterrence is attributed both to the willingness of states to employ nuclear force and to the unwillingness of states to employ nuclear force, to the belief that there are no interests over which states are prepared to initiate thermonuclear war and to the belief that there are interests over which states are prepared to initiate thermonuclear war (Osgood – Tucker, 1967: 344n).

The reduced credibility of the nuclear threat under conditions of mutual deterrence is also reflected in the development of the strategic doctrines of the superpowers. The initial period of over-reliance on nuclear weapons epitomized in the doctrine of 'massive retaliation' has yielded to the notions of 'flexible and graduated response' and 'limited war', implying a more balanced view of the potentialities as well as the limitations of the nuclear option.[3]

Nuclear deterrence has thus turned into a kind of 'intra-war' deterrence: the deterrence of escalation (cf. George – Smoke, 1974: 32). This revised version of deterrence is, however, not exempt from paradoxes either. Specifically, the emphasis on limited war and the 'conventional option' tends to encourage the initiation of such conflicts and thereby to degrade the deterrent value of nuclear weapons. To increase the feasibility of limited war is to deprive nuclear capabilities of their ability to deter a wide range of aggressive behavior (cf. Knorr, 1966: 97 – 98).

> In fact, paradoxically, improved capabilities for selective or graduated response by the defender may at times increase the likelihood that the initiator will challenge deterrence by a low-level move. This would follow if the initiator were led to believe that the defender would confine his initial response also to a low level, thus making it possible for the initiator to calculate and control the risk of his opening move (George – Smoke, 1974: 531n).

Vis-à-vis allies and 'spheres of influence'

The paradoxes of 'basic deterrence' are compounded by the problems associated with the extension of the 'nuclear umbrella' to the superpowers' respective allies. Superpower exercise of power within their alliances rests upon a *promise* of protection from an attack by the other side.

The question 'protection from what?' results in uncertainty among both protectors and protected. To the protector it is a question of commitments: which areas can and should I protect, and under which circumstances will the opponent take my threat of retaliation seriously? The protected, on the other hand, have doubts over the protector's readiness in an emergency to accept the risk of colossal destruction for the sake of lending protection to an ally. They want the opponent to be convinced that the protector's threat of retaliation is sincere, yet at the same time want the protector to retain his freedom not to carry out the threat. The nuclear umbrella is the only protection they have against a nuclear attack; yet, by placing themselves under the umbrella they become pawns in the superpower game and run the risk of getting involved in conflicts of no immediate pertinence to their own interests and of becoming targets of nuclear attack from the other superpower.

A conflict which, from the viewpoint of the superpowers, might be considered a limited war could well constitute a total catastrophy to the alliance partners. De Gaulle once said: 'It is possible to imagine that on some awful day Western Europe should be wiped out from Moscow and Central Europe from Washington' (quoted in Kahn, 1960: 31).

For the protected allies a crucial — but so far unresolved — question is naturally how much influence they have regarding the use of the umbrella. The British have, for instance, coined the expression 'no annihilation without representation'. To the superpowers, however, centralized control of the nuclear capabilities is a primary concern. Yet crisis management requires control not only over capabilities but also over alliance partners. Have the superpowers, then, been able to translate their nuclear hegemony within their respective alliances into power vis-à-vis their allies?

China and France of course represent the most obvious failures in this respect. They have pointed to one possible solution to the dilemmas and uncertainties plaguing superpower allies by withdrawing from the community under the 'nuclear umbrella' and developing their own nuclear capability. And they have thereby served as catalysts of centrifugal tendencies within the alliance systems.

Several observers have pointed out that the existing alliance arrangements have not necessarily made the superpowers more powerful vis-à-vis their allies. Ulam, for example, holds that 'in many cases it is the superpowers which are being exploited, and their weak allies and clients...are the exploiters' (Ulam, 1971: 155). And Keohane (1971: 161) employs the simile of an elephant yoked to a team of lesser animals, and concludes that 'alliances have in curious ways increased the leverage of the little in dealings with the big'.

Superior military force cannot guarantee small-state compliance with superpower interests, and relative weakness does not entail only liabilities for the small state, but also creates certain bargaining assets. Different strategies are available to small allies: a policy of 'blackmail out of weakness' means threatening collapse and possibly realignment if not aided sufficiently; a policy of 'limited independence' implies a threat by a small ally that it might have to reconsider its policy and move in the direction of neutralism if its needs are not met; and a 'superloyal' strategy implies being 'more religious than the Pope' and thus being able to challenge superpower policies without questioning the basic thrust of superpower doctrines (Keohane, 1971: 168 – 171).

Why, then, can small allies be relatively influential in their dealings with the superpowers? Keohane suggests that it is the superpower policies of global involvement and crusading spirit that have presented small allies with bargaining power. 'Leaders who believe in domino theories not only have to talk to the "dominoes", they have to listen to them and believe them as well' (Keohane, 1971: 163).

It might be added that hostility toward the other camp has been the chief bond tying the alliances together. As superpower relations have moved in the direction of détente, alliance cohesion has become increasingly problematic and smaller allies have increased their freedom of action.

We thus encounter a commonly observed paradox of alliances in the nuclear age: although alliance partners obviously add little to the security of the nuclear superpowers and may indeed be considerable liabilities, alliance commitments continue to be an important aspect of superpower policies (see, for example, Knorr, 1966: 153 – 158, Nash, 1975: 55 – 56).

The mutual realization of this superpower dilemma seems to have resulted in a common status quo orientation, involving a tacit understanding on 'spheres of influence': each accepts, and agrees to abstain from interfering or exercising influence within, regions dominated and penetrated by the other (cf. Kaufman, 1976: 9 – 11, Doran, 1976: 11 – 12).

In Ulam's words (1971: 377 – 378), 'there is a point, in the nuclear age, beyond which your enemy's troubles become a source of apprehension'.

> Although both superpowers try to stimulate centrifugal forces among each other's allies, neither wishes to see the emergence of new centers of military power — least of all nuclear power — that might endanger its own management of power. To this extent each has an interest in the other's preponderance within its coalition (Osgood – Tucker, 1967: 171).

The superpowers' spheres of influence have therefore increasingly turned into 'Al Capone alliances' (Keohane, 1971: 180): remaining a faithful ally protects the small state not primarily against external threats but rather against the superpower itself. As demonstrated by Franck and Weisband, the verbal justifications by both superpowers of recent interventions within their respective East European and Latin American spheres of influence are remarkably parallel. The symmetries extend even to the arguments offered in repudiating the other superpower's intervention, thus creating an impression of 'a classical ballet with the two powers in the second movement neatly changing roles and dancing each other's steps' (Franck-Weisband, 1972: 97). Each superpower has enunciated a doctrine of limited sovereignty, reserving the right to intervene in states within their spheres of influence which are not complying with the norms of the bloc, especially by tolerating the expansion of an alien ideology.[4]

Even if this tacit understanding among the superpowers has tended to reduce the foreign policy role of the member states of the spheres of influence, it does not exclude the possibility for these to break out of the superpower orbit by following one or a combination of the strategies outlined above, as demonstrated by the examples of Yugoslavia and Cuba or, to a lesser degree, Rumania and Peru (cf. Kaufman, 1976: 116 – 145).

Vis-à-vis the non-aligned world

Whereas nuclear capabilities can be translated into threats to the other superpower and into promises to superpower allies, they cannot form an effective basis for either threats, promises, or prescriptions vis-à-vis states outside the superpower orbit.

Nuclear threats/warnings cannot be made credible for at least two major reasons. First, the asymmetry between the stakes involved and the threatened measures is glaring. It is common wisdom that mosquitoes are not most effectively killed with heavy artillery. In addition, the stabilized mutual deterrence relationship among the superpowers has strengthened and universalized an expectation of the non-use of nuclear weapons. With both superpowers paralyzed by mutual fear of their nuclear arsenals, the opportunities for limited and localized violence have increased rather than diminished. Hence the commonly observed paradox that 'though the weapons of mass-destruction grew more and more ferociously efficient, the revolutionary guerilla armed with nothing more advanced than a rifle and a nineteenth-century political doctrine has proved the most effective means yet devised for altering world power balance' (J. Bowyer Bell, as quoted in Knorr, 1966: 144). One crucial difference between conventional 'limited war' involving the superpower blocs and guerilla 'sub-limited war' outside the superpower spheres of interest is therefore that the threat of escalation into nuclear war is far less credible — and hence far less deterring — in the latter case.

A promise of nuclear protection by a superpower is not likely to impress non-aligned states either, as the dilemma of smaller allies referred to above has become increasingly obvious and thus has tended to increase the perceived utility of remaining non-aligned. And promises of nuclear aid from the superpowers are ruled out by the common US and Soviet interest in preventing nuclear proliferation, manifested in the test-ban and non-proliferation treaties. Ironically, this mutual superpower interest does not seem likely to arrest nuclear proliferation. Non-nuclear states have repeatedly pointed to the paradox of the superpowers spending enormous sums on ever more sophisticated nuclear weapons while at the same time trying to convince non-nuclear states of the minimal value of nuclear weapons for them. A number of 'threshold' states have refused to sign the non-proliferation treaty, and India may well be the first in a row of states outside the superpower orbits going nuclear. Moreover, owing to the mutual superpower interest in preventing proliferation, the threat of becoming a nuclear power or the mere fact of being known to be capable of becoming one may enhance the capacity of the threshold states to extract concessions or support from the superpowers (cf. Hoffman, 1968: 45).

Nor are prescriptions from the superpowers necessarily effective. Both superpowers have tried to capitalize on their non-colonial record and anti-imperialist ideals in their efforts to establish authority among Third World countries. However, these countries have become increasingly convinced that they are dealing with 'anti-imperialistic imperial superpowers', to use Niebuhr's (1964) pertinent expression. And today a growing number of Third World states are adopting China's perspective of a superpower condominium detrimental to smaller states.

As a result of these tendencies, the superpowers are sometimes influencees rather than influencers in their relations with the non-aligned world. Even the 'non-decision-making' power (Bachrach–Baratz, 1962) of the superpowers appears to be eroding, as North-South issues tend to take over the previously predominant role of East-West issues on the agendas of international forums, notably the UN.

CONCLUSIONS

The advent of the nuclear age has thus far resulted in neither the 'pax atomica' of optimistic forecasts nor the Armageddon of doomsday prophecies. Rather, the great war and the genuine peace have been buried together, as predicted by the French strategist Beaufre (1966: 101). Similarly, the nuclear superpowers have turned out to be neither omnipotent nor impotent. Instead, superpower attempts to exercise power have underlined the limitations of nuclear capabilities.

Many of the apparent paradoxes of superpower stem from the aforementioned difference between capability analysis and analysis of power exercise processes. Several observers maintain that nuclear weapons have destroyed the previous direct correlation between military capabilities and political power (see, for example, Nash, 1975: 23). 'The paradox of contemporary military strength is that a gargantuan increase in power has eroded its relationship to policy', says Kissinger, adding that nuclear capability 'no longer translates automatically into influence' (Kissinger, 1969: 59, 60).

These lines were, incidentally, quoted with approval by his Soviet colleague Arbatov (1970).

I would argue that there has never been any direct, one-to-one relationship between military capability and political power. Capability measures were perhaps previously more satisfactory indicators or approximations of power, as in the pre-nuclear age the contest of wills depended more than now on estimates of relative military capabilities and less on estimates of intentions, determination, and risk-taking propensities. Nuclear weapons, however, have dramatically unveiled the fallacy of equating potential power (power bases) with actual power (successful power exercise).

By invalidating the traditional continuity between threats and the overt use of the weapons on which the threats rest, nuclear weapons have elicited widespread and strong expectations of their non-use. Such expectations go a long way toward explaining the observed limitations in the superpowers' exercise of power. It is, in other words, not the credibility of the nuclear *capability* that is reduced, but of the *intention* to use this capability. Hence, the limitations of the seemingly boundless power base.

> Once it became clear that neither of the two rivals wanted to use (or could easily use) precisely that supply of power that made it one of the 'superpowers', once it became clear that, being in a bottle, the two scorpions had lost some of their sting, other beasts decided they had their chance (Hoffmann, 1968: 35).

On the other hand, it would be erroneous to conclude that nuclear weapons confer no political power whatever to the superpowers. First, nuclear threats have, in fact, been employed for political purposes. Milton Leitenberg, in a comprehensive study of nuclear threats and alerts in the postwar era, notes twenty-three American and fourteen Soviet cases (Leitenberg, 1977). Although these nuclear threats have ostensibly been directed at several different target states, it seems obvious that they have, in essence, been 'signals' to the other superpower, constituting elements in a mutual 'convention of crisis management' (cf. Bell, C., 1971). The effectiveness of such threats is hard to establish. Have they decisively affected the outcome of international crises? In other words, can they be characterized as successful power exercises?

Secondly, and more important, a distinction should be made between the *specific* and *diffuse* role of nuclear capabilities as power bases (cf. Goldmann, 1978: 146 – 147). The specific role is based on the potential use of nuclear weapons; the diffuse role refers to the fact that relative military strength affects the outcome of conflicts or bargaining situations between states even when military confrontation is never contemplated. In this way the superpowers may be able to modify the behavior of smaller states without ever sending any power messages based on nuclear weapons. As the use of nuclear capabilities becomes increasingly constrained, the symbolism of nuclear capabilities becomes more important.

As witnessed by proliferating statements by Chinese and small-state representatives, the notion of omnipotent superpowers, or 'nuclear overlords', ruling the world in 'condominium' is prevalent in the contemporary world. By the same token, prestige considerations loom large among other states having acquired or striving for nuclear status. The diffuse or symbolic role of these weapons is seen to enhance the general power position of their possessors.

Thus, both the limitations and the potentials of nuclear capabilities as power bases bring the psychological dimensions of power exercise to the forefront. And once we focus on these psychological dimensions, it becomes imperative to be precise as to *who* exercises power *over whom to do what*.

Who exercises power over whom?

Another look at superpower influence attempts in the light of this question gives rise to several comments. First, it is abundantly clear that the 'absolute' weapon does not confer upon its possessor any absolute power. Superpower relations with one another as well as with other groups of states have to be analyzed in terms of *relative* power — just as interstate relations in general may be seen as mutual influence attempts or *bargaining situations*. In other words, in most bilateral or multilateral relations the superpowers act as influencer as well as influencee, as sender as well as receiver of power messages. In this connection it might be noted that the relative success of power exercise in their mutual relations seems to have undermined the superpowers' ability successfully to exercise power over other actors. As the symmetrical relationship of mutual deterrence has opened up the possibility of mutual destruction and thus made for a relatively stable 'enemy-partner' relationship (Aron, 1967: 536ff), the resultant expectations of non-use of nuclear weapons has made it considerably harder for the superpowers to base power messages to other states on their nuclear superiority.

Furthermore, while the global involvement of the superpowers is to a considerable extent a function of their nuclear capabilities, this very diversity of activity has resulted in 'the malady of too many pies', reducing the effects of the superpowers' considerable lead in capability over weaker states (Spiegel, 1972: 13).

Another observation elicited by the who-whom question concerns the homogeneity of the actors. By the same token as the internal unity/disunity of the influencer is regarded as a component in the influencee's credibility calculus, the internal unity/disunity of the influencee is an important condition for the success or failure of the influencer's power exercise. An analysis of mutual influence attempts between states or groups of states thus needs to take into account parallel intracoalition and/or internal processes of power. For instance, as discussed in detail by Mack (1975), asymmetric conflicts tend to trigger different internal processes in the stronger and weaker protagonists: increased unity in the case of the weaker state, divisive domestic conflicts in the stronger state. The Vietnam War is an obvious case in point.

This, in turn, points to a distinction not always upheld in abstract analyses of international power: that between power *within* a state and the power *of* the state itself.[5] The French language conveniently has different terms for these two aspects of power: *pouvoir* and *puissance*, respectively (cf. Aron, 1967: 49). While the impact of nuclear weapons on the *puissance* of the superpowers, as we have seen, is ambiguous, these new weapons have no doubt increased the *pouvoir* of superpower decision-makers, having, in Schurmann's words, 'created the need for a god' and contributed to an unprecedented centralization and expansion of executive power within the superpowers (Schurmann, 1974: 12 – 13).

Power to do what?

A first distinction to be made in connection with military capabilities is that between the power to hurt — to destroy treasured things, to inflict pain and grief — and the power to seize and hold forcibly; between punishment and victory. Nuclear weapons have made it possible to do monstrous violence to the enemy without first achieving victory. The power to hurt thus represents a kind of bargaining power: the *threat* of damage, or more damage to come, can make the enemy comply (cf. Schelling 1966: 1 – 34). But, as we have seen, the threat of nuclear damage is not effective against all kinds of opponents or in all kinds of situations.

Another more general distinction can be made between power exercised to make an adversary do something desired and power exercised to keep him from doing something undesired. Even though this difference is often observed, the terminology differs: 'dissuasion-persuasion' (Singer, 1963), 'denial-gain' (Hoffmann, 1968), and 'deterrence-compellence' (Schelling, 1966) are some of the concepts used. Whereas a deterrent threat is passive, relinquishing the initiative to the other actor, a threat that compels usually requires that punishment be administered *until* the other acts rather than *if* he acts. The deterrent threat may be combined with a promise of rewards administered until the opponent changes his behavior, and the compelling threat with a promise of rewards *if* he changes his behavior (cf. Schelling, 1966: 69 – 71). The distinction is especially important in the superpower context: nuclear weapons may be effective in *deterring* an opponent but are less useful for compelling others. Moreover, as cogently demonstrated by George and Smoke (1974), while deterrence of strategic war can be said to have been successful thus far, deterrence of limited war and 'sub-limited conflict' has failed in most cases.

Finally, the relevance and usefulness of nuclear capabilities of course varies with *issue-area* (cf. Chapter 4 in this volume) and *situation*. For instance, as we move from the military-security issue-area and from crisis to non-crisis situations, it becomes increasingly difficult to base power messages on nuclear weapons.

The broader conclusion following from this analysis is that assertions about states 'possessing power', 'being powerful', or 'being a power' as well as analyses attempting to measure state capabilities tend to raise more questions than they answer. Focusing on the exercise of power is suggested as one possible way of addressing these questions. And, as illustrated by the paradoxes of superpower, the exercise of power can be seen as a dynamic communicative process involving complex psychological dimensions.

NOTES

1. I have adopted D.V.J. Bell's 'linguistic paradigms' in a somewhat modified form. Specifically, I have avoided Bell's labels of power, influence, and authority statements, respectively, which, in my opinion, only tend to add to the ambiguity of the terms involved. Instead, I have preferred a terminology derived from bargaining theory.

2. Although the term itself is an anathema in Soviet political language, the deterrence idea is generally accepted. For instance, one Soviet writer on diplomacy speaks of 'compelling imperialism, by threatening its ruin, to accept peace and peaceful coexistence' (Deborin, 1963: 49), and Khrushchev once gave a vivid expression of the deterrence idea:

> The tiger is a beast of prey and will remain one as long as it lives, but everyone knows that a tiger will never attack an elephant... To continue the simile, it must be said that the Soviet Union, the countries of the socialist world, are today a much tougher proposition for the imperialists than the elephant is for the tiger (quoted in Tucker, 1963: 213).

3. Again, short of adopting the American terminology, Soviet nuclear strategists have gradually accepted the basic premises of American strategic thinking; and the development of Soviet strategic doctrine has been closely related to the American development with certain time lags (see, for example, Dinerstein, 1962; Wolfe, 1964; SIPRI, 1971: 197–199).

4. It should be noted that while the Soviet sphere of influence, as manifested in the 'Brezhnev doctrine', coincides with the Warsaw Treaty alliance, the main American sphere of influence does not comprise NATO states but rather Latin America, according to official doctrine as well as detached analysis (cf. Franck–Weisband, 1972; Doran, 1976; Ray–Gochman, 1976). Yet some repercussions of the doctrine of limited sovereignty have been discernible in the American discussion about possible Communist regimes in Italy, France and Portugal.

5. Deutsch's analysis of international power (1968: 21–39) represents one prominent — but by no means the only — example of the failure to observe this distinction.

REFERENCES

ARBATOV, G. A. (1970) 'American Foreign Policy on the Threshold of the 1970's', *Soviet Law and Government*, 9, no. 1. (Reprinted in M. A. Kaplan (ed.) *Great Issues of International Politics*. 2nd edn. Chicago: Aldine, 1974.)

ARON, R. (1967) *Peace and War: A Theory of International Relations*. New York: Praeger.

BACHRACH, P. and M. BARATZ (1962) 'Decisions and Nondecisions: An Analytical Framework', *APSR*, LVII: 632–642.

BEAUFRE, A. (1966) *Modern strategi för krig och fred* (Original: *Introduction à la stratégi*). Stockholm: Prisma.

BELL, C. (1971) 'The Adverse Partnership', in C. Holbraad (ed.) *Super Powers and World Order*. Canberra: Australian National University Press.

BELL, D. V. J. (1975) *Power, Influence, and Authority*. New York: Oxford University Press.

—— (1976) 'Political Linguistics and the Study of Power'. Paper presented to the XVII Annual Convention, International Studies Association, 25–29 Feb. 1976, Toronto.

BURNS, A. L. (1971) 'Introduction', in: C. Holbraad (ed.) *Super Powers and World Order*. Canberra: Australian National University Press.

DAHL, R. (1957) 'The Concept of Power', *Behavioral Science*, II (July).

DEBORIN, T. A. (1963) 'Novyi istoricheskii etap v razvitii sovetskoi vneshnei politiki i diplomatii' (The New Historical Stage in Soviet Foreign Policy and Diplomacy), in: V. Z. Lebedev (ed.), *O sovremennoi sovetskoi diplomatii (Contemporary Soviet diplomacy)*. Moscow: Izdatelstvo IMO.

DEUTSCH, K. W. (1968) *The Analysis of International Relations*. Englewood Cliffs: Prentice-Hall.

DINERSTEIN, H. S. (1962) *War and the Soviet Union*. New York: Praeger.

DORAN, C. F. (1976) *Domestic Conflict in State Relations: The American Sphere of Influence*. Beverly Hills: Sage.

FOX, W. T. R. (1944) *The Super-Powers*. New York: Harcourt, Brace and Co.

FRANCK, T. M. and E. WEISBAND (1972) *Word Politics: Verbal Strategy Among the Superpowers*. New York: Oxford University Press.

GADDIS, J. L. (1972) *The United States and the Origins of the Cold War, 1941-1947*. New York: Columbia University Press.

GEORGE, A. L. and R. SMOKE (1974) *Deterrence in American Foreign Policy: Theory and Practice*. New York: Columbia University Press.

GOLDMANN, K. (1978) *Det internationella systemet: En teori och dess begränsningar*. Stockholm: Aldus.

HERZ, J. H. (1959) *International Politics in the Atomic Age*. New York: Columbia University Press.

HOFFMANN, S. (1968) *Gulliver's Troubles, or the Setting of American Foreign Policy*. New York: McGraw-Hill.

JERVIS, R. (1970) *The Logic of Images in International Relations*. Princeton: Princeton University Press.

—— (1976) *Perception and Misperception in International Politics*. Princeton: Princeton University Press.

KAHN, H. (1960) *On Thermonuclear War*. Princeton: Princeton University Press.

KAUFMAN, E. (1976) *The Superpowers and Their Spheres of Influence*. London: Croom Helm.
KEOHANE, R. O. (1971) 'The Big Influence of Small Allies', *Foreign Policy*, no. 2 (Spring, 1971): 161 – 182.
KISSINGER, H. A. (1969) *American Foreign Policy: Three Essays*. London: Weidenfeld and Nicolson.
KNORR, K. (1966) *On the Uses of Military Power in the Nuclear Age*. Princeton: Princeton University Press.
LEITENBERG, M. (1977) 'Threats of the Use of Nuclear Weapons Since WW II'. Paper presented to Symposium 'Armaments, Tension, and War' at Hanaholmen, Finland, 26 – 28 Sept. 1977.
MACK, A. (1975) 'Why Big Nations Lose Small Wars: The Politics of Assymetric Conflict', *World Politics*, 27, no. 2.
NASH, H. T. (1975) *Nuclear Weapons and International Behavior*. Leyden: A. W. Sijthoff.
NIEBUHR, R. (1964) 'The Social Myths in the "Cold War"', *Journal of International Affairs*, 21: 40 – 56.
OSGOOD, R. E. and R. W. TUCKER (1967) *Force, Order and Justice*. Baltimore: Johns Hopkins.
RAY, J. L. and C. GOCHMAN (1976) 'Capability Disparities in Latin America and Eastern Europe'. Paper prepared for 1976 IPSA Congress in Edinburgh, 15 – 21 Aug.
SCHELLING, T. C. (1963) *The Strategy of Conflict*. New York: Oxford University Press.
—— (1966) *Arms and Influence*. New Haven: Yale University Press.
SCHURMANN, F. (1974) *The Logic of World Power*. New York: Pantheon Books.
SHERWIN, M. J. (1975) *A World Destroyed. The Atomic Bomb and the Grand Alliance*. New York: Alfred A. Knopf.
SINGER, J. D. (1963) 'Inter-Nation Influence: A Formal Model', *APSR*, LVII: 420 – 430.
SIPRI (1976) *Armaments and Disarmament in the Nuclear Age: A Handbook*. Stockholm: Almqvist & Wiksell.
SPIEGEL, S. L. (1972) *Dominance and Diversity: The International Hierarchy*. Boston: Little, Brown.
TUCKER, R. C. (1963) *The Soviet Political Mind*. New York: Praeger.
ULAM, A. B. (1971) *The Rivals. America and Russia since World War II*. New York: The Viking Press.
WOLFE, T. W. (1964) *Soviet Strategy at the Crossroads*. Cambridge: Harvard University Press.

4 Capabilities, Issue-Areas, and Inter-State Power

Olav Knudsen
University of Oslo

INTRODUCTION

The aim of this chapter is to formulate tentatively certain theoretical ideas on how variation in issue-areas might affect the relationship between capabilities and power in international politics.

Just as some people consider it a service to humanity not to have children, I have resolved not to offer any *original* definition of power in the following. Instead, I should like to call attention to the fact that some definitions of power may be converted into, or simply regarded as, propositions capable of empirical testing.

The point that social science definitions often incorporate propositions about empirical relationships is perhaps rather obvious, yet it is not so frequently made (exceptions are Ayer, 1936:126 — 128; Selltiz et al, 1962:485n; Zetterberg 1965: 35 - 39; Nagel, 1975:175). One of the examples most familiar to international-relations specialists is probably the use of 'anarchy' as a defining characteristic of international systems.

Propositions, the thrust of which are seemingly obvious or well established, may over time acquire the form of definitions which we often accept without much further thinking. In the power literature this seems to be the case where *capabilities* are concerned: power is (in one way or another) said to be a matter of capabilities.

Author's note: In addition to participants in the ECPR planning session in Louvain-la-neuve, April 1976, I am indebted to Arild Underdal, Tor Chr. Hildan, and an anonymous reviewer for constructive, critical comments.

Of course, many of the general works on international politics properly discuss the cirumstances under which such assumptions may be valid (e.g. Morgenthau, 1948 and 1962:47–70; Sprout and Sprout, 1962: 136–189, 213–296, 365–391; Aron 1966:47–70; Holsti, 1972:158–171; and notably Knorr, 1975: passim). Nevertheless, it is hard to see how much of the literature on international politics over the years could have been written without this convenient simplification. As K. J. Holsti (1972:159) and others have indeed suggested, our lack of hesitation to use terms like 'super powers', 'great powers', and 'small powers' seems to indicate that the assumption is considered reasonably tenable in the field.

Even so, contrary ideas have been circulating in political science for years. Familiar examples are the notion of a *conversion* process transforming capabilities into effective power, the idea of *issue-specific power*, and the observation that power in international organization fora has become increasingly *incongruent* with power on the outside. But until recently very little use has been made of these 'revisionist' ideas in actual international-relations research. It may even be said that students of international politics have long shied away from any kind of analytical research involving power: We didn't know what to do with it other than to show *who had it*. The mindless measurement fad in the earlier years of behaviorist enthusiasm reinforced this inclination. Power could easily be measured in terms of GNP, steel production or other approximations resting on the power-capability assumption. Thus, the strength of the convention linking inter-state power to capabilities led to a massive begging of the questions one really should ask of power: *What are the sources of power under varying circumstances and conditions? What is the nature of the relationships between different types of power and power resources?*

The 1970s have brought a new wave of empirical studies, undertaken in many countries, which have raised these questions once more — explicitly or implicitly — with reference to international phenomena. A solid stock-taking of this new research is found in Keohane and Nye's recent book (1977) in which a variety of theoretical and empirical threads are gathered, synthesized and academically legitimated — the latter achievement being not the least important in this connection.

Keohane and Nye have illuminated the central questions in 'floodlight' fashion. In contrast, the present chapter offers a 'spotlight' approach to the power-capability problem, following a quite simple design. The traditional assumption is restated in the form of a theory. Subsequently, two alternative elaborations are shown to entail empirical expectations conflicting with the one derived from the traditional theory. The expectations are then tested empirically. In a final section, some important further implications are discussed.

Before the theories are presented, I will clarify the concepts of *capabilities* and *power*. In particular, making theories out of power definitions forces me to formulate a definition of power which is not logically implied by the independent variables of the theories. Bertrand Russell's analysis of power (1938 and 1946) is still in many ways a stimulating piece of work, and his definition of power is as clear as it is timeless: 'Power is the production of intended effects' (Russell, 1946:35).[1] Using this as my starting point, then, I shall define 'interstate power' as *a state's degree of achievement — by its own efforts — of goals which apply, in part or total, to conditions beyond its jurisdiction*. The definition does involve some significant problems of measurement, to which I shall return at a later stage. It should be noted, on the positive side, that Russell's way of solving the definitional problem has the particular advantage of not presupposing that power is *only* a matter of controlling others' behavior. (I am referring here to 'the Dahl tradition'; see, for example, Dahl (1957) and Singer (1963).) By no means all foreign policy goals held by national governments are achieved (or are achievable) by controlling the behavior of particular other governments or foreign political actors. Creating and maintaining particular *states of affairs* abroad are notable among the phenomena I am thinking of here.[2] Hence, power should not be reduced analytically to merely being a matter of inducement or deterrence (Wagner, 1969:3 – 4).

The term 'capabilities' also requires definition. Capabilities are here defined as resources of whatever kind — physical, human, intellectual — a government may choose to employ, or not employ, to aid it in the pursuit of its external goals. Hence, although the concept is broadly defined, it may be distinguished from other factors favorable (or unfavorable) to the actor in a situation in that *capabilities are restricted to those factors which may be applied to goal-seeking activities when the actor so desires.* Capabilities are subject to the actor's discretion. Normally, then, the concept refers to those resources that are within the government's effective jurisdiction. Thus, typically stochastic, situational (i.e. transient) factors, which may in decisive moments be more favorable to some actors than to others — and hence may be a sort of 'power resource' — are excluded here. In its general outline this concept of capabilities conforms pretty well with the ideas of Jones (1954), whose elaborations I find quite useful.[3]

Note that capabilities may refer either to particular resources or to the sum of all resources. To avoid confusion, therefore, in what follows the term 'capabilities' will denote the *sum* of all resources available to a state[4] when nothing else is said.

A THEORY OF GENERAL CAPABILITIES AND POWER

In order to get a clearer perspective on the different lines of thought applied to capabilities and power, I shall here map out the barest essentials of the theoretical elements and relationships.

There are four elements involved which are often related to each other in different ways by different authors. These elements are:

Capabilities (C): theoretical concept/variable.
Power (P): theoretical concept/variable.
Capability indicator(s) (CI): observable phenomena claimed to be adequate representations or measures of C.
Power indicator(s) (PI): observable phenomena claimed to be adequate representations or measures of P.

Now let us have a brief look at some more or less familiar ways of relating these elements to each other. One position, which to most of us would seem rather extreme, is to say that

$$C = P$$

and although I cannot offhand quote anybody on it, I do think I have run across this view at one time or another. More common is probably this one:

C is one of the defining characteristics of P.

Both positions may be presented along with the claim that

$$CI = PI$$

(strictly justified only in the first case) which is also often set forth without any of the prior statements — a much-used solution for analysts in a hurry to say other, more important things.[5]

A proper capability theory must define the elements of the pairs $C-P$, and $CI-PI$, independently of each other (i.e. independently within each pair). In skeleton form, such a theory would say '*C* is (in some further specified way) a cause of (or produces) *P*', which logically implies the empirical statement '*CI* is (in some further specified way) correlated with PI' (see also Keohane and Nye, 1977:53).

For a more complete formulation I shall use the following theoretical variables:

Power — as already defined, i.e. 'inter-state power' (*P*).
Ability of a state to apply physical coercion to other states (*AC*).
Capabilities of a state — the sum of human and non-human resources at its disposal, i.e. the sum total of its capabilities as defined above (*C*).

The following statements constitute axioms of the theory, i.e. axioms '...in the sense of an untested (or untestable) assumption, rather than...an assumption the truth of which is taken for granted' (Blalock 1969:11):

A.11: P is a direct, linear function of AC — and AC alone.
A.12: AC is a direct linear function of C.

The time relationship of these variables is $C-AC-P$.

(Linearity is here postulated simply as a convenient initial assumption.) From these two axioms is derived the theorem

P.11: P is a linear function of C.

However, a second and for my purposes crucial proposition is this:

P.12: P.11 holds true for all issue-areas of a state's foreign relations.

This requires a definition of issue-areas:

An issue-area is conceived as a cluster of functionally interrelated issues, i.e. unresolved situations concerning the distribution of a particular value or a set of correlated values, involving two or more actors (here: states), and having two or more possible different outcomes to which the actors attach different degrees of desirability or preference.[6]

Proposition P.12, in other words, states that capabilities are *generally effective* and not restricted to particular issue-areas in foreign policy, such as for instance military security (see Keohane and Nye, 1977:30, 43, 49 – 50). There are two (and possibly more) plausible ways of arriving at this proposition. The most obvious way, perhaps, is to claim that P.13 can be derived directly from the axioms.

But P.12 (and P.11) may also be advanced on the basis of another line of reasoning, which would restrict the proposition(s) historically to the industrial era and link ability to coerce in international politics with industrial development (see Knorr, 1975:38 and 45ff). In this view — or some variety of it — coercive capability may not be equally effective in all issue-areas, but the achievement of strong coercive capability requires the development of industry to a high level of sophistication and maximum diversity. Hence.

capabilities for a wide range of different activities are *by-products* of a quest for coercive capability. As indicated, this line of argument may be set up in a number of different ways, among which is also found the view of Organski (1958). P.12 may also be derived from the rank-theoretical statement that an actor which ranks high on one dimension will tend to rank high on all dimensions (see Galtung, 1966).

The empirical implication of P.11 and P.12 put together is that in any given issue-area of foreign policy, those states which score high on *CI* will also score high on PI, *when PI is measured specifically for that issue-area* (henceforth denoted *PI'*). Conversely, no state should score high on *PI'* which does not also score high on *CI*.

A THEORY OF TASK PERFORMANCE AND POWER

The alternative theory is one which negates the theorem P.12 above (see Keohane and Nye, 1977:29 – 30). That in itself, however, does not tell us very much. More specifically, this theory holds that capabilities cannot be isolated from tasks; that the concept of capabilities must be related to the concepts of *task* (or task type) and *task performance*, which in turn must be seen in relation to issue-areas (Keohane and Nye, 1977:50).

From this perspective, we can formulate a first axiom of this second theory: which is that:

A.21: Power, i.e. the achievement of preferred outcomes, in an issue-area is a direct function of the extent or quality of task performance for a (specified) limited range of tasks.

Futhermore, the theory claims that:

A.22: The importance of a given type of task (*T*) will vary from issue-area to issue-area.

Tasks have to do with short-range, specific, practical, governmental objectives (sub-goals) which must be reached in order to make progress towards whatever goal the state has set itself in the issue-area. Some objectives are of the kind which must be continuously sought, others may be 'one-shot affairs'. The term 'task' here embraces the concrete governmental activity(-ies) undertaken as well as the objective.[7]

The axiom does not claim that *all* tasks will be different if we compare any two issue-areas in international politics. Rather, the theory holds that a given task is more relevant to *some* issue-areas than to others, and that a given issue-area may involve the performance of only some tasks out of a larger range of tasks.

Tasks may be performed well, less well, or not at all, and so it seems appropriate to regard *task performance* as a matter of degree. It is a central claim of the theory that

> A.23: A given type of capability is not equally effective in the performance of all task types.

This statement introduces the concept of a capability's performance effectiveness (E) which may be defined as the amount of increase or improvement in the performance of a given task resulting from the employment of (a given amount of) the capability concerned. To perform a given task well, in other words, it is necessary to have the 'right' capabilities[8] (see also Knorr, 1975:50ff, 62ff, 76, 83 – 85, 93).

From the foregoing statements we may derive a theorem which, in plain language, says that power in a given issue-area is a (linear) function of the performance effectiveness of the actor's capabilities in that issue-area. More precisely:

> P.21: P' is a (linear) function of the sum over all capabilities of the products of performance effectiveness (E) and amount of the capability (C) possessed, summed in turn over all task types relevant to the issue-area.

The notion of linearity is not derivable from the axioms, and its presence in the theorem is therefore questionable — but also in principle testable.

We shall refer to an empirical indicator of E as EI. Another theorem which may be derived from the axioms above is that

P.22: When *EI* is substituted for *E* in the statement P.21, this gives a better predictor of *PI'* than *CI*.

At this point we have a fairly precise statement of our second theory. Any thought of serious testing, however, will stumble over the lack of indicators for the terms involved. But my ambitions for the present are more modest. I shall be content if it is possible to test two contradictory empirical statements against each other. And indeed, the second theory does imply an empirical statement which contradicts that of the first, namely

States ranking high on *CI* will not necessarily rank high on *PI'*.

The reservation ('not necesarily') refers to the fact that the theory, as stated, does not exclude the possibility of the specific capabilities subsumed under CI being the 'right' capabilities for the issue-area in question.

A THEORY OF POWER IN ROUTINE, MUTUALLY BENEFICIAL TRANSACTIONS

The same empirical statement may also be derived from a different theory involving issue-areas, but in this case the theory is based on a distinction between what is claimed to be fundamentally different *types* of issue-areas.

If we consider the totality of interaction between national societies, including governmental interaction, it is possible to identify some of these activities as what might be called *routine, mutually beneficial transactions*. More specifically, the characteristics of this type of international (or better: transnational) activities may be spelled out as follows:

— the activity in question should involve more than one national jurisdiction;
— the activity should be one of exchange;
— the activity should be continuous, in the sense that transactions are likely to be frequently repeated and that any two parties are likely to meet again to repeat their dealings.

- the exchange should involve expectations of some extent and kind of *benefit or gain* to the participants;
- the participants should in principle be free to enter and withdraw from the transactions, and change transaction partners, if they so choose; and
- participants may be private individuals, firms, voluntary associations, etc. or they may be public agencies.

Examples of such activities are international trade, international transport, international clearing arrangements for foreign exchange and payments, international reinsurance arrangements, agreements for the international exchange of technical or scientific information, etc.

Obviously, these transaction types may be described concretely in terms of the *values* involved in the activity, e.g. money, goods, transportation, information, etc. When disputes arise between states as to the distribution of the concrete values involved, an *issue*-area — in our terminology — becomes 'activated', as Rosenau would have put it (see e.g. Rosenau, 1966:81). For most transaction types there is a corresponding issue-area, usually concerning the public control, regulation, and supervision (and so also manipulation) of the activities involved. Thus, governments may in practice be involved both as participants in transactions and as actors in the issue-area. Whether participants are governmental or not, the theory is presented here with the simplifying assumption that a government will consider the interests of 'its' national participants in the transactions to be an integral part of its own interests in the issue-area. It is clear that this assumption does not always hold, but it is nevertheless indispensable here to make the analysis manageable.

The theory may be introduced by way of the following axioms:

A.31: The chief motivation for governmental behavior in issue-areas of this type is the desire to protect and maximize the benefits which the nation derives from the transactions concerned.

A.32: The derivation of benefits in routine, mutually beneficial transactions is a function of the predictability and continuity of the transactions.

We can derive from the axioms the theorem:

P.31: Governmental behavior which interferes with the predictability and continuity of transactions will be avoided in issue-areas of this type (see Knorr, 1975:215–216; Keohane and Nye, 1977:40).

A third axiom states that

A.33: Behavior which applies AC (i.e. coercion, as defined above) will interfere with the predictability and continuity of routine, mutually beneficial transactions (see Knorr, 1975:125–126).

From P.31 and A.33 we derive

P.32: Behavior which applies AC will be avoided in issue-areas of this type (see Keohane and Nye, 1977:103, 119–120).

To continue it is necessary to 'borrow' from the theory of general capabilities.

A.12: AC is a direct linear function of C.

With 'power in the issue-area' (P') still defined as the achievement of preferred outcomes in the issue-area, axiom A.31 and theorem P.32 lead further to

P.33: P' is not a function of AC,

which also implies

P.34: P' is not necessarily a function of C.

On this basis one arrives again at the empirical expectation that states ranking high on CI will not necessarily rank high on PI' for an issue-area of this particular type; and conversely, states ranking high on PI' are not necessarily expected to rank high on CI.

But the theory still leaves us without much of a clue as to the sources of power in such issue-areas. In fact, the theory involves a possible source of confusion in that it deals simultaneously with two sets of activities: transactions and issue-area activities. Both involve participants striving to achieve preferred outcomes, yet the term 'power' refers here only to the activities of governments in issue-areas. Why? Because empirically speaking the achievement of preferred outcomes in transactions can rarely be ascribed to power phenomena *alone*, but is often the result of market forces or similar phenomena beyond the control of individual participants. It may also be a combination of market forces and power.[9]

Power in issue-areas dealing with routine, mutually beneficial transactions therefore has to do with the efforts of a government to affect the *conditions under which the transactions take place* to make them more favorable to the derivation of national benefits. Hence, there is no simple cause-effect relationship between the activities of governments in the issue-area, and the benefits realized from the transactions. The promotion of the doctrine of free trade and the doctrine of free commercial shipping are examples of rather successful governmental efforts of this kind.

Returning to axioms A.31 and A.32, if we add

> A.34: The greater the *relative* benefits derived from the transactions (i.e. relative to national benefits derived from *other* activities), the stronger the desire to protect and maximize those benefits,

we can derive the proposition:

> P.35: The greater the relative benefits derived from the transactions, the stronger the desire to maintain the predictability and continuity of the transactions.

Finally, paraphrasing Hernes (1975:35) we introduce

> A.35: The more intense one's desires, the greater the power[10] of those who can grant or deny them,[11]

and arrive at

P.36: Power in an issue-area of this type is a partial negative function of the relative benefits derived from the transactions.

P.37: Power in an issue-area involving routine mutually beneficial transactions is a partial function of the ability to unilaterally alter the benefits accruing to others.

In other words, power in these issue-areas is a joint function of the unimportance of the transactions to the actor himself and the importance to others of transacting with him.[12] Empirical indicators of the benefits derived from these kinds of transactions are likely to be hard to come by, but we should expect such an indicator (BI) to be correlated with an indicator of power in the issue-area (PI').

PROCEDURES OF MEASUREMENT

The theories require that we establish empirically which are the high-scoring states in terms of CI and PI'. The question of what is meant by a 'high' score is impossible to answer definitely, and a cut-off point which does not seem excessively arbitrary must be found. An important consideration in this regard must be the possible effect of the cut-off point on the results obtained. In the present case the greater the number of states included in the high category the easier it would be to disconfirm the general capability theory. I have chosen the nice, round figure of 10 as what I consider a reasonable number, but will also show what the results would be with a smaller number. (With a greater number, it seems, the idea of a high score would gradually become rather vague.)

As for the particular measures chosen, I propose to use, for CI, the composite world power rating developed by Cox and Jacobson (1973:437ff). This index combines GNP, GNP-per-capita, population, nuclear capability, and prestige by a special weighting procedure explained in detail in the source. It may be of interest to note that the ten high-ranking states in 1967 according to the Cox/Jacobson ratings are identical with the ten high-ranking states by GNP alone in 1964 (Taylor and Hudson, 1972:306), although the specific ranks among them are different. Other indicators, or other ways of constructing indices, could of course have been employed.

However, since we know (Cox and Jacobson, 1973:437ff; Petrén, 1976:58 – 62) that several of them yield the same top ten states with differences only in specific ranks, the present measure is fully adequate for my purposes.[13] (The theories do not require any ranking *within* the high-categories.)

Measures of power in the issue-area of shipping, by contrast, cannot simply be looked up in the literature. ('Shipping' is here defined as the international commercial carriage of goods by sea, and activities related to this, such as the determination of freight rates, procurement of cargo, shipbuilding, etc. Further elaboration on the 'borders' of this issue-area is found in Knudsen, 1973:13 – 24.) In what follows *PI* will be represented by a measure of 'influence in shipping' whose correspondence with the concept of 'power in an issue-area' (as previously defined) is not completely satisfactory. Nevertheless, the results have certain qualities — on which further comment is found below — which may allay some otherwise justifiable doubts. In any case, the measurement procedures do require some explication.

The method of assessing influence chosen here is the *reputational method*: the interviewing of presumably well-informed persons. The main rationale for using the reputational method should normally be the *inaccessibility* of the political process itself. That is also the case here. Raymond Wolfinger, in a thoroughgoing and, at first glance, almost devastating critique of the method, claims that it is useful only 'as a systematic first step in studying a city's political system rather than a comprehensive technique for discovering the distributions of power' (Wolfinger, 1963:704). That may be true for studies at the micro level, but even here his assertion may be somewhat overstated. It ignores the problem of accessibility, and even at the local level it may presumably be difficult at times to uncover influence structures by more direct methods (Merton, 1968).

The processes of interaction between governments have always been marked by secrecy and incomplete information as to what actually takes place. To get at influence structures in international politics the researcher thus has little choice but to employ indirect methods.

On certain conditions the reputational method seems to offer considerable promise. The conditions demanded by Wolfinger are that the judges must have exceptional knowledge of the processes they are evaluating; that issue-areas must be taken into account; that it must be clear to respondent as well as interviewer what is meant by 'influence'; and that the discovery of a group of influentials says nothing about whether they form a cohesive group (or elite), or are in opposition to each other. A few problems not raised by Wolfinger will also be considered.

The reputational method relies on interviews with 'well-placed judges', to use Robert Dahl's phrase, to ascertain who is influential in a given context. But:

> The big disadvantage of the method is that it puts us at the mercy of the judges — and how are we to determine who are the best judges? Even seemingly well-placed observers can be misled by false reputations; they may attribute great power where little or none exists (Dahl 1963:52).

This aspect is fairly well taken care of in the present case. The judges chosen were all delegates to a specialized committee of UNCTAD dealing exclusively with shipping matters. There is, of course, no *guarantee* of expertise and insight implicit in this. Some information on the personal background of the 34 judges (from as many countries) would be appropriate for clarification. First of all, one might ask whether the judges generally had a high or low status within their country's delegation to the Committee on Shipping. Here, the respondents were grouped in three categories: *representative* (i.e. head of delegation), *alternate representative*, and *other* (predominantly advisers). Of the 34, 19 were representatives, 15 were alternate representatives, and none were found at the lower level. Considering that the choice of specific respondent was left up to each delegation, this result must be considered quite satisfactory.

A more important question would still be the extent of actual shipping expertise among the respondents. In response to a question on their professional status *apart from* their specific assignments to the Committee on Shipping, 19 described themselves as government officials working exclusively with shipping matters in the home country, and 4 respondents gave their place of work as the department of trade or foreign affairs in the home country. In other words, 23 out of 34 had come from their home country to Geneva for the sole purpose of attending the session of the Committee on Shipping. (Presumably, if there had been no particular need for expertise, the government would have used a member of its permanent mission in Geneva instead.) The remaining 11 respondents were stationed at the permanent UN mission in Geneva, or at embassies in neighboring countries. The overall picture is that of a quite adequate level of expertise in shipping, and of a most satisfactory level of formal rank in their delegations, among the 34 judges.

As to the method itself, the specific procedure employed was to ask the respondent, within the framework of an interview (in ten cases a questionnaire had to be used instead of the interview), *which countries he felt were the more influential ones in the Committee on Shipping.* In the overwhelming majority of cases there was no indication that 'influence' was a concept foreign to the respondent. On a few occasions, however, a further explanation of what was meant proved to be necessary. The standard elaboration used in such cases was *effectiveness in persuading other countries to adopt or support their positions, or in raising support for draft resolutions.* (Wolfinger, 1963:706 – 7 also comments on this.)

Six of the 34 did not answer the question on influence, but only one refused outright. The other five gave various evasive replies.

All told, from a methodological point of view the assessment of influence in shipping must be deemed fairly successful and as falling within the general standards of acceptability for that kind of research task (Best, 1960; Keohane, 1965; Jacobson, 1967; Miles, 1970). The complete rankings are given in Appendix A. As is shown there, two different ways of processing the respondents' answers yielded somewhat different results. Still, the top ten states were the same in both cases, which fulfills the present requirements.

TESTING

To recapitulate, the general-capabilities theory expects that states ranking high on *CI* (indicator of general capabilities) will also rank high on *PI* (power in a specific issue-area). The expectation of the two other theories is that this is not necessarily so. The results are shown in Table 1.

TABLE 1

Distribution of states ranking among the world's ten highest on general capabilities (CI) and on influence in international shipping (PI').

(Data for CI from 1967, for PI' from 1968.)

		Influence in international shipping (PI')*	
		High (ranks 1-10)	Lower (ranks 11-)
General capabilities (CI)*f*	High (ranks 1-10)	United Kingdom** United States** India** Japan**	USSR** France** China West Germany Italy Canada
	Lower (ranks 11-)	Norway Netherlands Brazil** Sweden Denmark Pakistan	(excluded)

* Influence by reputation among delegates to UNCTAD Committee on Shipping. Interviews and questionnaires.
** States ranking among the top ten on influence in UNCTAD generally, as measured by Nye (1973:362) in 1968-69. (Positive and negative influence combined.)
f General capabilities measured by Cox and Jacobson (1973:442) in an index of world power combining GNP per capita, population, nuclear capability, and prestige. For scoring rules, see Cox and Jacobson (ibid.).

There can be little doubt about the outcome: our confidence in the general-capabilities theory is weakened by the test, whereas our confidence in the two others is strengthened. Furthermore, the results are not affected by the cut-off point: if we restrict the high group to five states, there will still be three of those high on *PI* which should not be there according to the general-capabilities theory. Even going down to three leaves two out of three states in contradiction of this theory. On the other hand, Table 1 also shows that the measure of influence employed here does not simply tap the *general* influence of states in the affairs of UNCTAD, as measured by Nye.

The design of the experiment has a basic flaw, however, since it does not help us solve the question *which of the two remaining theories is 'better'*? We are still left with the intriguing question of sources of influence in this issue-area (or in issue-areas of this *type*, covering routine, mutually beneficial transactions). In principle, the theories as stated have already set the stage for a further test, if only adequate indicators for *EI* and *BI* can be found. However, I shall have to save that task for a later occasion.

CONCLUDING REMARKS: SOME FURTHER IMPLICATIONS

We are apparently left with theories two and three in a state of competition. But it is also possible, as I shall argue here, that they may be mutually compatible. The theory of task performance emphasizes the ability to bring about desired *states of affairs*, whereas the theory of mutually beneficial transactions stresses the ability to change others' behavior. In international shipping the task performance aspect of power may perhaps be found first of all in *maritime expertise* (technological and economic), while the potential for inducement or deterrence of others may reside in a favorable position in the *transaction network of shipping*. I should like to attach some further comments to these hypotheses.

Returning to the theory of power in routine, mutually beneficial transactions, it will be recalled that theorems P.36 and P.37 taken together suggest what are likely to be the *bases* of power. However, where the *exercise* of power is concerned, P.31 indicates a probable preference among participating governments for methods of conflict resolution, and for ways of exercising power, which are quiet, predictable and not disruptive of ongoing transactions. Now, if power bases such as those specified in P.36 and P.37 were to be *put into use*, the consequences would certainly not be compatible with P.31. In most political systems such problems lead to the development of *institutionalized* and *legitimized* power relations. In other words, the theory may be elaborated to predict that power relations are likely to become institutionalized and legitimized in such issue-areas, at least among those countries which have the greater (rather than smaller) interests to protect — and no matter how much their interests may be in conflict with each other.[14] The incentives for institutionalization and legitimization are (1) the consequences flowing from disrupted transactions, and (2) the relative importance of the transaction type to each government.

Institutionalization refers both to the establishment of intergovernmental organizations and agreed procedures for conflict management, to the development of international law and — not to be forgotten — to agreed procedures for the normal, daily conduct of transactions (Keohane and Nye, 1977: 19 – 22). Maritime transport provides striking examples of such processes, with cooperative bodies such as the Maritime Transport Committee — a formal structure — and the more exclusive Consultative Shipping Group, which is set up as a tightly sealed informal organ, both under the larger umbrella of the OECD. International shipping, moreover, has a highly developed system of international law, and standardized international practices (promoted by IMCO) for navigation, safety, bills of lading, charter parties, insurance, environmental protection, etc. (Knudsen, 1975).

Legitimization refers to a tendency on the part of the participating governments to accept, with little or no questioning, that those states which ostensibly possess relevant power bases (like those described in the combination of P.36 and P.37) should have a greater voice in the running of things than others.[15] Aron quite nicely points out how this worked in the European Concert (Aron, 1966:58), and Keohane and Nye demonstrate the same point in rich detail for their issue areas of 'ocean affairs' and 'monetary relations' (1977: passim, but esp. ch. 3 and 6). This tendency, likewise, is well illustrated in the handling of maritime transport affairs in the OECD (Knudsen, 1975).

Finally, both legitimization and institutionalization, to the extent they occur, would probably make the political system of a given issue-area rather insensitive to changes in the power base. One would expect a time-lag between changes in power base and corresponding changes in institutions and legitimacy, and the resultant incongruence might contribute to the occurrence of disruptive crises in the system (Keohane and Nye, 1977:52, 55 – 56). In international shipping, the ability to provide transport (cargo space) appears to have been the main base of power from the introduction of steamships until about the middle of this century. Since then, however, there has been a trend of increasing oversupply of cargo space, combined with an increasing willingness of governments to manipulate the allocation of outbound (in many cases also inbound) cargo in favor of national-flag vessels. Gradually, in other words, the power base in shipping has shifted from control of cargo space to control of the cargo flow — making *volume of seaborne trade* the new, chief power resource in shipping.

It should be observed that when I interviewed delegates to the UNCTAD Committee on Shipping in 1969, there had been no serious challenge to the established power structure — which may also account for the results obtained at that point. However, a major crisis in OECD shipping cooperation erupted in 1973 over the UN proposal to regulate liner shipping cartels. The first preparations for this *UN Code of Conduct for Liner Conferences* were started in 1970 — one year after my interviews. In the subsequent negotiations and finalizing votes during the winter 1973 – 74, the OECD countries were consistently split down the middle: shipowning nations on one side, trading nations on the other. In the end, the formerly powerful shipowning nations were unable to prevent the adoption of an important international legal instrument whose very spirit seemed contrary to their interests. Thus, the Code may conceivably turn out to be the first important step towards the institutionalization of a new power structure based on trade volume rather than shipping tonnage.

The story of shipping will not be elaborated further. It seems to suggest, however, that the theory of routine, mutually beneficial transactions holds some promise for the understanding of nonviolent, inter-state power relations. The next step should be to bring it to bear on issue-areas of a comparable type.

APPENDIX A: THE STRUCTURE OF INFLUENCE IN SHIPPING IN 1969

The evaluation of the chosen judges regarding the influence of states in shipping affairs can be processed in several ways. Two of them will be presented here. In each case the respondent was asked to name the three or four most influential states, whereupon he was told to rank those mentioned among themselves. A considerable number of delegates objected to the latter part of the question: they were willing to indicate several influential states, but not to say who among these were most influential. Thus, the simplest procedure is probably to rank the countries according to the number of times they were mentioned. This is done in Table A.1.

The other way of processing the responses concerning influence is to use the rankings performed *by the respondents*. As mentioned, many delegates objected to the request to rank influential states among themselves. However, ten respondents did comply with this request, and their ranking therefore forms the basis of the second ranking list (see Table A.2).

The difference between these two influence rankings should be made clear. In the first one (Table A.1), all states mentioned as influential were ranked on the assumption that those which are mentioned more frequently are likely to be more influential. In the second ranking list (Table A.2), the states were ranked by a special computation of ranks which had been assigned to them by each respondent separately.

The procedure for this computation in Table A.2 requires some explanation.

Although no more than 13 states were ranked by any one of the ten respondents, a total of 21 states were mentioned by them altogether. It was therefore assumed that there were 21 states each to be assigned a place on the ranking list. For each of the ten rankings yielded by the respondents, each single state was given a new score equal to 20 (i.e. 21 minus itself, or equal to the number of

TABLE A.1

Rank of states by attributed influence in shipping affairs, 1969. (Number of times mentioned by 28 respondents; maximum attainable score = 28.)

Rank	Country	No. of times identified as influential
1	United Kingdom	23
2	Brazil	20
3	Norway	18
4	USA	15
5.5	India	14
5.5	Netherlands	14
7	Japan	12
8	Sweden	10
9	Denmark	9
10	Pakistan	8
11.5	France	6
11.5	USSR	6
13.5	West Germany	5
13.5	Ghana	5
15	Indonesia	4
16.5	Chile	3
16.5	UAR	3
19.5	Italy	2
19.5	Ivory Coast	2
19.5	Nigeria	2
19.5	Poland	2

Source: Interviews with delegates to the 3rd session of UNCTAD's Committee on Shipping, April 1969, and questionnaires to delegates not interviewed. The questionnaires were all completed and returned in the period June-December 1969.

TABLE A.2

Rank of states by attributed influence in shipping affairs, 1969. (Attributed rank, by ten respondents.)

Rank	Country	Influence score (maximum = 20)	Number of times explicitly ranked (maximum = 10)	From Table A1: rank by number of times mentioned
1	United Kingdom	13.9	8	1
2	Norway	12.1	8	3
3	Netherlands	11.7	8	5.5
4	USA	10.9	7	4
5	India	10.2	8	5.5
6	Brazil	9.2	7	2
7	Sweden	7.4	5	8
8	Japan	6.6	5	7
9	Denmark	5.7	4	9
10	Pakistan	5.2	4	10
11.5	France	4.7	4	11.5
11.5	West Germany	4.7	3	13.5
13	USSR	4.3	3	11.5
14.5	Poland	2.1	2	19.5
14.5	UAR	2.1	2	16.5
16.5	Italy	1.8	1	19.5
16.5	Liberia	1.8	1	—
18.5	Ghana	1.6	1	13.5
18.5	Greece	1.6	1	—
20.5	Chile	1.0	1	16.5
20.5	Indonesia	1.0	1	15

Source: as in Table A1.

states *lower* in rank than itself) minus the number of other states ranked equally high or higher by that respondent. For example, one respondent ranked seven influential states as follows: 'Norway, UK, and the Netherlands are the three most influential states. Japan follows closely behind these three. Greece is somewhat less influential, but is more influential than Sweden and Denmark.' On this basis, Norway, UK, and the Netherlands each got a score (20-2) = 18 (i.e. 20 minus two other states ranked equally high; none were ranked higher). Similarly, Sweden and Denmark each received the score (20 − 6) = 14, (i.e. 20 minus 1 ranked equally high and 5 ranked higher).

For each state the scores it received from all ten respondents were summed and divided by 10. (See also the right-hand column in Table A.2, showing how many of the ten respondents mentioned each state.)

Also, the reader will observe that four states (Ivory Coast, Nigeria, Liberia and Greece) are present in only one of the two listings. There are two reasons for this. First, in Table A.1 states mentioned only once were excluded to guard against those mentioning themselves. In Table A.2 this requirement was dropped to avoid excluding entire rankings. Secondly, the ten respondents for Table A.2 mentioned only 21 states as influential, while the twenty-eight respondents for Table A.1 mentioned 24 states.

Because of the way in which the ranks were computed for Table A.2, it can be described as a weighted version of Table A.1. *Both* the frequency with which states were mentioned *and* the ranks which were attributed to them go into this measure. It is therefore likely that Table A.2 gives the most accurate picture of the distribution of influence in shipping (to the extent that influence in the Committee on Shipping is not significantly different from influence in shipping otherwise).

The most important difference between the two tables is the lower rank of Brazil in Table A.2 — for the rest the two lists are remarkably similar. Brazil's lower rank here is supported by comments made by several delegates during the interviews, to the effect that there is more 'bark than bite' to Brazil's influence. This may be a kind of phenomenon likely to be glossed over by the pure frequency measure: Brazil's high level of activity makes it easy to notice, but that says nothing about its relative influence. (Among the less developed members of the Committee on Shipping, Brazil has been the most outspoken critic of the policies of traditional, Western maritime powers.)

APPENDIX B: THE COX/JACOBSON POWER RATINGS FOR 1967 (Excerpts)

Rank order	Country	Score
1	United States	26
2	USSR	24
3	France	20
5	China	19
5	Japan	19
5	United Kingdom	19
7	Western Germany	18
8	Italy	17
9.5	Canada	16
9.5	India	16
11	Sweden	14
15	Australia	13
15	Austria	13
15	Brazil	13
15	Netherlands	13
15	Spain	13
15	Switzerland	13
15	Yugoslavia	13

Source: Cox and Jacobson (1973:442).

NOTES

1. This is an early (although certainly not the first) version of the 'power-over-outcomes' approach. The leading statement of this version of power theory currently seems to be that of Coleman (1966). A more recent alternative formulation is found in Nagel (1975), emphasizing the causal aspect (further discussed in Chapter 9 of the present volume). Applications to international politics research are discussed in Hart (1976).
2. Obviously, the more complex the outcome, the more difficult it is to trace it analytically to any particular actor. 'Power over outcomes' thus may be viewed fruitfully in causal terms as a partial coefficient: social outcomes are usually caused by a multiplicity of factors, and the causal effects of the efforts of a particular actor will often be only one of these (see Nagel, 1975). When the efforts of the actor in question are only weakly related to the outcome it seems less meaningful to speak of 'power'.
3. See also Knorr (1975:38, 45ff).
4. The concept of *sanctions* is not going to be much use here. Nevertheless, I should like to comment on the relationship between the two terms. If we have a situation involving two actors and two or more possible courses of action to which the actors attach different degrees of preference, we may define *sanctions* as whatever element actor A is (independently) able to introduce in the situation with the effect of *altering the preferences* of actor B. When the terms are defined in this way, the concept of capabilities subsumes that of sanctions; i.e. 'capabilities' is a broader concept. One may also note that the concept of sanctions thus defined is more appropriately used in connection with power defined as the modification of the behavior of others which, as pointed out, is narrower than the power definition chosen here.
5. Knorr (1975) gives a comprehensive discussion of the $C-P$ relation. See also Chapter 7 in this volume.

Cox and Jacobson (1973) have a more sophisticated way of bolstering their use of $CI = PI$. In their appendix on measuring power, they state their position thusly:

> 'Power' is used here in reference to states. It is the potential of a state for wielding external influence. *Power is conceived as a function of a number of component factors*: the amount of resources, the extent to which these resources can be effectively mobilized to exert influence, skill in using resources, and willingness to use them (1973:437). (Emphasis added.)

It seems then that Cox and Jacobson prefer to state the relationship between C and P in the form of a proposition which, being part of the definition, actually plays the role of an axiom: it is *assumed* to be tenable and so will not be tested in that particular study. Just a few paragraphs later, however, they demonstrate the strength of their belief in its tenability, when the component factors of which 'power is...a function...' are referred to as 'the components of power' (ibid.). I consider this a slip-of-the-pen which only goes to show how easy it is to make intellectual 'short circuits' in this area. Cox and Jacobson then proceed to use GNP, percapita GNP, population, nuclear capability, and prestige as indicators of their 'components of power'. (Their approach will also be used here, except that here it will represent the term *CI*. See below.)

6. Formulation partly borrowed from and partly inspired by Rosenau (1966) and by Hernes (1975): see the latter's definition of HENDELSE (event) on p. 28. See also Coleman (1966) who gives Hernes his point of departure.

7. Examples of tasks are the negotiation of agreements with other states (found in most issue-areas); the monitoring of legal and administrative practices in other countries regarding, for example, sea-borne trade, which is a standard task of OECD countries' shipping policies; the conduct of military manoevers which is a task of military security policies; the production of military weaponry which is a task of the same issue-area; the control and supervision of amounts of catch and types of gear used, which are tasks of fisheries policies; the keeping of month-by-month statistics which is a crucial task in several economic issue-areas such as foreign trade and monetary policies; and the tracing of the origin of components of imported goods which is a task of foreign trade policies under free trade agreements.

8. Strictly speaking, the theory at this point should introduce both a typology of tasks and a typology of capabilities. I have no good excuse for my neglect here, except that for the present purposes it is possible to do without it.

9. See also note 2 above. Note that Knorr does not consider power to be involved in such activities (Knorr, 1975:80 – 81, 135). Still, he discusses such phenomena briefly under the heading of 'market power' (Knorr, 1975:100 – 101).

10. Note that 'power' here is used in a narrower sense, i.e. as the ability to modify the behavior of others.

11. Cf. Keohane and Nye (1977:11); 'Less dependent actors can often use the interdependent relationship as a source of power in bargaining over an issue and perhaps to affect other issues.'

12. Another dimension, which perhaps should have been included here for greater clarity, is the *availability of alternatives*, both to the power holder (P.36) and to others (P.37). Where P.37 is concerned, however, this consideration may be said to be covered implicitly by the formulation 'ability to unilaterally alter the benefits accruing to others'. Keohane and Nye stress the importance of this point — in their terminology the 'vulnerability dimension' (Keohane and Nye, 1977: 13ff).

13. In a cluster analysis of 171 'power indicators' for the late 1950s and 190 for the early 1970s, Petrén found GDP to be the first-entering indicator in the main cluster at both time cuts. Among the other indicators in this cluster were *investment, energy consumption, energy production,* and *defense expenditures* (Petrén, 1976:41 – 52). Her ten main 'conventional power indicators' yield nine of the ten top-ranking states according to Cox and Jacobson (Petrén, 1976:61).

14. Keohane and Nye have made this question of *international regimes* a central theme of their book, and develop a theory of regime change which is much more elaborate than the ideas sketched here. However, I have reservations to their analysis, particularly that of the oceans case, in which they assume that the relevant capabilities for issue-specific power are *naval* capabilities. This is an oversimplification which brings them into problems when explaining certain regime changes, especially the one in 1967. Analytically, the problem stems partly from an

imprecise definition of 'issue area' (many 'oceans issues' are hardly *functionally related* at all, which is politically much more important than 'perceived' linkages), and partly from their lack of attention to the significance of the *functional applicability* of a power resource to the activities of an issue area. In the oceans case, two new and highly relevant power resources are thus insufficiently recognized by the authors: on seabed issues, technological capability to exploit seabed resources; and on 'navigation' issues, political willingness to manipulate cargo flows by the nationality criterion (Keohane and Nye, 1977: ch. 3 and 6). My own argument in the present chapter is therefore different from theirs, in that issue-specific power resources are held to be those which enable the actor to manipulate the activities concerned *directly*. Indeed, Keohane and Nye undermine their own analysis from the start by showing that naval force has only limited applicability in peaceful ocean affairs.

15. Cf. Goldmann's concept of 'diffuse power', Chapter 1 in the present volume.

REFERENCES

ARON, R. (1966) *Peace and War*. New York: Doubleday & Co.
AYER, A. J. (1936) *Language, Truth and Logic*. Harmondsworth (England): Penguin Books (Pelican Books) edition 1971.
BEST, G. (1960) 'Diplomacy in the United Nations'. Unpublished Ph.D. dissertation. Northwestern University.
BLALOCK, H. M., Jr. (1969) *Theory Construction*. Englewood Cliffs, N.J.: Prentice-Hall.
COLEMAN, J. (1966) 'Foundations for a Theory of Collective Decisions'. *American Journal of Sociology*, 71:615 — 627.
COX, R. W. and K. JACOBSON (1973) 'Appendix A. The Stratification of Power', in: Cox and Jacobson (eds.) *The Anatomy of Influence*. New Haven: Yale University Press.
DAHL, R. A. (1957) 'The Concept of Power', *Behavioral Science*, 2:210 – 215.
—— (1963) *Modern Political Analysis*. Englewood Cliffs, N.J.: Prentice-Hall.
GALTUNG, J. (1966) 'International Relations and International Conflicts: A Sociological Approach'. Transactions of the Sixth World Congress of Sociology. Evian.
HART, J. (1976) 'Three Approaches to the Measurement of Power in International Relations', *International Organization*, 30:289 – 305.
HERNES, G. (1975) *Makt og Avmakt*. Oslo: Universitetsforlaget.
HOLSTI, K. J. (1972) *International Politics* 2nd edn. Englewood Cliffs, N.J.: Prentice-Hall.
JACOBSON, H. K. (1967) 'Deriving Data from Delegates to International Assemblies', *International Organization*, 21:592 – 613.

JONES, B. (1954) 'The Power Inventory and National Strategy', *World Politics*, 6:421 – 452.
KEOHANE, R. O. (1965) 'Political Practice in the United Nations General Assembly'. Unpublished Ph.D. thesis. Harvard University.
—— and J. S. Nye (1977) *Power and Interdependence: World Politics in Transition*. Boston: Little, Brown.
KNORR, K. (1975) *The Power of Nations. The Political Economy of International Relations*. New York: Basic Books.
KNUDSEN, O. (1973) *The Politics of International Shipping*. Lexington, Mass.: D. C. Heath & Co.
—— (1975) 'Political Engineering in Liner Shipping: The Code of Conduct for Liner Conferences', *Arkiv for sjørett*, 12:577 – 543.
MERTON, R. K. (1968) *Social Theory and Social Structure*. Revised edition. New York: Free Press.
MILES, E. (1970) 'The Logistics of Interviewing in International Organizations', *International Organization*, 24:361 – 370.
MORGENTHAU, H. J. (1948 and 1962) *Politics Among Nations*, 3rd edn., 2nd repr. New York: Knopf.
NAGEL, J. (1975) *The Descriptive Analysis of Power*. New Haven: Yale University Press.
NYE, J. S. (1973) 'UNCTAD — Poor Nations' Pressure Group', in: Cox and Jacobson (eds.), *The Anatomy of Influence*. New Haven: Yale University Press.
ORGANSKI, A. F. K. (1958) 'The Power Transition', reprinted in Rosenau (ed.), *International Politics and Foreign Policy*, 1st edn. New York: Free Press of Glencoe, 1961.
PETRÉN, K. (1976) 'Maktstrukturens huvuddrag. En kvantitativ analys av 20 maktindikatorer'. UI Research Reports, UI-76-2. Stockholm: Utrikespolitiska Institutet.
ROSENAU, J. N. (1966) 'Pre-Theories and Theories of Foreign Policy', in: R. Barry Farrell (ed.), *Approaches to Comparative and International Politics*. Evanston, Ill.: Northwestern University Press.
RUSSELL, B. (1946) *Power. A New Social Analysis*, 5th impr. London: Allen & Unwin.
SELLTIZ, C. et al. (1962) *Research Methods in Social Relations*. New York: Holt, Rinehart & Winston.
SINGER, J. D. (1963) 'Internation Influence: A Formal Model', *American Political Science Review*, 57:420 – 430.
SPROUT, H. and M. Sprout (1962) *Foundations of International Politics*.Princeton, N.J.: Van Nostrand.
TAYLOR, C. L., and M. C. HUDSON (1972) *World Handbook of Political and Social Indicators*. New Haven: Yale University Press.
WAGNER, R. H. (1969) 'The Concept of Power and the Study of Politics', in: Bell, Edwards, and Wagner (eds.), *Political Power*. New York: Macmillan – Free Press.

WOLFINGER, R. E. (1963) 'Reputation and Reality in the Study of Community Power', in: Polsby, Dentler and Smith (eds.), *Politics and Social Life*. Boston: Houghton Mifflin Co.

ZETTERBERG, H. L. (1965) *On Theory and Verification in Sociology*. Totowa, N.J.: The Bedminster Press.

5 Tension Between the Strong, and the Power of the Weak: Is the Relation Positive or Negative?

Kjell Goldmann
University of Stockholm

INTRODUCTION

It has become common to point out that East-West détente is a mixed blessing. Soviet – American cooperation to dominate the world was one of Charles de Gaulle's visions.[1] More recently Olof Palme, the former Swedish Prime Minister, has become known for emphasizing that détente is problematic for smaller states. We are, according to Palme, living 'in a time when the hegemony of the superpowers grows stronger and stronger', and détente between them may mean 'a threat to the independence of the small nations'.[2] Such fears seem to have become widespread.

Suggestive episodes from recent history are easily recalled, as are analogies in other contexts than the international one; consider for example how the position of the consumer is affected by the formation of a producers' cartel, or the extent to which the influence of the FDP is determined by the relations between the SPD and the CDU/CSU. At a theoretical level similar ideas have been applied to international systems by Galtung-inspired peace researchers (Wallensteen, Vesa and Väyrynen, 1973: 14 – 17).

The argument, obvious as it may seem, becomes less persuasive if one recalls that not so many years ago the opposite thesis was put forward by many people: that the Cold War had forced most states into the orbit of one superpower or the other, and that this fact had deprived them of much of their independence. The present essay takes as its point of departure what the two views have in common: the assumption that it is a significant aspect of the power structure of a social system whether relations between its leading components are essentially cooperative or essentially conflictful. The object is to clarify how and why this may be the case. Neither a formalized theory nor systematic empirical evidence will be reported here, but the essay may be seen as the first step towards such a theory and such empirical research.

The concept of power is used here in the way explained in Chapter 1 of this volume. The possession of power is seen as a disposition and hence as a general hypothesis about the relation between one actor's preferences and another actor's behaviour: the statement 'A has power over B' implies the prediction that if A prefers B to do x, then B will actually do x. A's control of B's behaviour is the essence of this way of defining the concept 'the possession of power'. Power in this sense can be seen as a quality that is distributed among the members of a social system; at least if the distribution of power is relatively significant, enduring, and simple we may refer to it as the system's 'power structure' (see Chapter 1, second section).

The common way of identifying international power structures is to examine what was called in Chapter 1 the 'power base' of the members of the system. By A's power base in relation to B is then meant those characteristics of A, of the relation between A and B, and of the larger system in which A and B are components, which lead to A's possessing power over B. The power base of an actor consists of a number of 'power base elements', abbreviated PBEs. It was suggested in Chapter 1 that our main problem, when trying to identify international power structures, is the primitivity of our knowledge about power bases. In particular, even when we can take it for granted that a phenomenon may function as a PBE, we rarely know much about to what extent, under what circumstances, and in what respects this phenomenon will actually provide an actor with power over others. The present essay may be seen as a modest contribution to the task of improving our 'power base theories'.

The power of the small state is the 'dependent variable' in the following discussion, and the nature of the relations between the Great Powers is the 'independent variable'. It has been debated whether 'small state' is a useful concept and whether it is possible to distinguish meaningfully between 'Great Powers' and 'small states' (Amstrup, 1976). In the context of the present analysis this is a marginal problem, however. The essay is concerned with systems in which power is distributed in such a way that a few members have much more power than all the others; we assume that the international system is of this type; and the question we ask is how the size of the power gap between great and small, strong and weak, is affected by changes in the nature of the relationship between the great, the strong. No harm is done by using the familiar terms Great Powers and small states to denote the strong and the weak in the international system. However, in order both to simplify the text and to suggest that the analysis may be applicable to social systems consisting of other components than states, the symbols S_i and W_i will frequently be used to denote a Great (= Strong) and a Small (= Weak) Power, respectively.

The expression 'the *power* of the weak' refers not only to the 'offensive' but also to the 'defensive' power of small states; this distinction was introduced in Chapter 1. It is common to discuss the position of small states vis-à-vis the Great Powers in terms of the 'freedom of action' or the 'freedom of movement' of the former; our concept 'defensive power' is largely synonymous with these notions, and the question of how the nature of the relations between the Great Powers may affect the freedom of action of small states is thus at the heart of the essay.

So much for the dependent variable. The independent variable has hitherto been described in loose terms as the 'nature of the relations' between the Great Powers and the like. From now on the term 'tension' will be used, defined in the following way: tension exists between two actors, or coalitions of actors, to the extent that they expect conflict behaviour to occur between them.[3] The question we ask concerns how increases and decreases in tension between the Great Powers affect the international system's power structure.

It should be pointed out that we are not simply comparing the power effects of Great Power collusion with those of Great Power collision. That would have been a trivial undertaking. One of the reasons why tension is interesting as the independent variable is that the relation between détente and collusion is less than self-evident. Whether détente implies large-scale collusion is uncertain, and that collusion may occur in periods of high tension is well known; the combined Soviet and American pressure on Israel in November 1956 is a dramatic illustration of the fact that the gap is sometimes narrow between collision and collusion.[4]

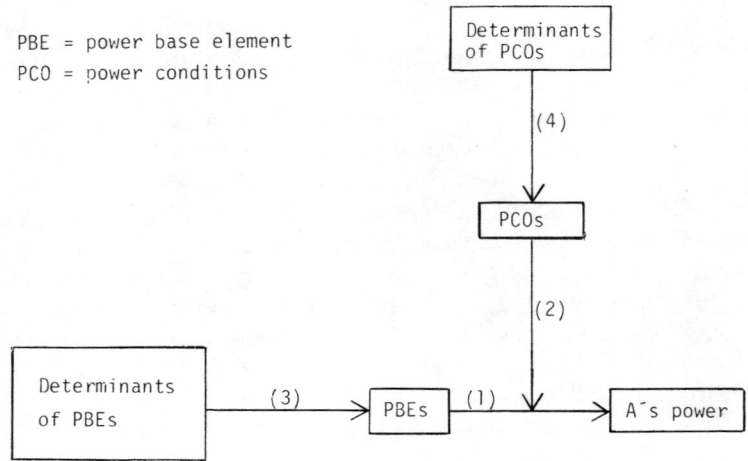

Figure 1.
A framework for the analysis of power bases.

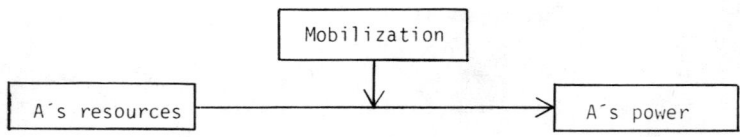

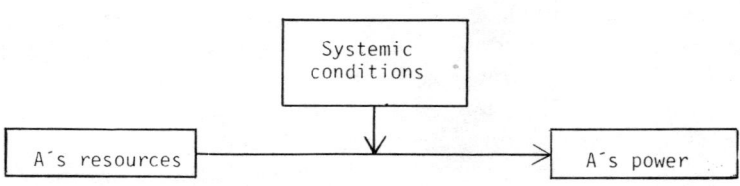

Figure 2.
Two common models.

The present study is an example of a type of analysis in which the question is how the power structure of a system is affected by a given phenomenon. It may be useful to point out that the relation between the dependent and the independent variable in such a study may be not of one but of four types. Figure 1 suggests a scheme for the analysis of PBEs. The main object of the figure is to emphasize that a given phenomenon functions as a PBE for an actor A in relation to other actors only if the 'power conditions' or PCOs are the appropriate ones. Put differently, the extent to which a PBE actually gives A power (arrow 1 in Figure 1) depends on various PCOs (arrow 2 in the figure); it is the interaction between PBEs and PCOs that makes other actors behave in the way A wants. The two most common applications of this idea are probably those shown in Figure 2: the notions that the 'resources' of an actor provide him with power only if they are mobilized, and only if conditions in the system are the appropriate ones.

Suppose now that we want to improve our understanding of how the power structure of a system is affected by some phenomenon x. Bearing in mind the generous way in which the concept of power base has been defined here it is in most cases possible to regard x as a PBE; the main object of one's analysis then becomes to identify the relevant PCOs. But it is not necessary to treat x as a PBE. Sometimes it is useful to regard x as a PCO in relation to other phenomena that are seen as PBEs. Or x may be treated neither as a PBE nor as a PCO but rather as a determinant of PBEs or PCOs (arrows 3 and 4 in Figure 1).

The fact that it may be unclear whether x belongs to one box or the other in Figure 1 illustrates the ambiguity of the concept of power base. This ambiguity may be a serious problem for a researcher interested in describing the power base of an actor. It is less problematic for a study of the present type. The question asked here is how x affects the power structure of a system and not whether x is part of somebody's power base. For our present purposes the significance of the analytical framework in Figure 1 does not lie in its distinguishing between the boxes but in its emphasizing that the effects of x should be taken into account regardless of whether x belongs to one box or the other.

In the present essay tension between the strong is our x. Most people think of this variable as one of the 'systemic conditions' in

Figure 2, i.e. as a PCO determining the extent to which the strong can use their strength against the weak. The level of Great Power tension may also be thought of as a PBE of strong as well as of weak actors; an example is the suggestion that high tension between the Great Powers may be actively exploited for offensive purposes by small states. Great Power tension may even be conceived of as a 'background variable', i.e. as a determinant of what we think of as PBEs or PCOs; a simple idea of this kind is the hypothesis that the higher the tension between the Great Powers, the larger their military capabilities are likely to be. There are many ways in which Great Power tension may affect small state power.

TENSION AND POWER IN A BIPOLAR SYSTEM

A bipolar system can be defined as one in which two leading members, S_1 and S_2, are much more powerful than all the others.[5] In this section we shall limit ourselves to discussing how variations in tension between S_1 and S_2 may affect the power of W_i, i.e. of every other member of the bipolar system. We shall then, in the next section, consider the application of the analysis to systems that are not bipolar.

It seems possible to summarize most suggestions about how the level of tension between Great Powers affects the power of small states in the form of four hypotheses.

The deterrence hypothesis: the higher the tension between S_1 and S_2, the more effectively they deter each other from using their resources against W_i, and the larger in consequence is the power of W_i.

The coalition hypothesis: the higher the tension between S_1 and S_2, the less likely they are to form a coalition against W_i, and the larger in consequence is the power of W_i.

The neutralism hypothesis: the higher the tension between S_1 and S_2, the more likely W_i is to be able to play off one of them against the other, and the larger in consequence is the power of W_i.

The polarization hypothesis: the higher the tension between S_1 and S_2, the more bipolarized the system is, and the *smaller* in consequence is the power of W_i.

The deterrence hypothesis is rooted in traditional balance-of-power thinking. The coalition hypothesis is the one proposed by Palme and others; it can in fact be regarded as a supplement to the deterrence hypothesis, and they will be discussed together below. The neutralism hypothesis is familiar from the role ascribed in the 1950s and 1960s to some Third World nations; Egypt is a typical case. The polarization hypothesis was popular during the Cold War, as pointed out in the introduction; it is of particular interest because it appears to contradict those hypotheses that prevail today.

The deterrence – coalition hypothesis

Traditional international relations theory assumes that the main factor limiting the ability of S_1 to control others is the existence of S_2, and vice versa. According to the deterrence hypothesis, the significance of this limitation varies with the level of tension between S_1 and S_2. High tension between the strong deters each of them from using more than marginal resources against the weak, and détente therefore weakens a major restraint against the exercise of power by S_i over W_i.

The deterrence mechanism works in two ways. High tension deters both by making it risky to exercise power over W_i and by making it necessary for S_1 and S_2 to set aside most of what they have for use against one another. Détente from both points of view means that W_i becomes more exposed; W_i is no longer protected by the rivalry between S_1 and S_2.

Arguments of this kind are usually made in terms of military capabilities and confrontations. Sweden is one of those countries whose security policy assumes that because of the fact that the Great Powers are chiefly preoccupied with each other, only marginal resources can be used against third parties. The higher the tension between the United States and the Soviet Union, the more plausible this assumption may appear to be; it has, as a matter of fact, been pointed out in Sweden that mutual force reductions in Central Europe would make forces available for deployment elsewhere and that Scandinavia might therefore become more and not less exposed due to this manifestation of détente. But precisely because the deterrence hypothesis has a military flavour it is important to point out that it can be broadened to encompass 'civil' as well as military power. It is tempting to generalize the hypothesis by suggesting that attention is the resource which may be more or less available for use against W_i. Attention is critical for the exercise of power, and the higher the tension between S_1 and S_2, the more of its attention S_1 and S_2 must allocate to their mutual relation, and the smaller in consequence is the amount of attention they can allocate to third parties.[6] This is one way in which tension between the strong may reduce the power gap between them and the weak.

The deterrence hypothesis is illustrated in Figure 3. The horizontal, solid line represents what is true by definition: i.e. that the more resources available to S_i, the larger his power over W_i. The vertical, solid line represents the deterrence hypothesis: i.e. the higher the tension between S_1 and S_2, the smaller the proportion of S_i's resources that can actually be brought to bear on the relation with W_i. The broken arrows indicate two kinds of feedback, both of which represent qualifications of the hypothesis that we must now consider.

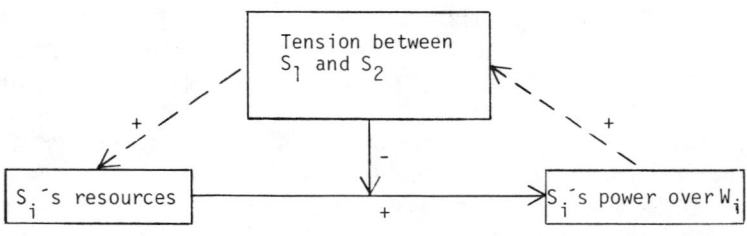

Figure 3.
The deterrence hypothesis.

First, the deterrence hypothesis assumes that the resources available to S_1 and S_2 are independent of the level of tension between them. This is not necessarily the case. At least in some contexts it may be an equally plausible hypothesis that détente would actually decrease the amount of resources available for use against other actors, be it the chief rival or some weaker opponent. This may be true even with regard to intangible PBEs like attention: détente may cause both S_1 and S_2 to devote more attention than earlier to internal matters, thereby decreasing the total amount of attention available for their external relations.

Secondly, the deterrence hypothesis assumes that the level of tension between S_1 and S_2 is unaffected by their exercising power over W_i, and this assumption may also be venturesome. There may be something to be said in favour of the contrary idea, namely that if S_1 or S_2 were to actually exploit détente to the detriment of W_i, tension between S_1 and S_2 would increase again; not only high tension but also the risk of an increase in tension may deter the strong from exercising power over the weak.

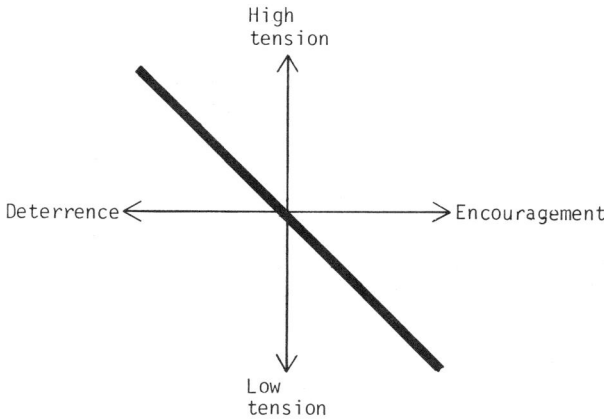

Figure 4.
The deterrence and coalition hypotheses combined.

The qualifications are by no means fatal to the deterrence hypothesis, but they suggest that its applicability may be more limited than may appear to be the case at first sight.

We now turn to the coalition hypothesis, which concerns the extreme case when S_1 and S_2 not only abstain from deterring each other but actively cooperate against W_i, pooling their power bases into an overwhelming concentration of power. The power gap between strong and weak is now at its maximum, and the system approaches unipolarity (cf. Wallensteen, Vesa and Väyrynen, 1973:17). It seems fruitful to regard the coalition hypothesis as a mere continuation of the deterrence hypothesis, an idea that is illustrated by the straight line from north-west to south-east in Figure 4. The x-axis in the figure represents the effect of S_1's power on S_2's power over W_i: 'deterrence' to the left of *origo* and 'encouragement' to the right of *origo*. The y-axis represents the level of tension between S_1 and S_2. Most of the north-west quadrant corresponds to the deterrence hypothesis, and most of the south-east quadrant corresponds to the coalition hypothesis. In the *origo* area there is the intermediate situation in which, on the one hand, S_1 and S_2 respect each other's spheres of interest but, on the other hand, active cooperation against third parties is unlikely.

However suggestive it may seem, the coalition hypothesis is not without its problems. Human experience suggests that lasting and far-reaching coalitions between all the strong members of a social system against all its weak members, a quasi-permanent alliance of topdogs against underdogs, is in fact not very probable. Cooperation between the topdogs is more likely to be limited in scope and time; the further we are to the south-east in Figure 4, the more limited and temporary the coalition is likely to be, and the smaller in consequence is the extent to which S_i's power over W_i is actually affected by a change in tension between S_1 and S_2. However deep the détente, the United States and the Soviet Union are hardly entering an area in which they will habitually act in common to control all the essentials of world politics; this notion, utopian or nightmarish, seems unrealistic.

Now a proponent of the coalition hypothesis like Olof Palme does not go this far. Palme appears to take it for granted, as most of us do, that rivalry between the two superpowers will continue to exist. The US and the USSR do have one interest in common, however: to avoid nuclear war. The implication of détente, according to Palme, is that Washington and Moscow have agreed 'to keep a careful eye on all the crises in the world that could ultimately lead to nuclear war'. They claim that they have 'the right, and almost an obligation, to intervene if a local conflict tends to develop into a world conflagration'. This way of thinking amounts to 'a moral justification of the predominance of the superstates... It is particularly essential that we should be very aware of the dangers it can involve for the small nations'.[7]

Even with this limited version of the coalition hypothesis there is a problem, however. The relation between superpower cooperation to prevent nuclear war on the one hand and the level of tension between them on the other, is unclear. An example of superpower collusion has already been mentioned: simultaneous American and Soviet pressure on Israel in 1956. This incident did not occur after a long period of détente but at the height of a major international crisis. 'Munich 1938' symbolizes a similar event. Indeed, it can be argued that high tension is as likely as low tension to bring about collusion; this may be more difficult to organize in the former case than in the latter, but the incentives may on the other hand be stronger. It is in fact an open empirical question whether détente between S_1 and S_2 makes collusion against W_i more or less likely. The straight line in Figure 4 should perhaps be substituted by a

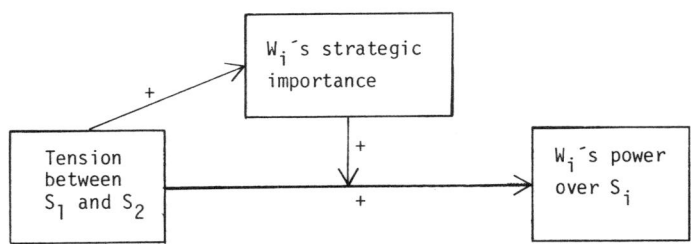

Figure 5.
The neutralism hypothesis.

curve showing that both very high and very low tension are likely to encourage the formation of a coalition between S_1 and S_2.

The neutralism hypothesis

The deterrence — coalition hypothesis is à la mode. The neutralism and the polarization hypotheses are survivals from the Cold War.

It is of course a most obvious idea that a conflict between the strong can be exploited by the weak. Conflict between S_1 and S_2 can be part of W_i's power base. The more intense this conflict, i.e. the higher the tension between S_1 and S_2, the larger the power of W_i. The label 'neutralism' is used here for want of a better term. It may be somewhat misleading: all neutralist nations do not attempt to play the Great Powers off against one another, and some nations that are not neutralist do.

The neutralism hypothesis is illustrated in Figure 5. The figure suggests that the extent to which W_i can successfully exploit any given level of tension between S_1 and S_2 is a function of the 'strategic importance' of W_i. This statement, although not meaningless, is less informative than it may appear to be. It is clear that some small states are more important to the Great Powers than others but we have little systematic knowledge of the factors determining the strategic importance of a country. Figure 5 contains the additional suggestion that W_i's strategic importance is a positive function of the degree of tension between S_1 and S_2; the latter variable may be seen not only as a PBE of W_i but also as a determinant of an important PCO.

There is no need to go into details about the model in Figure 5; the idea behind the neutralism hypothesis is familiar to everybody. The chief problem with the hypothesis is also well known: if it is true that the higher the tension between S_1 and S_2, the more there is to exploit for W_i, it may also be true that the higher the tension between S_1 and S_2, the more risky it is for W_i to exploit this conflict. The net result is not always an increase in W_i's power. We shall soon return to this matter.

The polarization hypothesis

So far we have discussed some arguments supporting the opinion that the level of tension between the strong is positively related to the power of the weak. It is now time to discuss the opposite possibility. What I have chosen to call the 'polarization hypothesis' is illustrated in Figure 6. Its main features are, first, the suggestion that there is a mutually reinforcing relation between the level of tension between S_1 and S_2 on the one hand, and the degree of bloc-building or bipolarization around them on the other, and, secondly, the idea that bipolarization tends to increase the power of S_1 over W_i.[8]

According to the polarization hypothesis there are two interacting reasons why bipolarization is a likely consequence of an increase in tension. On the one hand, the higher the tension between S_1 and S_2, the more important it is for both of them to control W_i; they will both have an interest in building blocs. On the other hand, this very desire on the part of S_1 and S_2 to control W_i may make it necessary for W_i to seek the protection of one of S_1 and S_2 against the other; W_i will also have incentives for bloc-building.

Then, how is the degree of bipolarization related to the power of S_i over W_i? The argument we call the polarization hypothesis runs roughly as follows. In general, inter-bloc tension makes a high degree of intra-bloc solidarity necessary, and this is bound to imply adaption on the part of W_i to the preferences of the respective bloc leader S_1 and S_2. In particular, the basic characteristic of the situation in a highly bipolarized system is that W_i has a security problem

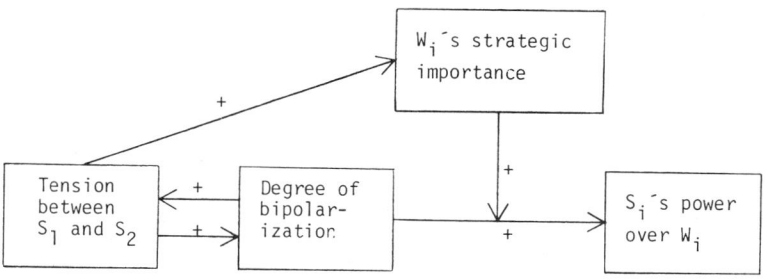

Figure 6.
The polarization hypothesis.

which can be solved only by means of an alliance with S_1 or S_2, and this dependence of W_i on S_i is a PBE for the latter in relation to the former. And the power effects of bipolarization are not limited to those who feel compelled to join one camp or the other. Non-aligned actors may be less dependent on one of S_1 and S_2 because of their not being aligned to him, but they may at the same time be more exposed to the other of the two leading actors in the system. In a highly bipolarized system even the non-aligned minority is likely to find their freedom of movement circumscribed by the high level of tension between S_1 and S_2, and between their respective blocs. It is added in Figure 6 that the extent to which the power of W_i is affected by changes in tension and in the degree of bipolarization is a function of W_i's strategic importance, exactly as according to the neutralism hypothesis.

From the point of view of the polarization hypothesis détente between the strong is no problem for the weak. Détente rather means that the weak are liberated from the constraints inherent in a highly bipolarized situation.

One problem with the polarization hypothesis is that it may be open to question whether S_i and not W_i gains in power from bipolarization. After all, by getting S_1 involved in the situation W_i may gain in power vis-à-vis his chief opponent S_2; high tension between S_1 and S_2 may be a prerequisite for S_1's power base being available to W_i for use against S_2. Polarization is not necessarily an asset of the strong against the weak. This is part of the general problem that the four basic hypotheses are not fully compatible with one another. It is to this incompatibility that we now turn.

Preferences versus capabilities

The essence of the controversy can be specified with the help of Figure 7. This figure is a variation on the set of triangles commonly used to illustrate a key theorem of structural balance theory: that a triad is stable if either none or two relations are negative, and unstable if one or all three relations are negative (e.g. Healy and Stein, 1973: 49–53; Wilkinson, 1976: 66–68). Here however our interest is not in stability but in power. In Figure 7 a plus sign indicates low tension and a minus sign high tension. Cases a and b in the figure illustrate two possible situations in which W_i may find itself as a consequence of low tension between S_1 and S_2. Cases c, d, and e represent three possible positions of W_i when tension between S_1 and S_2 is high. Case b represents the coalition of the strong against the weak, case c the neutrality of the weak in a conflict between the strong, and case d the coalition between weak and strong. One school of thought assumes that high tension between S_1 and S_2 implies case c and low tension case b; the other school of thought maintains that high tension implies case d and perhaps case e, and low tension case a.

The two views need not be contradictory in a strict sense; if one is correct the other is not necessarily completely false. In part the hypotheses complement rather than contradict each other. If we start with the obvious, there is a common element in the neutralism and polarization hypotheses: they both assume that the importance of W_i to S_i is a function of the level of tension between S_1 and S_2. Being important to S_i is an asset for W_i by the neutralism hypothesis and a problem for him by the polarization hypothesis. Both may be true. One and the same actor may both lose and gain from détente. High tension between the strong tends to make the weak dependent on the strong — but also to make the strong dependent on the weak. High tension between the strong implies that W_i has much to gain from playing off S_1 against S_2 — but also that this game is risky. Détente does reduce the likely gains, but

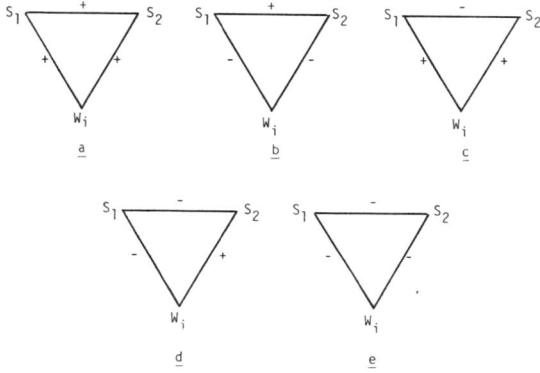

Figure 7.
Five structures of tension and détente.

also the likely risks. The neutralism effect is likely to dominate in some contexts or with regard to some actors, and the polarization effect in other contexts or with regard to other actors. It is a task for further research to identify and systematize the PCOs making one effect or the other the dominant one.

The neutralism and polarization hypotheses are thus concerned with the effects of tension between S_1 and S_2 on the preferences of S_1 and S_2. The deterrence-coalition hypothesis, by contrast, is a hypothesis about their capabilities. The problem of the compatibility of the hypotheses is reminiscent of a well-known example of how changes in capabilities and incentives may tend to neutralize each other: the classical security dilemma. Defensive measures by A against B, such as an increase in armaments or joining an alliance, may increase not only the capability protecting A but also B's incentives for undertaking measures perceived as threatening by A; the net outcome for A's security is uncertain. Similarly, détente between the strong may not only increase the resources the strong can use against the weak but also decrease the importance the former attach on the latter; it is not clear under what conditions the net result will be a decrease in the power of the weak and under what conditions it will be an increase — or even whether it is meaningful to talk of a 'net result'.

Can the question be answered by way of empirical enquiry? This will not be easy. The empirical study of how PBEs and PCOs interact to produce power is difficult. The chief problem concerns the operationalization of the dependent variable. The opinions of qualified judges (cf. Saaty and Khouja, 1976, and Chapter 5 of this book) and similarity in UN voting and other behaviour (e.g. Deutsch, 1967: 237 – 238) are among the indicators that may come to mind. It is certainly worthwhile to search for the predictors of such phenomena, but the validity of both operationalizations is unclear. It can be shown for example that there is a positive correlation between the level of East – West tension in Europe and the propensity of UN members to vote with the United States,[9] and that there is a negative correlation between the level of East – West tension in Europe and the propensity of Swedish governments to voice criticism of the US (Goldmann, 1976: 291 – 309). But it is open to question what conclusions can be drawn from such findings about the way in which tension between the strong affects the power of the weak. In case studies of foreign policy decision-making it may be easier to give the dependent variable a convincing operational interpretation; Brecher's study of foreign policy decision-making in Israel is an example of research containing much thought-provoking material for the analyst interested in PBEs and PCOs, including Great Power tension seen as a PBE or a PCO (Brecher, 1974). But the other side of the coin is that the problem of generalization becomes acute: it is possible to find historical examples, even within the limits of Brecher's study, supporting virtually any hypothesis one may have about how tension between S_1 and S_2 affects the power of W_i and hence difficult to answer questions about which effect is the dominant one.

In summary: there are significant theoretical arguments and of course considerable historical evidence suggesting that the level of tension between the strong may significantly affect the power of the weak. Our problem is that the theoretical arguments partly contradict each other and that systematic empirical research designed to answer questions following from this contradiction is difficult to carry out, due in particular to the difficulty of operationalizing the dependent variable. The level of tension between the two leading members of a bipolar system is likely to be an important aspect of the system's power structure in the sense that changes in tension will lead to important changes in the distribution of power. But the nature of the latter changes varies with third variables in a way that is largely unknown. It may in fact be misleading to ask for a simple answer to the question put in the title of this chapter: whether the relationship is positive or negative.

TENSION AND POWER IN A NON-BIPOLAR SYSTEM

It is striking the extent to which bipolarity has been taken for granted in the debate about the effects of détente — striking against the background of the widespread belief that it is becoming increasingly misleading to characterize the system as bipolar. It is frequently maintained that new superpowers — China, Japan, the European Community — are emerging; such a process, leading to an increase in the number of 'poles', may be called the *multipolarization* of the international system. It is also commonly suggested that 'civil' power is becoming more and military power less important, and that the distribution of civil power is becoming increasingly different from that of military power; this process may be termed the *multidimensionalization* of the international system's power structure. Finally, it is often pointed out that international relations are to an increasing extent carried out by actors other than national governments and that this fact may have significant consequences for the ability even of superpowers to control the system; paraphrasing a term that has become familiar in recent years we may call this third process of change the *transnationalization* of the international system.

It is not the object of this chapter to discuss whether multipolarization, multidimensionalization, and transnationalization are in fact taking place. *If* they occur the system is becoming non-bipolar; the purpose of this section is limited to considering how such a change might affect the relation between tension and power.

The effects of multipolarization

Suppose that the international system is tripolar rather than bipolar. Sociological theory suggests that triads have a built-in tendency to become dyads and that the chief question concerns who will be the isolate (Wilkinson, 1976). In other words: the nature of the bilateral relations between S_1, S_2, and S_3 is of major consequence for the distribution of power among the three leading members of the system. This fact by itself implies that the pattern of tension between S_1, S_2, and S_3 is a significant aspect of the system's power structure.

Here we are concerned with the way in which the power of W_i is affected by changes in this pattern, however. Multipolarization adds to the complexity of the matter because of the fact that high tension in one bilateral relation between Great Powers may coexist with, and even help bring about, détente in another such relation. This is an additional reason why a change in tension between the strong may affect the power of the weak in quite complex ways.

The concept 'bipolar subsystem' may aid in clarifying the matter.[10] If the number of Great Powers exceeds two, the system can be divided into subsystems defined in terms of pairs of leading members; if the system is tripolar there are three such subsystems which may be called the S_1S_2 subsystem, the S_1S_3 subsystem, and the S_2S_3 subsystem. The membership of W_i in such a subsystem can be defined in terms of interaction, both positive and negative, between W_i and S_i. In Figure 8 the x-axis represents interaction with S_1 and the y-axis represents interaction with S_2. A number of imaginary components are plotted in the figure. We may say that in order to be a member of the S_1S_2 subsystem W_i must have at least some interaction with both S_1 and S_2. Strictly speaking this means that only components located in *origo* or on one of the axes fail to qualify for membership. It may seem more reasonable to think of subsystem membership as a matter of degree. Or it may be useful to define a threshold between membership and non-membership, of the kind suggested in Figure 8.

Note that W_i may belong to one, to none, or to several bipolar subsystems depending upon his interaction with S_i. Some components to the left and below the border-line in Figure 8 may belong instead to the S_1S_3 subsystem or the $S_2 S_3$ subsystem. And

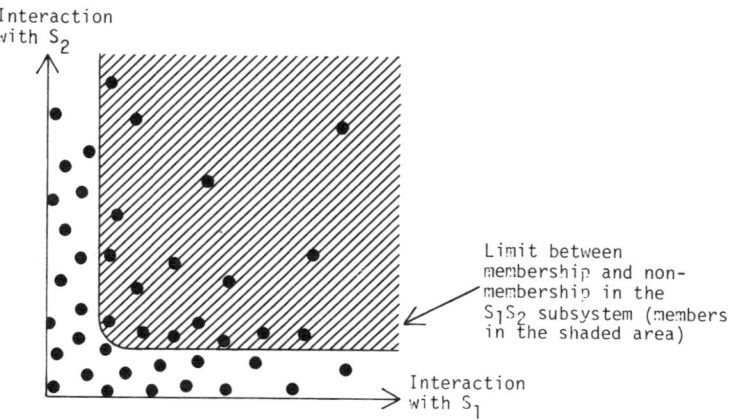

Figure 8.
Illustration to the concept of "bipolar subsystem."

some components that are clearly members of the S_1S_2 subsystem may belong to other bipolar subsystems as well. In the current international system Sweden may belong primarily to the US – USSR subsystem, the Philippines to the US – China subsystem, and Mongolia to the USSR – China subsystem; India may be a member of all three subsystems; and if there is a state isolated enough not to belong to any of these three bipolar subsystems Nepal may be an example.

The question now is whether the above analysis of the relation between tension and power in bipolar systems holds also with regard to bipolar subsystems of non-bipolar systems. In the absence of empirical evidence it may be suggested a priori that the analysis should be qualified in one respect. The qualification concerns the coalition hypothesis. It was suggested above that in bipolar systems Great Power collusion could realistically be expected only in extreme circumstances such as those outlined by Palme. Matters may be different in bipolar subsystems. Not only in triads but also in systems with more than three leading members there may be a built-in tendency to polarization; coalitions are to be expected, and the only question is who will join forces against whom. Far-reaching and lasting coalitions between the two leading components may be rare in bipolar systems, but they may be common in bipolar subsystems of non-bipolar systems. The applicability of the coalition hypothesis may therefore be greater in a non-bipolar system than in a bipolar one.

It has been suggested here (1) that there may be a negative relation between tension in one bilateral relation between Great Powers and tension in another such relation and (2) that bipolar subsystems may overlap. If we combine these ideas we realize how complex the effects of a change in tension between the strong may be for the power of the weak. The recent history of Vietnam provides us with an example. The United States found it necessary to commit itself militarily in Vietnam at a time when the Cold War was still intense, and this intervention contributed to making Hanoi dependent on Moscow and Peking; such developments are to be expected in periods of high tension, according to the polarization hypothesis. Hanoi's dependence on the USSR and China was however mitigated by the fact that tension was high also between these two powers; to at least some extent Hanoi managed to play one off against the other, which is what the neutralism hypothesis predicts. But in the early 1970s tension decreased both between the United States and the Soviet Union, and between the United States and China; détente may have helped pave the way for American withdrawal by decreasing the strategic importance of Vietnam — the polarization hypothesis again. At the same time tension between China and the Soviet Union also seems to have decreased to some extent, which may have deprived Hanoi of a useful PBE — the neutralism hypothesis. This loss may have become particularly significant in the face of Soviet-American quasi-collusion to make Hanoi accept a cease-fire — the coalition hypothesis.[11] A simple answer can hardly be given to the question of how détente between the Great Powers affected the ability of North Vietnam to attain her objectives.

The effects of multidimensionalization

The belief is becoming widespread that international relations analysts have tended to underrate the significance of 'civil' power, particularly 'economic' power, and that they have therefore tended to provide a simplistic analysis of the international system's power structure; the point is taken up in other chapters of this volume. It has become common to make a distinction between 'military Great Powers' and 'economic Great Powers', with the Soviet Union as the prime example of the former and Japan as an extreme instance of the latter. This distinction in effect suggests a more basic one between an international security system and an international economic system dealing with different issues and having power structures that overlap only in part. This hypothetical discrepancy between the military and the economic power structures is the main example of a broader process, which is here called multidimensionalization. Assuming that the distinction between the international security system and the international economic system is fruitful the question is to what extent our basic hypotheses about tension and power are relevant not only to the former but also to the latter.

Only tentative speculation is possible on this point too. The hypotheses about coalitions and neutralism seem to be at least as relevant to economic systems as to security systems; we have already mentioned the possibility that there lurks behind the notion that the current détente is problematic for small states an analogy with the position of the consumer in a market that is becoming less competitive due to the formation of a producers' cartel. Are the deterrence and polarization hypotheses equally applicable to economic systems? The answer is uncertain. On the one hand it seems possible to identify economic analogues with the deterrence and polarization mechanisms. On the other hand it appears a plausible guess that these mechanisms are less significant in economic systems than in security systems. I am inclined to hypothesize that in economic systems the relation between tension and power is likely to be positive, whereas the matter is more uncertain with regard to security systems.

It should be emphasized that the international economic system and the international security system are interdependent; the links are so numerous that the very distinction between them may be misleading. I hope to be able to return to this matter in another context. Suffice it here to point out that if it is true that a process of multidimensionalization is under way, this does not necessarily imply that changes in tension between the leading members of the *security* system (the 'military Great Powers') are without consequence for the power of the small states in the *economic* system. Suppose that S_1 is an essentially military Power like the Soviet Union, that S_2 is a predominantly economic Power like Japan, and that S_3 is strong in both respects, as the United States. Suppose, furthermore, that there is a negative relationship between, on the one hand, the level of tension between S_1 and S_3 and, on the other hand, the level of tension between S_2 and S_3; for example, S_2 and S_3 might be economic rivals but at the same time security allies vis-à-vis S_1. Détente between S_1 and S_2 would lead to increased economic competition between S_2 and S_3 and would therefore affect the power of the smaller members of the S_2S_3 subsystem and not only those of the S_1S_2 subsystem. It is tempting to speculate that the relation between tension and power is predominantly negative in security systems and predominantly positive in economic systems; if this is the case, détente between S_1 and S_2 would lead to the optimal outcome from the point of view of W_i.

The effects of transnationalization

It is sometimes suggested that the process we call transnationalization is of major consequence for the power structure of the international system.[12] This issue deserves an essay of its own; significant aspects of the problem are discussed in Chapter 9 of the present volume. Here, I shall limit myself to mentioning a few ideas directly related to the problem of how tension between the strong affects the power of the weak. We have two questions to consider: does transnationalization reduce the power of the strong to such an extent that tension between the strong becomes a significantly less important determinant of the power of the weak than previously? And, to what extent is it necessary to revise the four basic hypotheses in the light of the possibility of transnationalization?

The answer to the former question is not self-evident. Transnationalization may seem bound to decrease the power of governments. It is traditionally taken for granted that all resources that can be ascribed to a nation can in fact be mobilized by its government and be used for the purpose of exercising power, and that all the external relations of a country can be manipulated by its government and consequently function as PBEs when the need arises; it appears that transnationalization undermines this assumption. But it can also be argued that the main consequence of transnationalization is the creation of an increasingly sophisticated and extensive set of PBEs available to governments in case of need; a multinational corporation, for example, is not necessarily a new actor usurping some of the power of its home government but may equally well be a bridgehead for or an agent of this government. A third, intermediate view also seems possible: transnationalization does imply a loss of 'civil' power on the part of governments, but this is likely to be compensated for by a return to prominence of military power. This is merely to scrape the surface of a vast problem; the only point I am making is that the consequences of transnationalization for the power structure of the international system is a more intriguing matter than it may appear to be at first.

With regard to the tenability of the four hypotheses suggested in this paper, at least one aspect of transnationalization is worth considering. Whatever the effect of transnationalization on the 'size' of the power base available to a government, such a process may increase the difficulty of mobilizing this power base. Inspired by Keohane's and Nye's analysis of US – Canadian relations (Keohane and Nye, 1974), Barbara Haskel has reflected upon the conflict between the United States and Sweden over the Vietnam War; she suggests that a government, in this case that of the United States, can exploit a network of transnational relations for the purpose of exercising power only in extreme and unusual circumstances (Haskel, 1976). This may imply that the more transnationalized a nation's external relations are, the more important is tension as a determinant of the power of the nation's government. It was pointed out above that one problem with the deterrence hypothesis is the possibility that the power base of S_i may be a positive function of the level of tension; we now add that transnationalization may increase the significance of this possibility and hence decrease the significance of the deterrence hypothesis. One effect of transnationalization on the way in which tension between the strong affects the power of the weak may thus be to increase the likelihood that this relation will prove to be essentially negative, as people were prone to believe in the 1950s, rather than essentially positive, as is often suggested today.

NOTES

1. See for example his press conference on 10 November 1959 (*L'année politique 1959*, 1960: 633 – 638). See also Sjöberg (1972: 14 – 19).
2. *Documents on Swedish Foreign Policy 1974* (1976:53). For a critical analysis of the so-called Palme doctrine see Kleberg (1977).
3. For a detailed discussion of this definition see Goldmann (1974: 13 – 27).
4. See in particular Brecher (1974, ch. 6).
5. With regard to this definition, see Goldmann (1974: 102 – 6).
6. The idea of regarding the allocation of attention as a key variable has been borrowed from Deutsch and Singer (1964). One of their hypotheses is that a low degree of attention implies a low probability of war; a common objection is that a low degree of attention may increase the probability of unintentional war; empirical research is needed to settle the issue. Similarly, against the suggestion that the power of W_i is a negative function of the amount of attention S_i can allocate to W_i can be set the common notion that détente between S_1 and S_2 will make it possible for them to devote enough attention to the problems of W_i to do something about them; détente is to the advantage of developing countries. In this case too empirical research would be useful.

Another objection against the hypothesis suggested in the text is that a decrease in the amount of attention allocated to W_i by *top-level decision-makers* in S_i may be compensated for at lower levels and that the power effects of this change are uncertain. The objection is of course inspired by the so-called bureaucratic politics paradigm. It raises the general issue of how A's power over B is affected by the level at which matters relating to B are handled within A. To my knowledge this is a matter that has so far not been explored in the scholarly literature. It does seem reasonable to suggest that more and 'stronger' PBEs can be mobilized by a President or a Prime Minister than by a Deputy Under-Secretary or an Ambassador, but this may be too superficial a view. The matter clearly deserves to be investigated.

7. *Documents on Swedish Foreign Policy 1974* (1976: 51 – 54).

8. With regard to the concept 'bipolarization' and its relation to tension, see Goldmann (1974: 107 – 74). With regard to the former, see also Wall (1975: 12 – 22).

9. Data on European tension are from Goldmann (1974: 225). Data on UN voting are from Rowe (1969:244). The product-moment correlation between the two time series was found to be 0.56. An experiment has also been made on the basis of Gareau's data on the propensity of UN members to vote with the US and the USSR (Gareau, 1969). If we compare the voting of the fourteen European UN members in the period 1947 – 55, a period of high European tension, with their voting in the period 1962 – 67, during which the average level of tension in Europe was lower, we find (1) that eight of these states showed a virtually unchanged degree of pro-US or pro-USSR voting, (2) that five of them were significantly less US-oriented in the latter period than in the former (France, United Kingdom, Sweden, Norway, and Denmark), and (3) that only one was more superpower-oriented in the latter period than in the former (Yugoslavia).

10. With regard to the concept 'bipolar subsystem', see Goldmann (1974: 113 – 14).

11. The example is inspired by an on-going study by Lars-Erik Lundin about Soviet assistance to North Vietnam and Egypt and its influence on the behaviour of the latter.

12. For representative statements along these lines see Nye (1975, 1976).

REFERENCES

AMSTRUP, N. (1976) 'The Perennial Problem of Small States: A Survey of Research Efforts', *Cooperation and Conflict*, 11: 163 – 182.

BRECHER, M. (1974) *Decisions in Israel's Foreign Policy*. London: Oxford University Press.

DEUTSCH, K. W. (1967) 'On the Concepts of Politics and Power', *Journal of International Affairs*, 21: 232 – 241.

—— and J. D. SINGER (1964) 'Multipolar Power Systems and International Stability', *World Politics*, 16: 390 – 406.

Documents on Swedish Foreign Policy 1974 (1976) Stockholm: Ministry for Foreign Affairs.
GAREAU, F. H. (1969) The Cold War 1947 to 1967: a Quantitative Study. Denver, Colorado: University of Denver.
GOLDMANN, K. (1974) Tension and Détente in Bipolar Europe. Stockholm: Esselte Studium.
—— (1976) 'The Foreign Sources of Foreign Policy: Causes, Conditions, or Inputs?', European Journal of Political Research, 4:291 – 309.
HASKEL, B. (1976) 'Det moraliserande Sverige', Internationella studier, 30 – 32.
HEALY, B. and A. STEIN (1973) 'The Balance of Power in International History: Theory and Reality', Journal of Conflict Resolution, 17:33 – 62.
KEOHANE, R. O. and J. S. NYE (1977) Power and Interdependence: World Politics in Transition. Boston: Little, Brown.
KLEBERG, O. (1977) 'De stora och de små — Olof Palmes syn på supermakter och småstater', in: Är svensk neutralitet möjlig. Stockholm: Liber.
L'année politique 1959 (1960) Paris: Presses Universitaires de France.
NYE, J. S. (1975) 'Transnational and Transgovernmental Relations', in: Goodwin, G. L. and A. Linklater (eds.). New Dimensions of World Politics. London: Croom Helm.
—— (1976) 'Independence and Interdependence', Foreign Policy 22:130 – 61.
ROWE, E. T. (1969) 'Changing Patterns in the Voting Success of Member States in the United Nations General Assembly: 1945 – 1966', International Organization, 23:231 – 253.
SAATY, T. L. and M. W. KHOUJA (1976) 'A Measure of World Influence', Journal of Peace Science, 2:31 – 48.
SJÖBERG, H. (1972) De Gaulles Europatankar. Stockholm: Rabén och Sjögren.
WALL, G. R. (1975) The Dynamics of Polarization. Stockholm: Department of Political Science.
WALLENSTEEN, P., U. VESA and R. VÄYRYNEN (1973) The Nordic System: Structure and Change, 1920 – 1970. Tampere: Tampere Peace Research Institute, and Uppsala: Department of Peace and Conflict Research.
WILKINSON, D. (1976) Cohesion and Conflict: Lessons from the Study of Three-party Interaction. New York: St Martin's Press.

II Interdependence and Power

6 The Concept of Interdependence: Its Uses and Misuses

Philip A. Reynolds
University of Lancaster

Robert D. McKinlay
University of Lancaster

The concept of a closed system may sometimes be of value in the natural or applied sciences. It can rarely be so in the social sciences. The billiard-ball model of relations among states had some very limited value for analysis at the macro or system level, but in black-boxing the state units it excluded important components of the interaction pattern even at that level. It made the assumption that states were sufficiently impermeable and uniform for variations in their behaviour resulting from variations in their internal processes or goals to be able safely to be treated as insignificant. The state sub-systems were effectively treated as closed. The student of comparative politics likewise habitually treated the state as a closed system, in that his analysis of the processes by which value allocations were made in a variety of polities typically excluded consideration of inputs from the international arena in which his polities were located. Interdependence is a concept that embraces a variety of modes of attack on the appropriateness of both these approaches.[1]

In this chapter we argue that although the literature on international interdependence has made a number of useful contributions, the general rather lax usage of the concept has led to a number of major difficulties. We shall examine some of these contributions, in each case calling attention to some of the main problems and qualifications which are frequently overlooked as a consequence of the focus on interdependence.

AUTONOMY AND DEPENDENCE

Let us take the question of autonomy first. In a purely legal sense states are of course autonomous. The fact of recognition by other states confirms for their properly-constituted authorities the legal right to regulate all affairs within the territorial limits which define the state. But equally obviously this de jure autonomy is de facto qualified by the extent to which entities outside the state are able to influence the authorities to do things they would otherwise not choose to do. Sovereignty is not independence. But does the absence of independence mean dependence? And what is interdependence to be taken to mean?

The NATO allies are dependent on the United States for their nuclear defence. The government of East Germany is dependent on Soviet support. Britain is dependent on a high level of world trade. These three familiar observations all have slightly different connotations, though with a common core of meaning. The dependence of the NATO allies derives from the perception of an external threat of a particular kind, and from the economic and technological incapacity of the European allies to meet it and/or their unwillingness to allocate the resources to develop the capacity that would be necessary to meet it. Dependence in this case therefore varies with the perception of the nature of the threat (an input from the alliance's external environment), with assessment of the ability and willingness of their United States partner to meet it on their behalf, and with the degree of preference for accepting this 'dependence' over withdrawing resources from education or roads or industrial development or any other desirable purpose. Thus, when France under de Gaulle perceived the Soviet threat to have diminished, and after Sputnik increasingly doubted the will of the United States to enter a nuclear exchange on Europe's behalf, the decision was taken to develop the *force de frappe* and restore France's 'independence'.

The dependence of Ulbricht and Honecker is of a rather different kind. Ulbricht was installed in power by the Soviet armies. Both the source of his support and the policies he sought to pursue were deeply unpopular. The June 1953 rising had to be suppressed by Soviet tanks, and in the subsequent years many of those who were able to voted with their feet and fled to West Germany, thus causing the Berlin wall to be built. The dependence in this case therefore was of a particular regime needing external support because it lacked sufficient internal support from its own people. But with the death of Ulbricht, with the coming to maturity of a new generation knowing no other regime, and with substantial economic growth in the past decade or so the degree of internal opposition has lessened, and the degree of dependence accordingly has also.

Britain's dependence on a high level of world trade means merely that when world trade is in recession the standard of living of the British people is likely to be affected more adversely than is that of other more nearly 'self-sufficient' peoples. Since about half Britain's food has to be imported (at the current level of agricultural activity, and with the quantity and type of food consumption to which the British people is now accustomed), and since almost all the materials required for British industry also have to be imported (apart from energy), when world trade declines and British exports have difficulty in finding markets unemployment necessarily rises and the standard of living is rapidly depressed (unless foreign fairy godmothers come to the rescue). But dependence in this case relates to the maintenance of particular patterns of economic activity and of expectations about standards of life which could in theory — though with difficulty in practice — be so transformed as to remove the dependence altogether.

The sources of dependence are thus widely variant. It may derive from some feature of a state's external environment (which the state may or may not be able to affect or change), it may derive from inadequacy of resources at the state's disposal (or from deliberate choices about resource allocation or expectations about standards of living), or it may derive from inadequate internal support to a regime. The three sources may of course frequently be related. But in all cases the effect of dependence is to limit the freedom of manoeuvre of the state's decision-makers, though the nature and variability of that limitation will vary with its source.

It is not to be assumed, however, that this dependence is one-way. The United States would not have joined the Atlantic alliance, and certainly would not have undertaken the major burdens of giving it strength, had successive United States administrations not perceived the alliance as being valuable to the United States. The more the alliance is valued by the United States, the more limited is the ability of the United States to use its nuclear umbrella to affect the behaviour of other members of the alliance, if the alliance were to be weakened thereby, and especially if it were seen by the Soviets to be so weakened. The freedom of manoeuvre of the United States in other parts of the world could likewise be limited by NATO, to the extent that action elsewhere weakened NATO by causing distrust or fear among the other allies, and this weakening was seen as more disadvantageous than refraining from the action that would cause it. In terms of our definition, therefore, there is mutual dependence, though it is not of course symmetrical.

Similarly in the case of Ulbricht the Soviet Union's freedom was not unlimited, although it doubtless came much nearer to being so. Stalin and his successors saw it as being vitally important that Germany should not be reunited under a regime associated with the Western capitalists and so hostile to themselves, and direct rule of East Germany was not a viable course of action in the long term. They therefore had need of German agents to do the job for them. The more efficiently Ulbricht did this the more difficult it became not to support him. His position would be without strength only if there appeared to be others in East Germany who would be able to do the job better than he could. The argument is illustrated by the events of 1968, if the reports are true of the part played by Ulbricht in persuading the Soviets to invade Czechoslovakia on the ground that if the Dubček reforms survived Ulbricht's position might become untenable.

Even in the most general case of dependence — that of Britain on a high level of world trade — the independence of others does not hold. Britain being a large world trader, ill-health of the British economy is a matter of concern to many other states, and for this reason the effects for Britain of trading recessions or of a declining British share of trade have repeatedly been reduced by assistance from other more fortunate or better run economies. Indeed, the British case well illustrates the strength of weakness, in that the more shaky the British economy became the more urgent became the pressures to give help, since its total collapse would produce consequences of unmeasurable magnitude which would almost certainly exceed the costs of supporting it.

These illustrations of different kinds of dependence suggest the general proposition that all dependence relationships involve mutual dependence, although it is likely that in the great majority of cases, if not all, the dependence of each on the other will be asymmetrical. But then what becomes of the notion of interdependence? If it means anything it surely means mutual dependence. But if all state relationships are of this kind, the notion must be intended to imply a change in the degree or nature or range or scope or complexity of mutual dependence that justifies the introduction of a new concept. Let us examine the literature from this viewpoint.

VARIETIES OF 'INTERDEPENDENCE'

Four main groups of enquiries may perhaps be identified. The first relates to processes of institutionalization at the global level, the second to ranges and types of transactions in the global arena, the third deals with ideas and problems associated with the notion of the global village, and the fourth seeks to identify linkage patterns between groups and behaviours within and outside state boundaries.

Institutionalization

That there has been a great increase in the number, membership and functions of intergovernmental organizations (IGOs) since 1945 is of course well known.[2] From the point of view of interdependence IGOs are significant in two ways. In the first place their growth both reflects and stimulates the development of international transactions which are seen to require monitoring and regulation. Thus, the IMF and GATT came into existence because of a recognition by decision-makers in leading countries that international monetary and trading transactions were now of such range and importance that allowing them to remain without regulatory mechanisms involved excessive risks for the economic well-being of their peoples. Once in existence, however (and this is the second consideration), such institutions, in order to perform the functions assigned to them, impose constraints on the freedom of manoeuvre of governments by, for instance, largely eliminating the policy option of tariff protection, or by setting conditions for the making of loans, or on occasion by acting as pressure groups, like UNCTAD and the Group of 77. The more the transactions which made the IGOs necessary develop and interweave, the less the option of withdrawing from an institution seems possible and the more the institutions in sustaining a common purpose (such as maximizing economic welfare) need to limit the options open to individual states. This is the argument: how far it is persuasive will be examined in the latter part of this chapter.

The growth of IGOs is matched and exceeded by the growth of INGOs (international non-governmental organizations).[3] The focus of interdependence in this case shifts subtly (and unnoticed). No longer is it a matter of governments being limited in their ability to make policy decisions without reference to other governments (as in the IGO case, though mediated through formally-constituted institutions): the limit here derives from the actions of agencies other than states, or from organizations whose main impact is upon the domestic environments of decision-makers. Thus, the control of sectors of economic activity within states by multi-national corporations gives them considerable power over government behaviour if these sectors are significant in terms of the size of the workforce or the critical nature of the product. Levels of investment and so of employment in particular industries or regions, international currency movements, even information flows on secret defence matters, may be difficult for governments to control; while the complexity of interlocking multi-national activities may lessen the ability even of groups of governments to implement policies, as the manoeuvrings of the oil companies in response to the oil crisis at the end of 1973 showed. Other INGOs, which now run into thousands, create an overlapping network of international memberships which can be used to promote simultaneous internal pressures, or can foster the emergence of loyalties to, for instance, a world community of scientists, and so undermine the level of acceptance of governmental decisions (on, for example, monopolizing discoveries which have both economic value and may contribute to the welfare of mankind). The development of INGOs is frequently cited as a manifestation of the growth of interdependence, and this illustrates the confusing umbrella-like nature of the concept: INGOs exemplify the emergence of actors other than states in the global arena, and they result from and stimulate increasing relationships among professional or interest

The Concept of Interdependence

groups in different countries, but they do not affect mutual dependence of states except to the extent that they create demands or constraints in decision-makers' internal environments. The implications of this argument also will be considered in the latter part of this paper.

The oldest institution at the international level is of course the diplomatic system. This is infrequently discussed in the interdependence literature, but it may perhaps be considered to bear on the question in two ways. In the first place the system depends on information flow. The number of states is now such that only a few can maintain representatives with all others, and may have to rely for information on 'friendly' governments, or on clearing agencies like the Commonwealth secretariat in London, or on the town meeting of the world at the United Nations in New York. The United Nations is seen by many states as being important because it is a highly cost-effective source of information; and since the perception of diplomatic representatives is usually influenced by the environment within which they work, the 'internationalist' atmosphere at Lake Success may well impart to information flow in the diplomatic system a degree of awareness of mutual dependence which might otherwise not exist. In the second place, the working of the system depends upon the acceptance of certain customs and norms, such as diplomatic immunity: this marries with the other aspects of institutionalization which have already been discussed to stimulate the slow emergence of commonly-accepted norms, values and goals at the global level. Economic growth, and economic and social welfare, are widely-accepted goals, while anti-colonialism, and opposition to racial discrimination, are widely-accepted principles. The more values of this kind command global adherence, the more perceptions of mutual dependence are reinforced, and freedom of manoeuvre of states is limited (though some, as always, very much more than others).[4]

Transactions

The second major group of studies that is mobilized behind the notion of interdependence deals with changes in the nature, quality and range of transactions in the global arena, mainly, but not entirely, among states. Resurrection of the term 'political economy' (prefaced by the adjective international) well illustrates this. Until recently many economists have been reluctant in their analyses to take explicit account of political and social variables that have not been susceptible to treatment sufficiently rigorous to satisfy economists' criteria. The real world has compelled a revision of this attitude. The politicization of international economic relations is seen in the assumption of control over economic policy-problems by high-level political actors, in the injection of international economic issues into domestic politics, and in the reduction of governments' control over instruments of economic policy and over outcomes.[5] Thus, the institutions established at the end of the Second World War, such as the IMF, are frequently buttressed or were virtually superseded in their operations by meetings among top decision-makers of the major economic states, meetings which bear witness to the general awareness that the economic fate of all is deeply affected by the economic fate of each. The manipulation of trading balances is subject to the influence not merely of the agreements and regulations of the GATT, but also to the internal political consequences of higher employment when it results from increased exports, or more unemployment when it is seen to be the consequence of imports. Trade union and Left-wing pressure for import controls in Britain is resisted by a Labour Government which perceives the interplay between Britain's importing policies and the import policies of other states, so that controls might bring retaliation which, given Britain's need for a higher level of world trade, could have consequences more serious for Britain than for other countries. This interplay between economic policies is not new: the argument is that its range and complexity are much greater, and the consequences of uncoordinated policies more fundamental. But even though some of the dangers may be warded off by cooperation, others such as world harvest failure, or new cartels among primary producers of essential commodities, or anticipations by currency dealers of future currency price movements, or major international cyclical movements, are outside the control of single governments, or even of many governments acting together. For all these reasons the freedom of manoeuvre of governments, and their ability to achieve objectives in that major area of political activity, economic welfare, are sharply limited, and the limits are mutually operative for all the major industrialized countries, though in varying degrees.

Closely linked to the tightened interweaving of international economic relationships is the technological imperative.[6] In part, technological peaks are to be scaled because, like Everest, they are there. But in the continuous struggle for economic growth (an all-but universally accepted goal which is necessary to greater economic welfare, internationally as well as nationally), advancing technology is the key both to improving productivity and to effective competition with rivals. But the costs of high technology in the form of investment, both human and material, are in many cases so large that even economies of the power of the United States cannot sustain all of them alone. For smaller economies, however, like those of West Germany, France or Britain, it is possible to push out the technological frontiers only by international collaboration. CERN, Concorde or the multi-role combat aircraft, and nuclear fusion, are only three of the areas in which pooled resources are seen to be necessary if projects are to be undertaken. Concorde well illustrates the effects on governments' freedom of manoeuvre. Long after it became clear not merely that the grossly underestimated costs of the project could never be recovered but that every flight the aircraft made would almost certainly produce a loss, production was still pushed ahead, partly because of the prestige that was seen to be involved, partly because neither government wished to incur the odium of cancellation, partly because the cooperative undertaking acquired significance as symbolic of Britain's commitment to Europe, and partly because of collaboration between the French and British trade unions in resisting the loss of employment that would have resulted from cancellation. The costs of research and development must continue to rise: mutual dependence, the argument runs, is for this reason inescapable.

The argument is interwoven with that relating to strategy.[7] There are two aspects. The first reflects the same cost-technology nexus. The multi-role combat aircraft mentioned above is an example of attempts at standardization of weapons systems within the NATO alliance, standardization seen as being required by the need to contain escalating costs of ever more sophisticated systems. Selection of a system involves bitter competition among the allies, but once a choice is made the dependence of each member of the alliance upon a system produced, and with spares supplied, by another state imposes cooperation upon them. The same process occurs within the Warsaw pact, although in this case the role played by the Soviet Union is even more pre-eminent than that of the United States in NATO.

The second aspect of strategic interaction derives from the nature and range of the weaponry itself. Each of the major alliances is aware that they can utterly destroy the other, and that the destruction could be wreaked even after an all-out onslaught had been launched and received. In these circumstances the freedom of manoeuvre of each is sharply limited, in terms of technological progress (lest it should be disastrously destabilizing, and perhaps particularly if done in secret), of types of weapons systems (civil defence measures, for instance, may appear to be preparatory to a pre-emptive strike), and of foreign policy behaviour generally which might carry the risk of escalation to nuclear confrontation. Interdependence here is surely at its highest.

Spaceship earth

The discussion so far has concentrated largely, though not wholly, on manifestations of interdependence among developed and industrialized states. The 'spaceship earth' literature has a different focus.[8] Its concern is with problems, mainly ecological in character, which demand a global and holistic approach for their solution. The earth's life systems, it is argued, are threatened by uncontrolled striving for economic growth, by economic imbalances, and by ill-considered technological development. Fertilizers or pesticides to increase food production lead to pollution. Advances in health and hygiene without appropriate changes in social habits and customs produce population explosions. Technological progress resulting in more wealth and employment for expanding populations increases pollution and hastens the rate of exhaustion of the earth's finite resources. Even renewable resources are ultimately finite, in that, for example, there is a limit to the amount of grain that can be produced from an acre of land. Uncontrolled competition for self-renewing resources can destroy them. Thus, the destruction of fish stocks resulting from overfishing exacerbates the problem of destruction of fish stocks from water pollution, which results from the need to dispose of industrial waste, which is the product of nuclear technology, which is necessary to produce more wealth for expanding populations, which need more food and fish to be kept alive. From arguments of this kind it is concluded first that there is a range of problems, vital to man's survival, which must be recognized as being global in character, and secondly that this recognition will be of no avail if matching economic and political structures are not created to deal with them. Interdependence here wears a different aspect: its concern is with the whole world, and not just with the developed states; and its focus is less on the freedom of manoeuvre of governments than on the need for supplementing or replacing them with machinery that can adopt a holistic and global approach to problems that are inherently of that character.

The blurring of the domestic-foreign policy distinction

The final group of enquiries that huddle under the umbrella of interdependence, questions whether the distinction between foreign and domestic policy can still validly be made. The questions are of two main kinds. In the first place it is suggested that policy outputs can frequently be better understood in terms of linkages between intra- and extra-state influences than in terms of the influence respectively of the domestic and external environments of state decision-makers on their policy choices.[9] Thus, analysis of the politics of economic policy-making in Italy would be seriously deficient if it did not take account of the relationship between the Italian Communist party and its ideological associates; while a study of French foreign policy which ignored the context of the Soviet-United States strategic relationship or the availability or otherwise of technical know-how possessed by foreign-owned subsidiaries on French soil, would likewise lack critically important elements. There is not therefore the contrast which was formerly assumed between demands arising within the frontiers of states, with which governments were competent and entitled to deal, and problems arising in the international arena, which had to be handled by discussion and negotiation among formally-equal agents: on the contrary, external issues may become important sources of domestic contention (as the Vietnam war, for example, became a domestic issue within the United States, and was itself much influenced thereby), and domestic questions may lead to external action (as India's foundation as a secular state made for lasting hostility to Pakistan, a state founded on a religious basis, and thus denying a tenet central to India's unity).

The second form of linkages that blurs the foreign-domestic distinction is institutional.[10] It used to be the case that external relations were almost exclusively reserved to a single government department, the Foreign Office or the Department of State. In Britain one of the distinguishing features of the Commonwealth was the right of High Commissioners to deal direct with other departments than the Foreign Office so that the Commissioners and their staffs had contacts throughout the machinery of government. By the early 1970s, however,

> all distinction between Commonwealth and non-Commonwealth governments had disappeared, and officials from the governments of European Community members were in direct and regular contact with their opposite number in Whitehall, not only through specialist attachés in London embassies but also through shared membership of intergovernmental committees and by telephone; able therefore to exchange views and to seek each other's support in bargaining with the other Departments of their own government (Wallace, 1975:111).

This is an example of 'transgovernmental relations', to use the term employed by Keohane and Nye, but it implies a limit on the freedom of manoeuvre of governments of a different kind from those identified previously. In so far as policy-choices are conditioned both by information flow and by lower-level or prior decisions, the existence of transgovernmental relations limits the range of courses of action that may be open to selection.

INTERDEPENDENCE AND POWER

The range and diversity of the interdependence literature should now be apparent. In the context of an analysis of power the questions that emerge are, first, what entities produce behavioural change, and secondly, are traditional definitions of capabilities still adequate? While it has long been recognized that the capacity to produce behavioural change is not precisely correlated with capabilities, nonetheless hierarchies of states are commonly assumed (such as superpowers, great powers, middle powers, small powers), and position in a hierarchy is determined by capabilities. The interdependence literature suggests a diffusion of power which makes any such hierarchy dubious. The variety of international actors and of international transactions produces a high complexity of cross-cutting issues and relationships. The interplay between external transactions and domestic repercussions may profoundly affect outcomes in the international arena. Salient components of capabilities, such as military resources, may be less able to produce desired effects, whether because of the unusability of nuclear power on account of unacceptable destructive capacities being equally balanced, or because political success is not the necessary consequence of military success. At the system level itself changes in the significance and distribution of different elements of capabilities have contributed to the emergence of many centres of power, not necessarily controlled by individual states, as instanced by the OPEC cartel. Thus, familiar state-centric, hierarchical, or centre-periphery models of the international system are replaced by the analogy of a cobweb (to use John Burton's term), where world society is conceived as an interwoven mass of transactional systems in which states are mere regulating agencies, and their boundaries are concealed from view (Burton, 1972). For Burton the concept of power becomes effectively redundant, because outcomes are the result of the working of, and interplay among, transactional systems, not of definable entities matching their capabilities against each other in order to achieve desired ends.

We would contend that the case as presented is overstated, and that the umbrella concept of interdependence is redundant, but that the questions raised about the sources of power and the nature of capabilities are important and need examination.

The case is overstated. As far as IGOs are concerned, their influence is very much a function of states' capabilities. Voting power in the IMF is related to size of contribution, which itself is largely dependent on GNP. While the IMF will often make loans only on conditions, these conditions are generally specified by receiving governments and the degree of constraint on their freedom that they will accept will depend on the degree of weakness of their economies. Under the GATT, tariffs have been generally reduced, but the constraint imposed by this varies with the degree of dependence of a state on trade, and on its ability to gain acceptance for informal methods of achieving the effects of tariffs, such as specifying standards of product. Military alliances such as NATO, involving a measure of integration of defence policy and weapons procurement, impose asymmetrical constraints to the point indeed that a state-member with a pre-eminent level of capabilities (such as the United States in NATO, or the Soviet Union in the Warsaw Pact) may well be able to make the alliance serve as an instrument of its policy and so act as an extension of its capabilities. The United Nations itself may often act as much as a tool of its state-members as a constraint upon them: thus the ability of the former colonial states to press forward the ideology of anti-colonialism was certainly increased by their growing numerical predominance in the General Assembly. Moreover, much of the activity that would seem to be the proper concern of international organizations is conducted outside them because of their frustrating political dynamics: witness Kissinger's 'peace-keeping' by shuttle diplomacy in the Middle East, or the meetings of finance ministers outside the context of the IMF. For all these reasons, therefore, while IGOs certainly impose some limits on freedom of manoeuvre on some states, these limits are widely variant in nature and effectiveness, and very often these organizations will serve primarily as a reinforcement to the capabilities of those states which in relation to the particular organization or issue are already the strongest.[11]

As far as INGO's are concerned it is evident that the consequences of the activity of many of them are trivial. As suggested earlier, they may serve in some degree to alter the domestic environments of decision-makers, but with some exceptions their effect either on capabilities or on objectives is likely to be minimal, and in no way can they be seen themselves as significant actors. Moreover, while the scope and volume of transnational activity expressed through INGOs has been increasing, so too has domestic activity: both may be argued to be reflections of more general processes such as economic growth and political mobilization. Deutsch's investigations of mail flows, for instance, suggested that mail flows had increased within states more than it had between them; and his more general indicator of boundaries of a community — intensities of communication within as compared with across an identified boundary — clearly shows states still to be salient.[12] Thus, although an international community of, say, physicists, may be seen to exist in their occasional meetings, in their reading of the same international journals, and in small degree in their resort to the same international foundations, nonetheless it remains true that most research activity is funded internally, that competition between national communities persists, and that numerous restrictions on the publication of certain types of research remain. National symbols and identification have not vanished — even within such an area as the European Community.[13]

Even those fashionable examples of the non-state actor, the multi-national corporations, can only act in interplay with the governments of the states in whose territories they are located.[14] Their operations remain subject to the laws, including the company laws, of the states where they are established; cooperation between corporation and government may often work to the advantage of both and so, percontra, antagonism may well be mutually disadvantageous; tactless or openly exploitative activity by a corporation can easily stimulate nationalist hostility; governments retain the ultimate sanction of nationalization or expropriation. Thus, while the often quoted observation that the annual sales of General Motors exceed the gross national product of all but a score or so states is clearly not without significance, in terms of outcomes in the international arena it is the mix of capabilities that is important, and the military, the legal, the political and the system-structure components have to be taken into account as well as the economic. No other entities as yet control so wide-ranging a mix of capabilities as states, and the degree of loss that a corporation can inflict (and so the amount of influence it can exert) depends on the centrality of its operations for a particular state or group of states in particular international conditions and at a particular time. Thus, the autonomous influence of oil companies has been reducing in this decade in consequence, from the one direction, of the progressive extensions of state control by the states where the oil exists, and from the other direction, as a result of the slow development of energy conservation policies and of alternative sources of energy by the consumer countries. It is also of course the case that 'multi-national' is from one point of view a misnomer, in the sense that the corporations are normally owned primarily by nationals of one country, and the proportion of nationals of that country employed in the corporation tends to increase as the management hierarchy is ascended. For this among other reasons a corporation may serve as a tool of the government of a country and like an international organization act as an extension of its capabilities.

The thrust of the argument about transactions is of a rather different kind. Here the case is not that other entities than states, and more significant entities, are operative at the international level, and these entities because of their international character destroy the near-total autonomy (except as it was limited by the power of other states) that states previously enjoyed: rather it is that the freedom of manoeuvre of states — and so their ability to affect outcomes — is limited by the irrefragability of the links that bind them together. This argument too is overstated. Formal control over those links is maintained by governments, and the question is whether their weakening or rupture would be more adverse in their consequences than maintaining them. Immediately this raises questions about moderating the effects of weakening links, and about time-scales. As far as economic matters are concerned, participation in an international economic system does not mean subordination to it: governments retain at their disposal a range of domestic policy actions in response to external influences, such as changing interest rates, altering tax structures, sponsoring export promotion, or borrowing internally or externally. Evidently the extent to which measures of this kind can enable a government to get round the constraints of the international economic system will vary with the nature of a state's international economic involvement, and with the level of internal support given to a political system despite unpopular actions. Furthermore, a nexus of economic ties, imposing constraints, by no means grows in a linear fashion over time. If short-term interest rates converge, short-term capital movements will lessen. Factor price equalization may lead to a decrease in the volume of international economic transactions. Such problems as those of insufficient international liquidity may be solved by the creation of new devices, such as SDRs. The politicization of economic issues already referred to may be partly a function of crisis, and so an intermittent rather than an established feature of relationships. The variables affecting the question of whether interdependence is increasing by no means operate consistently and in one direction.

Some observations already made are also appropriate for strategic transactions. In many cases their effect will to a greater extent be to increase one state's capabilities rather than to limit the freedom of manoeuvre of both, even though asymmetrically. The relationship is therefore likely to be more one of dependence than of interdependence; but even here the relationship may be broken at a certain cost, and in certain constellations of the international system, as the case of Sadat and the Soviet Union illustrates. Perhaps the most striking form of interdependence is that displayed in the strategic nuclear balance of terror between the United States and the Soviet Union, requiring as it does mutual caution in technological development, a high flow of information, and a shared understanding of fail-safe devices and control mechanisms on either side; but this is a unique relationship peculiar to the two major nuclear powers, it limits their freedom of manoeuvre in relation to each other but in other areas it does no more than impose care lest a stimulus to escalation might be created, and even this relationship might be transient in the admittedly somewhat unlikely event of an extensive agreement on nuclear disarmament.

The third type of transactions referred to, those of technology, relate very closely to the global village arguments. Technological ties were seen as being necessary partly in order to stay alive in the world of economic competition, and partly to maintain advance towards the all but universally-accepted objective of economic growth. But technology and growth have implications for the global village problems. Should the most pessimistic projections of the rate of exhaustion of the earth's resources come to seem persuasive, pressures will mount for abandonment of the goal of economic growth and for restrictions on advances in high technology in so far as these are seen as being required for growth or as causing environmental damage. The transactional ties resulting from the need for technological cooperation would thus be weakened, and competition would be sharpened.

The same conclusion may be arrived at from a more careful consideration of the global village arguments. They may be thought to be too deterministic and too undifferentiated. Population problems are certainly acute, but they are much more severe in Asia than they are in Africa or in Europe or in most of the Americas, in part because types of response vary. The implicit assumption that a disaster in one area, such as for example a major famine in India, must be global in its implications, by no means necessarily holds. The implication in the analysis that mankind lacks the adaptability to manage these problems as he has managed others in the past cannot be demonstrated. The importance of the global village arguments is therefore in their emphasis on the dangers of growing imbalances and hostilities, and so on the urgency of examining political, economic and social mechanisms and procedures at the international level to avert the danger of catastrophic conflict: these arguments are worthy of close attention, but they can be accommodated within the notion of interdependence only if the concept is stretched so far that it loses all precise meaning.[15]

There remains the question of transgovernmental relations, of linkages, and of the blurring of the distinction between domestic and foreign policy. There is no doubt that, although interplay between domestic affairs and external behaviour has always existed, there has been an important increase in the interpenetration of the two sectors, and in institutional arrangements that reflect it. But these developments are not uniform, universal or unchanging. Many questions of foreign policy have little domestic impact, and many issues in domestic affairs are well insulated from foreign policy. Because of variations from one state to another both in domestic circumstances and in the nature and extent of involvement in international exchanges, issues which for one state necessitate a close interweaving of domestic and foreign policy, for others can be handled almost entirely in one sphere or the other. The nature and extent of the interweaving of a state's domestic and foreign environments also vary over time: the phasing out of sterling as a major reserve currency is likely to reduce the effect of inputs from the international economic system on Britain's domestic economic policy, while rising oil prices will soon have a favourable rather than an unfavourable effect on the British economy. Although there clearly has been a significant growth in transgovernmental relations among some countries of the developed world, and particularly in the special context of the European Community, the phenomenon is to be observed only among a minority of states and can in no way be seen as a widespread manifestation of 'interdependence'. So denial of the billiard-ball model's rigid distinction between domestic and foreign policy does not entail at the opposite extreme acceptance of the assertion of the internationalization of domestic politics or the domestication of foreign politics. And the methodological failure effectively to integrate comparative politics and international relations should not be reified as a radically new international system.

SUMMARY AND CONCLUSION

The concept of international interdependence is clearly here to stay and, consequently, it would be futile to suggest that it should be eradicated from our research lexicon. Nonetheless, our conclusion from the foregoing is that unnecessarily imprecise usage of the concept has led not only to confusion but also to a number of misleading and essentially unsubstantiated conclusions on the nature of the power structure of the international system.[16]

Interdependence has come to be used to embrace such disparate phenomena that it leads to confusion and loss of understanding. Aggregating such phenomena as the growth of IGOs and the growth of INGOs distracts attention from the different factors that have led to the growth of these different organizations, and from the different effects and consequences of them. The concept as it is used tends to have deterministic overtones, and to imply linear progression, whereas in fact the process is not inevitable, and it is marked by discontinuities, asymmetries, and reversals. Writers using the concept often do not define it, but many clearly see it in terms of relation or transaction. But if all relations or transactions, as we have suggested, imply some mutual dependence, the concept of interdependence adds nothing unless it refers to mutual dependence of a wholly new range or nature or complexity. Writers who do suggest definitions use terms like 'sensitivity', 'responsiveness' or 'adaptation': these are concepts which merit exploration in their own right, but they may not help much with interdependence, since a state may, for example, adapt in its relations with other states in ways which may increase, decrease, or have nothing to do with mutual dependence. The blanket way in which the term is used obscures important differences so that an entity like, say, Australia, still operating very much as states used to operate half a century ago, is treated as being no different from an entity like, say, the United States whose territory serves as a resource-base for a wide variety of transnational systems.[17]

Within limits we can of course define concepts as we please. Definitions are neither true nor false, but they must at least be unambiguous. The conceptualization of interdependence is on the contrary marked by a high degree of ambiguity. For effective use of a concept the minimal requirement is to define it in such a way that we know who or what is interdependent and how such interdependence is manifested, so that we can then proceed to examine which factors precipitate interdependence and what are its consequences. Frequently, however, cause, consequence, and manifestation become inextricably mingled. The blurring of domestic and foreign policy, for example, can be seen as a manifestation, or cause, or consequence of interdependence with the result that the concept becomes not merely totally confusing, but also redundant.

The lack of precision in the use of the concept of interdependence means that interdependence frequently becomes synonymous either with a grand process, which is transforming the international system, or with a summary statement of the current state of the international system. It is the nature of all summary concepts that they must be rather overdrawn, but the danger of interdependence as a summary concept is that not only is it contentless, but it also has a number of misleading implicit connotations, the most common among these being cooperation and symmetry. Our discussion has shown, however, that the processes and phenomena identified in the interdependence literature may as well decrease as increase cooperation and symmetry. It was Rousseau's insight in Hoffmann's words 'that interdependence breeds not accommodation and harmony, but suspicion and incompatibility', an insight which many a married couple could confirm (Hoffmann, 1965: 62).

What then are the real questions to be asked? How are they best formulated? What is their relevance to the exercise of power? The analysis of power involves macro-analysis, since power in international relations is relevant and observable only in relationships in the international arena. Our concern is therefore with how outcomes are arrived at in the international arena. The literature which some now seek to wrap up in the single parcel of interdependence has from its various points of view contributed to the destruction of the notion that outcomes are to be understood in terms of interactions among largely autonomous states. It makes suggestions about new actors. It calls attention to limits on the freedom of manoeuvre of state decision-makers. These questions are surely relevant to the determination of outcomes. The problems to be explored then include the following. First, to what extent, and in relation to which issues, do new actors contribute significantly to outcomes? What processes are involved? In what varying degrees are states able to resist or control these new actors, or are compelled themselves to adapt their behaviour and their decision-making processes? What are the variables affecting their ability to resist or to accept adaptation? Secondly, what is the nature and effect of linkages between the domestic and external environments of decision-makers in limiting their abilities to influence outcomes? What types and questions of transactional networks may be identified and how do they differentially affect decision-makers' freedom of manoeuvre? What patterns of linked problem-investigating, information disseminating, or decision-making structures exist, and how far and to whom do they extend?

This is massive agenda for research. The questions are perhaps as important as any that may be devised, because they bear on the adaptability and suitability of existing structures to meet the demands that are being placed upon them. Inadequate adaptability puts survival itself in jeopardy. But enquiry must be based on precise and researchable questions: it will be hindered, not advanced, by woolly and redundant blanket concepts.

NOTES

1. The literature on interdependence is now mammoth. For a variety of illustrations of work focusing on interdependence, see Angell (1967), Bergsten and Krause (1975), Brown (1973), Cooper (1968), Katzenstein (1975), Keohane and Nye (1973), Mally (1976), Morse (1973), Nye (1976), Rosecrance and Stein (1973), Rosenau (1969-1972), Sprout and Sprout (1971), Tollison and Willett (1973), Young (1969).

2. For a variety of work on international organizations, see Bergsten (1976), Claude (1964), Cox and Jacobson (1973), Haas (1964), Huntington (1973), Meerhaeghe (1971), Nye (1971), Sewell (1966), Wallace and Singer (1970), Yalem (1965).

3. For a background review, see Skjelsbaek (1971). The most important of these organizations is the multi-national corporation, the literature on which is immense, though highly repetitive. For general reviews, see, for example, Behrman (1970), Dunning (1972), Kindelberger (1970), Paquet (1972), Vernon (1969-1971).

4. This point can be generalized in terms of the demonstration effect which was originally noted in the context of economic development by Nurkse (1953). Domestically, it has been used to explain why increases in consumption use up most of the increases in real income, while savings tend to remain relatively steady. While the demonstration effect domestically may act as a stabilizing influence which maintains expenditure and output, in the international context it introduces a destabilizing effect by changing tastes and patterns of consumption before a change in the allocation of resources. There is no reason why the demonstration effect cannot be generalized to a whole range of phenomena. In the same way that consumption patterns can be demonstrated, so too can economic policies, patterns of production and so on. For an interesting discussion of the international diffusion of values, see Nettl and Robertson (1968).

5. See, for example, Bergsten (1973), Bergsten, Keohane and Nye (1975), Cooper (1968), Hirsch (1976), Strange (1976).

6. For background literature see, for example, Brzezinski (1970), Drucker (1969), Ellul (1964), Galbraith (1969), Schwartz (1971).

7. Once again the background literature on which the arguments for interdependence draw is legion. See, for example, Baylis et al. (1975), Coffey (1971), Alting von Geusau (1976), Knorr (1966), Liska (1968), Melman (1971), Sarkesian (1972), Twitchett (1971).

8. See, for example, Alfven and Alfven (1972), Boulding (1971), Falk (1972), Meadows (1972), Mesarovic and Pestel (1975), Pirages and Ehrlich (1974), Sprout and Sprout (1971), Ward (1966), Ward and Dubos (1972).

9. See, for example, Hanrieder (1965-1967), Katzenstein (1976), Morse (1969), Rosenau (1966-1969).

10. See, for example, Hopkins (1976), Meltzer (1976), Nye (1976).

11. For further argument, see Cox and Jacobson (1973), Kay (1976).

12. See Deutsch (1960-1961), Deutsch and Eckstein (1961), Deutsch and Russett (1963). Recently Katzenstein (1975) has noted some qualifications to some of Deutsch's conclusions. Perhaps the most important measures are the ratios of

foreign to domestic transactions. While some indicators, such as trade as a percentage of GNP, show extensive external participation, others, such as telephone calls, do not. For example, Cherry (1971) points out that the ratio of internal to international calls in the US is 3400:1.

13. On the salience of national symbols, see Holsti (1970). In the context of the EEC, see Kerr (1973).
14. See the literature cited in note 3 and also Tharp (1976).
15. For a critique of the 'doomsday' studies, accusing them of overaggregation, simplification, and determinism, see Cole (1973) and Maddox (1972).
16. Other writers who have formulated qualifications and criticisms of interdependence include Calleo and Rowland (1973), Calleo (1976), Gilpin (1971-1975), Rosenau (1972), Tollison and Willett (1973), Waltz (1970). For one suggested reformulation of international interdependence, see Little and McKinlay (1978).
17. For further discussion of this theme see Vallier (1973).

REFERENCES

ALTING VON GEUSAU, F. A. M. (1976) 'Security in the Seventies, Changes, Issues and Policies', in: E. O. Czempiel and D. A. Rustow (eds.) *The Euro-American System*. Frankfurt: Campus-Verlag.

ALFVEN, H. and K. ALFVEN (1972) *Living on the Third Planet*. San Francisco: W. H. Freeman.

ANGELL, R. C. (1967) 'The Growth of Transnational Participation', *Journal of Social Issues*, 23 (1):108-129.

BAYLIS, J., et al. (1975) *Contemporary Strategy*. London: Croom Helm.

BEHRMAN, J. N. (1970) *National Interests and the Multinational Enterprise*. Englewood Cliffs: Prentice Hall.

BERGSTEN, C. F., ed. (1973) *The Future of the International Economic Order*. Lexington: D. C. Heath.

—— (1976) 'Interdependence and the Reform of International Institutions', *International Organization*, 30 (Spring): 361-371.

—— and L. B. KRAUSE, eds. (1975) *World Politics and International Economics*. Washington: Brookings Institution.

—— R. O. KEOHANE and J. S. NYE (1975) 'International Economics and International Politics: A Framework for Analysis', *International Organization*, 29 (Winter): 3-36.

BOULDING, K. (1971) 'The Economics of the Coming Spaceship Earth', in: J. P. Holdren and P. R. Ehrlich (eds.) *Global Ecology*. New York: Harcourt, Brace & Jovanovich.

BROWN, L. R. (1973) *World Without Borders*. New York: Vintage.

BRZEZINSKI, Z. (1970) *Between Two Ages*. New York: Viking Press.

BURTON, J. W. (1972) *World Society*. Cambridge: Cambridge University Press.

CALLEO, D. (1976) 'The Post War Atlantic System and its Future', in: E. O. Czempiel and D. A. Rustow (eds.) *The Euro-American System*. Frankfurt: Campus-Verlag.
—— and B. M. ROWLAND (1973) *America and the World Political Economy*. Bloomington: Indiana University Press.
CHERRY, C. (1971) *World Communications: Threat or Promise*. London: Wiley.
CLAUDE, I. L. (1964) *Swords into Plowshares*. New York: Random House.
COFFEY, J. I. (1971) *Strategic Power and National Security*. Pittsburgh: Pittsburgh University Press.
COLE, H. S. D., ed. (1973) *Thinking About the Future*. London: Chatto and Windus.
COOPER, R. N. (1968) *The Economics of Interdependence*. New York: McGraw-Hill.
COX, R. W. and JACOBSON, H. K., eds. (1973) *The Anatomy of Influence*. New Haven: Yale University Press.
DEUTSCH, K. W. (1960) 'The Propensity to International Transactions', *Political Studies*, 8 (2): 147-156.
—— (1961) 'Social Mobilisation and Political Development', *American Political Science Review* 55 (September): 493-514.
—— and A. ECKSTEIN (1961) 'National Industrialisation and the Declining Share of the International Economic Sector, 1890-1959', *World Politics,* 13 (January): 267-299.
—— and B. M. RUSSETT (1963) 'International Trade and Political Independence', American Behavioural Scientist 6.
DRUCKER, P. F. (1969) *The Age of Discontinuity*. London: Heinemann.
DUNNING, J. H. (1972) *The Multinational Enterprise*. London: Allen & Unwin.
ELLUL, J. (1964) *The Technological Society*. New York: Knopf.
FALK, R. A. (1972) *This Endangered Planet*. New York: Vintage.
GALBRAITH, J. K. (1969) *The New Industrial State*. Harmondsworth: Penguin.
GILPIN, R. (1971) 'The Politics of Transnational Economic Relations', *International Organization,* 25 (Autumn): 398-419.
—— (1975) 'Three Models of the Future', *International Organization*, 29 (Winter): 37-60.
—— (1975) 'Three Models of the Future', International Organization, 29 (Winter): 37-60.
HAAS, E. B. (1964) *Beyond the Nation State*. Stanford: Stanford University Press.
HANRIEDER, W. F. (1965) 'Actor Objectives and International Systems', *Journal of Politics*, 27 (February): 109-132.
—— (1967) 'Compatibility and Consensus: A Proposal for the Conceptual Linkage of External and Internal Dimensions of Foreign Policy', *American Political Social Review*, 61 (December): 971-982.
HIRSCH, F. (1976) 'Is there a New International Economic Order', *International Organization*, 30 (Summer): 521-531.
HOFFMANN, S. (1965) *The State of War*. London: Pall Mall.
HOLSTI, K. J. (1970) 'National Role Conceptions in the Study of Foreign Policy', *International Studies Quarterly*, 14 (3): 233-309.

HOPKINS, R. F. (1976) 'The International Role of the Domestic Bureaucracy', *International Organization*, 30 (Summer): 405-432.

HUNTINGTON, S. P. (1973) 'Transnational Organizations in World Politics', *World Politics*, 25 (April): 333-368.

KATZENSTEIN, P. J. (1975) 'International Interdependence: Some Long Term Trends and Recent Changes', *International Organization*, 29 (Autumn): 1021-1034.

—— (1976) 'International Relations and Domestic Structures. Foreign Economic Policies of Advanced Industrial States', *International Organization*, 30 (Winter): 1-45.

KAY, D. A. (1976) 'On the Reform of International Institutions', *International Organization*, 30 (Summer): 533-538.

KEOHANE, R. O. and J. S. NYE, eds. (1973) *Transnational Relations and World Politics*. Cambridge, Mass.: Harvard University Press.

KERR, H. H. (1973) 'Changing Attitudes through International Participation: European Parliamentarians and Integration', *International Organization*, 27 (Winter): 45-83.

KINDLEBERGER, C. P., ed. (1970) *The International Corporation*. Cambridge: MIT Press.

KNORR, K. (1966) *On the Uses of Military Power in the Nuclear Age*. Princeton: Princeton University Press.

LISKA, G. (1968) *Nations in Alliance*. Baltimore: Johns Hopkins University Press.

LITTLE, R. and R. D. McKinlay (1978) 'Linkage-Responsiveness and the Nation State: An Alternative Conceptualization of Interdependence', *British Journal of International Studies*, 4(3): 209-225.

MADDOX, J. (1972) *The Doomsday Syndrome*. London: Macmillan.

MALLY, G. (1976) *Interdependence*. Lexington: D. C. Heath.

MEADOWS, D. H. et al. (1972) *The Limits to Growth*. London: Earth Island.

MEERHAEGHE, M. A. G. van (1971) *International Economic Institutions*. London: Longman.

MELMAN, S., ed. (1971) *The War Economy of the U.S.* London: St Martin's Press.

MELTZER, R. I. (1976) 'The Politics of Policy Reversal', *International Organization*, 30 (Autumn): 649-668.

MESAROVIC, M. and E. PESTEL, (1975) *Mankind at the Turning Point*. London: Hutchinson.

MORSE, E. L. (1969) 'The Transformation of Foreign Policies', *World Politics*, 22 (April): 371-392.

—— (1973) *Foreign Policy and Interdependence in Gaullist France*. Princeton: Princeton University Press.

NETTL, J. P. and R. ROBERTSON (1968) *International Systems and the Modernisation of Societies*. London: Faber and Faber.

NURKSE, R. (1953) *Problems of Capital Formation in Underdeveloped Countries*. Oxford: Blackwell.

NYE, J. S. (1971) *Peace in Parts*. Boston: Little, Brown.

—— (1976) 'Independence and Interdependence', *Foreign Policy,* 22 (Spring): 129-161.

PAQUET, G. (1972) *The Multinational Firm and the Nation State*. Toronto: Collier-Macmillan.
PIRAGES, D. C. and P. R. EHRLICH (1974) *Ark II*. San Francisco: W. H. Freeman.
ROSECRANCE, R. and A. STEIN (1973) 'Interdependence: Myth or Reality', *World Politics*, 26 (October), 1-27.
ROSENAU, J. N. (1966) 'Pre-Theories of Foreign Policy', in: R. B. Farrell (ed.) *Approaches to Comparative and International Politics*. Evanston: Northwestern University Press.
—— (1969) *Linkage Politics*. New York: Free Press.
—— (1972) 'Adaptive Polities in an Interdependent World', *Orbis*, 16 (Spring): 153-173.
SARKESIAN, S. C., ed. (1972) *The Military-Industrial Complex: A Reassessment*. Beverly Hills: Sage.
SCHWALTZ, E. S. (1971) *Overskill*. Chicago: Quadrangle.
SEWELL, J. P. (1966) *Functionalism and World Politics*. Princeton: Princeton University Press.
SKJELSBAEK, K. (1971) 'The Growth of International Non-governmental Organisations in the Twentieth Century', *International Organization*, 25 (Summer): 420-442.
SPROUT, H. and M. SPROUT (1971) *Towards a Politics of Planet Earth*. New York: Van Nostrand.
STRANGE, S. (1976) 'Interdependence in the International Monetary System', in: E. O. Czempiel and D. A. Rustow (eds.) *The Euro-American System*. Frankfurt: Campus-Verlag.
THARP, P. A. (1976) 'Transnational Enterprises and International Regulation', *International Organization*, 30 (Winter): 47-73.
TOLLISON, R. D. and T. D. WILLETT (1973) 'International Integration and the Interdependence of Economic Variables', *International Organization*, 27 (Spring): 255-271.
TWITCHETT, K. J., ed. (1971) *International Security*. London: Oxford University Press.
VALLIER, I. (1973) 'The Roman Catholic Church' in: Keohane and Nye (eds.) (1973), op. cit.
VERNON, R. (1969) *Sovereignty at Bay*. New York: Basic Books.
—— (1971) *Multinational Enterprise and National Security*. London: Institute for Strategic Studies.
WALLACE, M. D. and J. D. SINGER (1970) 'Intergovernmental Organisation in the Global System', *International Organization*, 24 (Spring): 239-287.
WALLACE, W. (1975) *The Foreign Policy Process in Britain*. London: Royal Institute of International Affairs.
WALTZ, K. N. (1970) 'The Myth of National Interdependence', in: Kindleberger (1972), op. cit.
WARD, B. (1966) *Spaceship Earth*. New York. Columbia University Press.
—— and R. DUBOS (1972) *Only One Earth*. Harmondsworth: Penguin.
YALEM, R. J. (1965) 'The Study of International Organisation 1920-65', *Background*, 10 (1): 1-56.
YOUNG, O. R. (1969) 'Interdependencies in World Politics', *International Journal*, 24 (Autumn): 726-750.

7 National Power in an Economically Interdependent World

Klaus Knorr
Princeton University

THE RELATIONSHIP BETWEEN POWER AND INTERDEPENDENCE

There are several forms of international power and of international interdependence, and complex relations between them. This chapter will focus on the question of how increasing international *economic* interdependence affects the military and economic power of states.[1]

In line with current usage in the academic literature, though not in the world of affairs, I perceive power as an effect rather than as the possession of means that may produce relevant effects. Power equals the achievement of preferred outcomes against actual or potential resistance. There are two principal mechanisms through which such power can come about. One is that of coercion which works directly on the other actor's intentions. Thus, A achieves power to the extent that his use of military or economic capabilities compels B to restrict his choices of action; and A may enjoy power when B, apprehensive of A's superior capabilities, restricts his choices even though A has made no demand. Through a second mechanism, A achieves power when he uses capabilities to revise or defend the status quo against B's will without attempting coercive influence. For example, A may simply seize territory from B or deny B's attempt to seize part of his territory; or A may deny an export of technology to B in order to keep him from becoming commensurately stronger, or he may give B economic aid in order to strengthen him.

Author's note: I received helpful comments on a first draft from Kjell Goldmann and my Princeton colleague Jeffrey Hart.

While power as an effect on other actors is thus generated only in particular relationships and situations, and the power resources or capabilities are not power strictly speaking, because many situational variables determine the outcome when these capabilities are used, or even whether they will be used, it is nevertheless the known possession of suitable means and of the will to bring them to bear that can achieve power effects by way of the anticipation of other actors.[2]

Broadly speaking, interdependence means that states are mutually dependent on one another for things valued by their populations. Commonly valued things are peace, security, power, income, employment, knowledge, ideology, cultural goods, etc. Interdependence encompasses both conflictive and cooperative interactions among states. The key question for this paper is how the economic dependencies of states on other states affect their capacity for achieving military and economic power. Dependence is the opposite of self-sufficiency. It implies potential vulnerability to events abroad that can jeopardize the receipt of values or worsen the terms on which their receipt is conditional. Interdependence, in this context, means that as one state A is dependent for valued things on another state (or other states), so that other state is also dependent for certain valued things on A.

Given this conceptualization, power results from a certain structure of interdependence and, in turn, restructures such interdependence between actors. Thus, international economic leverage which is the means toward achieving economic power, is inherent in an *asymmetry* of mutual dependencies. It arises when B is more dependent for something of value on A than A is dependent on B. Similarly, military power is achieved when asymmetry in military capabilities is exploited by the stronger actor or quietly adjusted to by the weaker one. The militarily weaker actor is more dependent on military peace just as in the case of asymmetric economic dependencies the weaker actor is more dependent on economic peace.

The immediate means toward achieving military power is national military strength which consists of military forces, in terms of qualitative as well as quantitative capabilities, and of the will and skill with which they will be employed in certain contingencies,[3] and the potential to increase forces in the event of protracted conflict. An important part is the perception of these things by other actors, for these perceptions (making allowance for alliances) will go far toward determining the dependence of such actors on peace, i.e. the absence of war or threats of war. The ultimate bases of military strength are: (1) national manpower and economic (including technological) resources; (2) the political will that causes a larger or smaller fraction of these resources to be allocated for military purposes; (3) the level of skill (in terms of statecraft) that determines the efficiency with which mobilized resources are transformed into suitable military capabilities; and (4) the national reputation for a disposition to bring force into play when vital state interests are frustrated by other states.

The immediate means toward achieving international economic power is national economic strength which consists of a high degree of control over things of great economic value to other states, and the will and skill with which this leverage is employed. Such economic strength is the greater, the greater the degree of control and the more urgent the demand of the target state for the economic value involved. As is the case in a military confrontation, superior strength is a *net* phenomenon also in an economic confrontation. Both sides may control things of economic value to the other. Superior leverage rests on sharp asymmetry in degrees of control over supply and intensities of demand. The bases of this strength are: (1) the national possession of suitable economic valuables (i.e. markets and sources of supply, including finance); (2) the political determination[4] to mobilize these assets for the exercise of economic power; and (3) the reputation for a disposition to exploit economic leverage in the pursuit of national objectives. For some analytical purposes it is useful to distinguish between 'active' and 'passive' economic strength. Active strength concerns economic leverage over vulnerable states; passive strength refers to the absence of leverage over oneself by other states, i.e. to low or no vulnerability. While states can rank high or low on either dimension, they can also rank high on one and low on the other. National economic wealth, it should be noted, does not equal national economic strength even though some of the ingredients of wealth may also be ingredients of strength. A poor undeveloped country may have great passive economic strength while great economic wealth may be associated with low passive strength, as is indicated by the current dependence of the rich industrial countries on foreign oil.

Exercises of military and of economic power usually differ in one respect important to this discussion. World wars have occurred in which a high proportion of sovereign states took active part. But it is far more frequent for two or a relatively small number of countries to participate in war or in military threat-making. Most states remain neutral because vital interests are not engaged or because war is dangerous and otherwise costly. The states resorting to military conflict therefore need to match their military strength only against that of the militarily opposing states or state. On the other hand, when economic leverage is wielded by withholding something of great value, the target state seeks, and under most circumstances receives, relief from other states that find it economically or politically profitable to supply whatever it is that the state attempting economic coercion withholds. Thus, when the Soviet Union imposed in 1958 an embargo on trade with and aid to a recalcitrant Yugoslavia, the Yugoslavs were able to expand trade with and procure aid from the United States and other Western nations. Similarly, Castro was able to turn to the Soviet Union when the United States cut off economic relations with Cuba. As a result, both attempts at exercising economic power failed. There are usually no neutrals in economic war. The state or states attempting economic coercion must therefore possess a very high degree of control over the world's supply of the economic good that promises to afford effective leverage. A state (or some states) attempting military coercion need control only such a fraction of world military capabilities as exceeds, or is perceived to exceed, the opponent's (or the opponents').

We must now clarify the relationship between economic interdependence (and its rise) and the dependencies that affect the ability of states to achieve military or economic power. International interdependence increased spectacularly after the Second World War in terms of vast increases in the volume of international trade and capital flows. But this global expansion per se tells us little about how increasing economic interdependence impinged on the power capabilities of states. First, global figures ignore large differences in the degree to which individual countries participated in the process. Some countries — for example the members of the European Community which entered a customs union — did more so than others. Moreover, though the foreign economic transactions of some countries expanded greatly after the Second World War, they did so from and to a comparatively low level. As a result of these two factors, there remain large differences between the aggregate economic dependence of states on the outside world. For instance, although Soviet foreign trade increased greatly since 1950, it is still comparatively low. In 1976, exports expressed as a percentage of Gross National Product were 4.3 and 2.7 for the Soviet Union and China respectively, 6.7 for the United States, and 12.1 and 22.0 per cent for Japan and the European Community. Secondly, while such aggregative measures have a bearing on power resources, far more important in this respect is, as we will see shortly, the fine structure of particular dependencies and interdependencies. The nature of exports and imports and the diversification of markets are obviously important factors.

EFFECTS ON MILITARY CAPACITY

We are now ready to explore the relationship between power and the high level of international economic interdependence that has developed and may continue to rise in the future. We will discuss the effects on military power first. This relationship was of keen concern to mercantilists and also to post-mercantilist planners who were interested in national military preparedness. The relationship is complex.

To the extent that international economic interdependence results from relatively free foreign commerce, i.e. from letting comparative production advantage determine trade, national resources are employed more productively. This effect per se redounds to the benefit of national military potential which tends to increase with labor productivity. (Because each state's economic potential is relative to that of others, this effect can be ignored to the extent that trading countries experience equal production advantages.) It is on this dimension that aggregates of foreign economic transactions, and their ratio to gross national product, are significant.

However, national military potential is also determined by the composition, as distinct from the level, of output and hence by the composition as well as the volume of foreign trade. It is this structural effect that worried the mercantilists. They wanted the resources essential to waging war to be under national control. Their ideal was self-sufficiency in war-essential things. To depend for them on foreign sources of supply was too risky.

Countries depend on imports, wholly or partly, on the supply of many things, typically consumer goods that, while benefiting consumer welfare (and indirectly and marginally perhaps also labor productivity) are inessential to the local production of military strength or to the subsistence of societies at war because there are local substitutes, because inventories can be made to last longer than usual, or because consumption can be postponed. Actually, regarding all imported goods, there are different degrees of 'essentiality' in these terms from zero to absolute. Even if a country imported all of its food or fuel, it could do with less than normal supplies in a pinch. The marginal intensity of demand (and need) rises with progressive reductions in supply. Post-mercantilist economists understand this more clearly than their predecessors, and they also understand that market intervention designed to bring about a degree of national self-sufficiency in anything vital to making war — fuel, raw materials, food, industrial capacity and technological knowhow — is economically costly. National independence in these things can usually be achieved only at the expense of forgoing the advantages of international specialization which, as we have seen, also tend to benefit military potential. The idea that autarchy in the production of things vital to warfare is ideal from the mercantilist perspective is actually fallacious. The optimum position would be one in which a country would unrestrictedly participate in the international division of labor by specializing, on the basis of comparative advantage, in the production of the very goods that are essential at time of war, and exchange these for things that are dispensable in wartime. That country would have a huge *potentiel de guerre* while other states would have correspondingly less.

What has been happening to national economic potentials for war during the past thirty years or so while international economic interdependence increased very much? We can assume that the increase affected in both ways the potential of countries that participated in it even though we cannot isolate and hence measure these effects. Labor productivity rose globally, did so spectacularly in the very open economies, and this development can be attributed in part to the expanding international division of labor. It is more difficult to speculate on the structural effects. They were probably slight in the case of countries that even now trade little abroad.[5] The fact that this holds true of both great communist powers — where it has been elite wisdom to shun and therefore minimize any vulnerable dependence on the outside world — is an important part of our answer. Growing economic interdependence has probably not reduced the ability of these countries to wage war.[6] On the other hand, nearly all other countries have become less capable — and the highly industrialized capitalist states have become incapable — of achieving self-sufficiency in the production of many things that are indispensable for national subsistence at time of war. Dependence on foreign raw materials and even food, and above all on foreign fuel, is extremely widespread. These national dependencies have arisen as a result of (1) depleted natural resources; (2) population growth; (3) large increases in requirements owing to industrial development, advanced technologies and income growth; and (4) international specialization promoted by a substantially open international economic order. The first three of these especially are not significantly reversible. Economic interdependence has increased sharply. However, the significance of this change on the ability of these nations to wage war is far from clear because other developments, mostly technological, impinge on this problem.

To begin with, modern technology, rather than international economic interdependence, has greatly reduced the economic possibility for national autonomy in armament production. At the present time only the United States and the Soviet Union are able to develop and produce all lines of highly sophisticated and complex weapons systems. This is so mainly because economies of scale tend to make anything but large outputs grossly inefficient. Even Britain and France can now afford to produce only a limited number of such weapon systems, and can afford that number only by exporting sophisticated systems to countries that are worse off in this respect. This means that all but a very few large and highly industrialized states depend in greater or lesser, but usually in greater, part on imports of this range of weapons. International specialization has vastly increased in the production of these major arms; and technological advance has thus engendered new international dependencies — indeed interdependencies — because the few exporting countries are themselves beneficiaries of this change.

At the same time, however, there has been no geographic contraction in the production of technologically less demanding weapons. On the contrary, Israel and South Africa have become important producers of armaments, and so have some larger developing countries (e.g. China, India and Brazil). Furthermore, the rapidly spreading technology of nuclear power production is associated with the development of national capacities for manufacturing some sort of nuclear explosives.

We have thus contradictory developments in the international dispersal and concentration of weapons production. Mercantilist considerations remain relevant to the manufacture of simpler arms and, of course, the many things, including food and fuel, that the military as well as civilian populations need in time of war. They also remain relevant to the proliferation of nuclear bombs in that governments wishing to pursue or preserve this option will not want to become dependent upon foreign technology and materials if this dependence restricts their freedom of choice.[7] On the other hand, regarding complex aircraft, missiles, ships, tanks, reconnaissance and communications systems, technological advances have come to overshadow mercantilist apprehensions. A country need not worry about self-sufficiency in, say, certain essential metals if factors of scale or lack of technological capacity prevent it from producing such sophisticated arms even in time of peace.

These developments do not, however, signify a commensurate diminution in the ability of states to wage and threaten war. Independence in the material bases of military strength is a decided advantage only when armed clashes are protracted, as happened in the First and Second World Wars. Dependence on foreign arms is no disadvantage when hostilities are so short that they can be conducted with prewar stocks. Prolonged wars are struggles of attrition in which, everything else being the same, the side weaker in material resources will lose. Dependence on foreign goods, including arms, does not necessarily result in such weakness: witness the long war of North Vietnam against South Vietnam and the United States. Self-sufficiency is no advantage, and may be a disadvantage on account of degraded productive efficiency, as long as foreign supplies are readily accessible. Yet there is the risk that the enemy may sever lines of supply by means of direct military action or by effectively threatening neutral supplying countries. The effect of increased economic interdependence on the military capacity of states then hinges on the likely mode of future warfare in this dimension.

In the past, advances in military technology have alternatively favored short or lengthy wars by conferring technical advantage on offensive or defensive operations. Nuclear technology has so far rendered defense close to hopeless, and *potentiel de guerre* is regarded as irrelevant in the event of strategic nuclear exchanges. Moreover, non-strategic warfare between states possessing nuclear arms, if it occurs at all, is assumed to be short because of the probability of escalation to the strategic level. NATO planning for war in Europe is based on the expectation that any military conflict would hardly last longer than a few weeks or months. In addition, most sizeable wars that have taken place since the Second World War have been brief,[8] e.g. the wars between Israel and Arab states, between India and Pakistan, and the war between China and India. There were, however, exceptions. One was the war in Korea and the other, the really big exception, was the American war in Vietnam which was a war of attrition, but one of attrition of will, not of material resources.

Short wars are perhaps also favored by another consequence of modern weapons technology although experience with this effect is so far limited and inconclusive. One would suppose that the stupendous quantum jump in the capacity of new arms (not only nuclear) to cause mass destruction over a brief time span would, if fully exploited, tend to generate a quick exhaustion of the will to fight — on one side or both. It is also possible that the will to fight will flag quickly in highly developed democratic societies which have abandoned traditional beliefs and attitudes that supported international warfare and have grown more aware of the full costs of this way of settling conflicts, even perhaps when they involve core security values.

If future wars are so short that they will be fought with existing stocks of weapons, then dependence on external sources of fuel, raw materials, food and arms is no handicap. Sufficient stocks of foreign weapons, however, can become a critical factor even when wars are short. The Arab-Israeli war of 1973 demonstrated that modern military encounters may consume weapons stocks at such a stupendous rate that any prolongation depends on the willingness and ability of foreign states to provide further supplies. Foreign sources of supply may turn out to be reliable, as was the experience of North Vietnam in its long struggle against South Vietnam and the United States. But such dependence is evidently a risk. Once prewar stocks of arms are depleted, the outcome of war may be affected by unequal rates of replenishment from abroad, and may be decided if only one side continues to receive replacements. This risk, even in the absence of protracted hostilities, is a consequence of increased international interdependence, not along broad economic lines but in the specific area of arms production. Nevertheless, the tendency of both kinds of dependencies to reduce the assured ability of states to wage war will be the stronger the more protracted is the warfare.

Even if the above hypothesis turns out to be valid, the tendency for future wars to be short may be upset by new developments and, in the shorter run, it may not be strong enough to prevail over contrary tendencies. Over the longer run, technology — which is ever changing — cannot be relied upon to favor the offensive and thereby make short military clashes more likely than prolonged ones. The invention of effective defense against nuclear attacks is not inconceivable, and experts are currently wondering whether some new precision-guided weapons (i.e. anti-tank, anti-ship, and anti-aircraft systems) may not come to favor the defenses. It is also possible that some of the new highly accurate weapons will reduce mass destruction to more bearable dimensions.

Of course, other factors than military technology affect the duration of warfare, and essential dependence on arms imports will not necessarily render future wars short even if we except low-key guerrilla fighting. As already intimated, foreign arms supplies may render countries able and willing to prolong war waged with imported weaponry.[9] It is also possible that countries will continue to wage war with simpler arms once they have expended their sophisticated equipment. However, some guerrilla fighting apart, such adaptability has not been observed so far. For example, the several wars between India and Pakistan showed a disposition to stop fighting once the expensive hardware had been shot up.

However, even if future hostilities turned out to be prolonged, it is not clear that the new economic dependencies will substantially affect the ability of states to conduct them. No such effect should be produced between belligerents whose dependencies entail approximately equal handicaps. If one side's dependence on foreign weapons in wartime seems riskier than the other's, that risk can be equalized by the establishment of alliances, adjustments in the accumulation of pre-war stocks, some expansion in domestic arms production, or by resort to military strategies that promise to force a quick decision.

To the extent states are able to produce arms themselves, we have already observed that increased economic dependence on the outside world for raw materials, fuel, etc. would be disabling only if that dependence included indispensable things the supply of which could be cut off during a protracted war. Again, even if some conditions should once more come to favor prolonged warfare in the future, countries suffering equal handicaps would not be disabled from fighting one another. And to the extent that the handicaps were perceived to be unequal, governments might do various things to make them less so. They could do this by means of stockpiling supplies of critical materials, protecting high-cost production of certain items, and by maintaining large inventories of armaments in time of peace. By resorting to such measures, countries could either diminish their dependence on the outside world, i.e. cut back international interdependence in selected critical areas, or they could render dependence less risky.

It should also be noticed that an opponent's military ability to cut, or threaten to cut, a country's lines of supply with the world abroad will — rare particular circumstances aside — loom like a grave risk only in the event of major conflagrations, especially a war between the Soviet Union and the United States, involving their allies — a conflict that would be *sui generis* in many ways.

Three conclusions appear indicated on this part of the discussion.

(1) Increasing international economic interdependence has hardly affected the war-making capacity of those states, including the Soviet Union and China, that participated little in the process or still cultivate low levels of economic transactions with the outside world.

(2) Increased economic interdependence has done little to reduce the *ability* of other states to fight wars with one another, especially short wars. And if these states so desire, they can diminish the risks that rising economic interdependence has created or magnified.

(3) Increased international economic interdependence has probably affected the mode of warfare, especially its duration, more than the war-making capacity of states.

These conclusions fit the information we have on the prevalence of military conflicts, military threats and military preparations during the past thirty years. This information does not suggest a noticeable global diminution in national resorts to force or in military spending. Within the global picture, however, the information also suggests some shift in these respects characterized by a relatively lower incidence in the highly developed capitalist countries and a higher one in the rest of the world (Knorr, 1977: 5-27).

EFFECTS ON INTERNATIONAL ECONOMIC LEVERAGE

For the sake of brevity I will discuss the effects of increasing interdependence on international economic power only with reference to the coercive use of economic leverage.[10] It follows from the introductory remarks that only a completely self-sufficient country is safe from all attempts at economic coercion. Such a country would possess the utmost passive economic strength. Conversely, a state that depends on foreign actors for the supply of all things vital to its subsistence and prosperity is highly vulnerable. It would have no passive economic strength whatever. The ideal position for an aggressive actor is a monopoly over the supply of something that is indispensable to all other states combined with its own dependence on the outside world solely for luxuries that can be done without.

One can rank cases of economic coercion on a continuum from very high to very low in terms of the costs of compliance to the threatened actor. These costs tend to be high when the attempt at coercion is, first, dramatic, i.e. when it precipitates, or occurs in the course of, a grave political crisis and is associated with a great deal of domestic and international publicity and, secondly, when it is directed across issue areas, e.g. when economic means are used to achieve political results as, for example, when the US Senate approved an agreement for enlarged trade with, and credit to, the Soviet Union conditional on greater freedom of emigration for Soviet Jews. (Issues are rarely dramatic when economic coercion is attempted for the achievement of some sort of economic gain.) Cases characterized by high costs of compliance are typically on the level of *haute politique*.

On the other hand, the costs of compliance tend to be low when the stakes of conflict are small and advanced in a routine manner and the attempt at coercion receives little or no publicity as, for example, when the receipt of additional economic aid is made conditional on the strengthening of anti-inflationary policy. Such attempts usually occur in the same issue area, i.e. low-level economic coercion is meant to achieve compliance in matters of economic policy.[11] They can be regarded as cases of 'low diplomacy'. The costs of compliance are determined not only by the disutility of whatever it is the target state is expected to do, but also by the experience of having to yield to a foreign threat. The sheer act of compliance is a loss to governments in terms of domestic as well as international standing. This is why the degree of publicity surrounding the coercive play is an important factor.

The distinction between cases of high and low diplomacy in international exercise of economic strength is important because the target state will yield only if the threatened economic deprivation exceeds the costs of compliance. In cases of high diplomacy, coercive attempts therefore have a chance to succeed only when they are based on very strong leverage in terms of degree of control over the supply of things of economic value, and of the target state's high intensity of need for them. In cases of low diplomacy, modest economic leverage can succeed.

Control over things of economic value — e.g. markets, sources of commodity supply, economic aid, technology and arms — is usually dispersed internationally. Very high degrees of national control occur very rarely. It is therefore not surprising that attempts at exercising economic power in matters of high diplomacy have seldom succeeded in the past (Knorr, 1975: vi-vii). The Soviet attempt in 1948 to coerce Yugoslavia into accepting Soviet hegemony by cutting off trade and economic aid was a typical case. Yugoslavia had been highly dependent on the Soviet Union and the Eastern European communist states for trade and aid. Yet Yugoslavia was able to switch trade to, and procure aid from, the West. She refused to comply. Similarly, Castro was able to turn to the Soviet Union and other communist countries when the United States imposed an embargo on trade with Cuba. Third states are apt to supply what the state attempting coercion is denying to the target country. A high degree of control over supply is, of course, achieved more readily when a number of states act together. Yet such cooperation is difficult to establish when the purpose of economic coercion is political (rather than when it is the extraction of monopolist or oligopolist profit). It is a rare coincidence when states that happen to share control over something of value as a result of geographic luck or similar technological development are united on the purpose of pursuing aggressive *political* objectives. OAPEC is exceptional. Even collective economic sanctions — under the League of Nations against Italy in the mid-1930s when it had invaded Ethiopia, and under the United Nations in recent years against Rhodesia — have failed because a few countries did not cooperate. On the other hand, attempts at economic coercion in matters of *low* diplomacy have been more frequent; indeed, they occur almost routinely as in bargaining over trade restrictions and between donors and recipients of foreign aid. Although we lack statistical studies, the impression is that these low-level pressures often succeed, at least in part. Since the costs of compliance tend to be low in these cases, neither a high degree of control over the supply of something of economic value, nor a highly inelastic demand is needed for coercion to become effective.

It is much more difficult to speculate about the effects of mounting international economic interdependence on the exercise of economic power than on that of military power because far less empirical work has been done on the international uses of economic leverage than on military threats and conflicts.[12] An increase of international interdependence is of course tantamount to a growth of mutual dependence but, per se, this need not increase coercive economic leverage. Only the emergence of greater asymmetries in mutual dependence can bring this about. It all depends on how the growth of interdependence is structured. International economic leverage would increase only if increasing interdependence were associated with higher degrees of national control over economic valuables, or if certain valuables became more indispensable to states depending on foreign sources of supply.

Evidently, much of the expansion of profitable international commerce involves goods that do not create a dependence on foreign supplies which can be exploited in important power plays. For instance, American imports of foreign automobiles, television sets and shoes have expanded sharply in recent years. To pose the possibility that foreign exporting countries would want to cooperate in order to withhold these goods for exerting pressure on the United States, boggles the imagination. But let us suspend disbelief and assume that this would happen. Little leverage would be generated because American consumers, owning large inventories of these durable goods, could postpone new purchases until American production is expanded to satisfy domestic demand. American consumers would have to pay higher prices but it is most unlikely that this prospect would lower the resistance of the country to foreign pressure.

No doubt, the Arab oil embargo in 1973-74 was a spectacular event in the use of economic leverage for attempting coercion in a conflict of high diplomacy, and there have been repeated threats since then, usually vague, that the Arab states might reimpose an embargo or press OPEC to fix oil prices at a higher level than desirable on strictly economic grounds in the event that the Arab-Israel dispute was not terminated by a settlement acceptable to the Arab states. It has also been hinted that the oil weapon might be unleashed again if the leading industrial states were insufficiently responsive to Third World demands for a new world economic order. In view of the continued dependence of the industrial states on foreign oil — a dependence that has been sharply increasing since 1973 in the case of the United States — the OAPEC countries no doubt command substantial economic leverage as long as they act in unison. Interdependence here is of large scope, of high degree and intensity, and of low reciprocity. This situation indicates a particular vulnerability that has developed as a result of the greatly increased dependence of many states on the major oil exporters. Moreover, because oil is so large a component of world trade (about one-fifth by value), one might infer that, on account of this one commodity situation alone, international economic leverage for coercive use in high diplomacy has vastly increased in just a few years. There was nothing like it before 1972.

Yet it is easy to exaggerate the potential of 'oil power'. The effectiveness of power plays is always context-determined. Any proportion of oil exports subjected to an embargo is likely to have less coercive effect in the future than it did in 1973 because of the absence of surprise and panic, and because increased inventories of oil in importing countries can be stretched out by means of rationing for a long time even if OAPEC instituted a total embargo. Therefore, a severe oil embargo would have to last a long time before crippling effects could be achieved. This, in turn, means that the costs to OAPEC members of imposing an embargo would be correspondingly heavy. These countries have also learned in recent years of unemployment and inflation in the industrial oil-importing countries that their prosperity is closely tied to the prosperity of the latter. None of these developments rules out a future embargo. The leverage is there, but it has diminished in the sense that a particular degree of coercive pressure now requires an embargo that is more severe and/or more prolonged than was the case in 1973. Employing the embargo has become more costly.

The question has been raised whether the progressive depletion of other non-renewable resources, on the one hand, and an expanding international demand resulting from world economic and population growth, on the other, may create similar supply dependencies in the future. The postulated trends are certainly plausible. But whether they foreshadow international scarcities that are highly exploitable is doubtful. Thus far, no study of particular commodity markets has suggested the likelihood of new international dependencies anywhere near as vulnerable as is the present dependence of many countries on foreign fuel. The case of oil looks to be unique in terms of a very high inelasticity of demand as well as span of control over supply. No need is as vital as that for energy. Regarding raw materials, the possibilities of substituting one material for another, of inventing technologies that reduce specific needs, of reclamation and of stimulating new, even if high-cost, production seem to serve as a constraint on monopoly power; and it would take a number of countries in every instance that would have to unite for other purposes than engineering a monopolist elevation of prices in order to establish great leverage for coercive attempts in conflicts of high diplomacy. Indeed, even the base of collective 'oil power' for use in high diplomacy depends on the persistence of unifying political objectives, and is threatened over the long run by the combined effects of conservation, the increased production of various fuels, and the rise of nuclear energy.

Control over food supplies does not at this time loom as a likely base for effective coercive power except perhaps occasionally with reference to some less developed countries visited by a series of poor crop years; and the political and moral costs of exploiting leverage over them would serve as strong restraints on potential surplus countries (i.e. the United States). Consumers in developed countries occasionally suffering disastrous agricultural conditions, such as the Soviet Union, can always choose to eat less meat and cheese for a year or so instead of having their government bow to economic pressure. The supply of manufactured goods will remain widely dispersed, and become even more so as industrialization proceeds in the Third World; and demand for these goods tends to be relatively elastic because consumption is more easily postponable than holds true for energy and basic food. The supply of high technology is more likely to yield at least fleeting monopolist power, but its consumption likewise can be postponed in a pinch and several sources of supply are usually available.[13] Control over the supply of sophisticated weapons systems is a still more likely candidate for the derivation of considerable monopolist power. To be sure, the competition between exporting states has so far set sharp limits to this potential leverage. But the practical difficulties for an importing country to switch from one supplier to another for arms that are not standardized do offer opportunities for coercive exploitation although leverage also in this case depends on the degree to which consumption is postponable — a factor that is governed by the security needs that importing states perceive to face.

Economic aid has figured frequently as another base of economic leverage of coercive pressure in conflicts of high diplomacy (Knorr, 1975: vi-vii). But coercive success has proved elusive. When the costs of compliance to the target state are substantial, it may prefer to forgo aid or to turn to alternative donors who are rivals for influence of the country attempting a power play. Indeed, in my historical work I have not come across a single case in which the withholding of economic aid, or the threat of doing so, succeeded in conflicts of high diplomacy.

All the bases of international economic power we have just discussed serve, of course, also when economic pressure is exerted in low-level diplomacy concerned with conflicts over trade or aid policy and similar things. Even small asymmetries in mutual dependence can be exploited when the stakes of conflict are small or moderate and do not arouse public concern. It is my impression — on the basis of anecdotal material and deductive reasoning[14] — that these low-level attempts at international coercion have been frequent, in certain relationships to the point of routine (i.e. in the relationship between the donor and the recipient of economic aid), and that the attempts have often been successful. Unfortunately, we know nothing about the precise magnitude of this practice. The very fact that these applications of economic leverage usually escape publicity impedes their numerical recording. It is impossible to observe any changes that may have taken place as international economic interdependence increased.

Nor is it fruitful here to derive hypotheses deductively. One might hypothesize that the rapid growth of this interdependence is bound to have multiplied bits of asymmetrical dependence that provide enough leverage for low-level exploitation. But it is also possible that most of this growth involved international exchanges that create no real dependencies, as when countries produce or even export as well as import the same type of article. It is also possible that whatever the actual (but unknown) relationship between growth of economic interdependence and low diplomacy attempts at economic coercion, it was overshadowed by exogenous developments, for example the entry into the international system after the Second World War of numerous poor and usually small states whose governments were eager to receive concessionary economic advantages from the highly developed countries or, for that matter, the practice of the latter states to give economic and technical aid to destitute less developed countries. I mention these examples only to explain why, in the absence of an empirical basis, it is not possible to say anything about the effects of rising interdependence on the distribution of international economic leverage capable of exploitation in low-level attempts at coercion.

The principal conclusions on changes in the bases of international economic power are as follows.

First, it is not the volume of international trade and finance but the emergence of particular patterns of asymmetrical dependencies that supplies a basis for the wielding of economic power. Secondly, the recent past has brought the rise of oil power which is formidable enough to lend itself to attempts at coercion in matters of high diplomacy. But this rise has been a singular event. No similar situation of high and cohesive control over an extremely vital good seems to be in the offing. Cases of great economic leverage have been rare in history. When they occurred, they resulted from unusual combinations of circumstances. Increasing international interdependence has not apparently made them less unusual. Thirdly, lack of empirical information precludes any generalization about changes in the bases of lesser economic leverage that might be associated with increasing international economic interdependence.

There are, of course, things countries can do to reduce whatever vulnerabilities to foreign coercion that growing economic interdependence has engendered. Within the limits of overall resource constraints and willingness to bear the opportunity costs of security measures, they can minimize riskful dependencies on economic valuables in the outside world or make such dependencies less dangerous. In the military area, countries can do the first by protecting the production of things regarded as vital to the degree of military strength that affords a viable basis for deterrence and defense. They can do the second by stockpiling critical materials and arms, by seeking assured access to foreign supplies within suitable systems of alliance, and by designing postures for deterrence and defense that do not depend on protracted effort. In the economic area, countries can also limit risky dependencies by protecting domestic production, and curtail the vulnerability inherent in such dependencies by maintaining large inventories of critical

goods and by diversifying foreign sources of supply. They can also conduct their economic life in ways making it independent of foreign favors.
There are to be sure limits to such adaptation. Those that are absolute depend on size and resource structure of countries. Others are fixed by the costs of security measures, especially those connected with forgoing some of the economic benefits yielded by unhindered international movements of goods, capital, technology, managerial skill and even labor. In this respect, societies are confronted by trade-offs capable of rational solution, within the constraints of uncertainties, as long as all types of marginal advantages and disadvantages are taken into proper account.

EFFECTS ON THE WILL TO USE POWER RESOURCES

Even if the recent increase in international economic interdependence had modified but not appreciably abridged national capacities for exerting military and economic power internationally, the question remains of whether this growth has diminished national *dispositions* to resort to coercive action when international conflicts of interest involve sufficiently high stakes. Even if increasing economic interdependence has done nothing or little to reduce the power resources of many states, these and non-economic interdependencies might have diminished their willingness to bring these resources into play.

The empirical record does not suggest on the global level any notable change in this direction. There have been plenty of military threats and conflicts and they do not exhibit a clearly observable trend. The absence of major hostilities among the great powers permits no contrary conclusion because such wars did not occur for prolonged periods of time before (e.g. from 1815 to 1870 and from 1871 to 1914). Moreover, levels of military expenditures and manpower have been high and rising since the early 1950s. It is true that the disposition to resort to force has strikingly declined, compared with previous behavior, in Western Europe and Japan, and provision for military defense in this set of countries has decreased relative to that in the rest of the world taken as a whole. But because the rest of the world has increased such provision in absolute terms one can speak only of a global shift, not of a global diminution. And once the Arab oil-exporting countries came to enjoy a rare degree of monopoly control over something vital to others, they lost no time in applying it for coercive purposes.

It is of course difficult in a dynamic and untidy world to detect newly emergent trends. Perhaps inchoate changes are in the making and government behavior in most of the world is lagging behind in adjusting to them. Indeed, some people have speculated about the international emergence of novel restraints, associated with rising economic interdependence, that impinge on the disposition to pursue coercive policies. Already the early free traders around the middle of the nineteenth century, in particular the Manchester School in England, predicted that free trade would not only render nations economically too interdependent to conduct war but also foster cosmopolitan leanings and identifications and thus make nations more peace-loving. And, more recently, what Stanley Hoffmann has called the modernist school of thought in international studies (1973: 3-25) has advanced the propositions that contemporary states are increasingly beset by common problems which, demanding cooperative solution, make the use of coercion irrelevant, and that the spread of transnational loyalties and the shrinking capacity of national governments condemn interstate conflicts, and national preparations for engaging them, to increasing obsolescence.[15]

Although it is hard to perceive a decline in the role of state government — national government seems only now to be coming into its own in most of the world — I do not doubt that growing economic interdependence along with other factors (especially rapid population growth and the exploitation of new technologies) has heightened incentives toward seeking cooperative solutions for a growing number of pressing international problems. Nor can it be doubted that there has been a spread of transnational and subnational identifications (although often associated with intense hostility toward other groups within and across national boundaries). Yet the modernist hypotheses that assert these developments as *dominating* traditional forms of behavior lack, so far at least, sound empirical foundations and cannot at this point be regarded as more than allegations or hopes.

It is surely safer to speculate about changes in the perceptions and attitudes of governments and elites which, although not dominating, nevertheless tend to restrain coercive attempts somewhat. United Nations declarations, for instance, record new normative sensitivities, however frail, that call for restraint in the use of force, and there has been the surfacing of sensitivities posing the responsibility of rich societies to help the poor — an attitude that should tend to inhibit the former from applying economic leverage against the latter for purposes of national gain.[16] It is to be noted, however, that such developments are not a consequence, certainly not directly, of growing *economic* interdependence.

It is also possible to approach the problem in a different way. Instead of only positing rather revolutionary changes in relevant attitudes among governments and elites, one can ask whether or not there has been some recent tendency for the utility of coercive attempts, whether by economic or military means, to fall off. When representing rational behavior, attempts at wielding military or economic power have always been restrained by an awareness of the costs, including risks, of doing so. This is why over most historical periods they were justified only by stakes of conflict commensurately high in the eyes of decision makers.

It so happened that the end of the Second World War also marked the end of an era during which a number of countries that were first to develop themselves economically and technologically acquired capabilities for coercive action so superior to those of the rest of the world that their employment was extraordinarily 'cost-effective' and hence possessed exceptional utility even when the stakes were low. Recent decades have brought two revolutionary changes on this score. First, a diffusion of national capabilities has greatly reduced the effectiveness and cheapness of coercive attempts by the former imperial states against members of the Second and Third Worlds. Secondly, a diffusion of political influence by means of progressive democratization within the leading industrial states has substantially complicated decisions on whether resorts to coercive plays are nationally worth while. Social groups that bear the main costs and can expect little if any gain from international aggression now have more influence than they enjoyed before. Additional changes, especially in the realm of military technology, have exerted congruent effects (see Knorr, 1966).

Again, however, although these changes have been momentous, they are not directly attributable to the growth of international economic interdependence. But this growth probably did contribute, if only modestly, to increases in the costs of engaging in coercive interaction. Conflict, whether economic or military, does disturb, if not suspend, productive economic exchanges, and this negative effect is apt to have grown perceptively, though not necessarily proportionately, with the rising level of economic intercourse. Certainly, to cite just one example, Arab statesmen understand that an oil embargo, heavy and prolonged enough to yield important coercive power, would be costly to their countries, not only in the short run but also in terms of basically weakening the national economies on whose prosperity they depend. This sort of perceived interdependence can be expected to caution restraint. It seems likely therefore that the elevated level of economic interdependence, and a growing understanding of its impingement of national welfare, have somewhat raised the threshold that must be crossed before attempts at international coercion appear to be worthwhile.

NOTES

1. Again, this limitation is not to convey that non-state actors are unimportant. International terrorists who do not act as agents of a state may present formidable quasi-military problems in the future if they acquire weapons of mass destruction and employ them coercively. In addition to international organizations, private multinational corporations have attracted a great deal of attention as wielders of economic 'power' which they can use in formal bargaining with host governments and for intervening in the political process of host countries by means of bribery and financial support to preferred political groups. However, state governments have been and are by far the most important wielders of power in the international system. Recent experience has shown that state governments in the Third World, as they become gradually stronger, tend to have the upper hand in any contest with multinational corporations. State sovereignty tends to win out in determining the conditions under which such business firms are allowed to operate. The bargaining

strength of these firms results essentially from the advantages that host governments perceive to derive from the local activities of foreign enterprises.

2. In roughly this sense, Kjell Goldmann speaks of the 'possession' of power as a 'dispositional concept' (see Chapter 1). In my own work (1975: 9-14), I have distinguished between 'putative' and 'actualized' power.

3. Note that this formulation makes military strength ultimately situational. Not all the military forces of a state may be available for, or suitable to, employment in particular situations, and logistical reach may be a factor. Even will and skill are apt to vary depending on the purposes and modes of employing force. On all these scores, for example, American military strength for waging war in Vietnam was far less than it would have been for defending the United States itself or even for participating in the defense of Western Europe.

4. The political will to mobilize and use resources for exercising power or, defensively, for putting up counter-power, links interstate politics with domestic politics.

5. A qualification is in order, however. A state guided by extreme mercantilist considerations might trade little with the outside world but import a few things essential to the production of military strength that cannot be produced at home. But such a state would be likely to stockpile such goods for use in emergencies.

6. This does not exclude the possibility that certain imports, if available, would not strengthen the power resources of these states. Thus, it is possible that the denial by the United States of exports to the Soviet Union of certain 'strategic' goods (e.g. highly sophisticated computer technology) disadvantaged the latter's armament industry.

7. Among the states that have recently refused American demands for full international safeguards against the diversion of nuclear facilities and materials to weapons production are Israel, South Africa, India, Pakistan, Brazil, and Argentina.

8. There has also been a great deal of minor fighting that is intermittent and prolonged, such as border skirmishes in Africa, and fairly prolonged interventions in civil wars, such as the Egyptian intervention in Yemen and the Iranian intervention in Oman. The extent to which these relatively low-level efforts were subject to material constraints is unclear. Yet even if they were, it was scarcely international economic interdependence that accounted for the constraints. On the contrary, the arms involved were largely supplied from abroad.

9. However, as the Yom Kippur War of 1973 demonstrated, there are countervailing constraints, especially when military stocks are being absorbed in battle at a very high rate. Inventories may be limited in supplier countries. There may be logistical bottlenecks, and supplier countries may perceive a political advantage in bringing the fighting to an end.

10. The analysis of the other uses is similar and presents no important special problems.

11. It is to be noted that there are cases in which these characteristics do not converge. For instance, financial aid to a country in serious balance-of-payments trouble may be made conditional on the adoption of remedial domestic policies which its government finds extremely difficult to enact for political reasons. The political

costs of compliance are then high even though interaction occurs in the same issue area.

12. There is not, paralleling the International Institute of Strategic Studies in the military field, a center that records and analyzes encounters of international economic power.

13. Dependence on foreign technology and materials in the development of nuclear energy is a special case. In the interest of minimizing the proliferation of nuclear weapons production, the United States has recently attempted to induce a number of countries to accept stricter international safeguards designed to prevent diversion of fuel materials to military programs, and has tried in particular to make countries forgo both breeder reactors that produce more weapons-grade plutonium than they consume and local plants for reprocessing spent fuel. So far this policy has encountered strong resistance, in part because some countries want to preserve the option of weapons development and in part because countries do not want to accept indefinite dependence on foreign countries for uranium or processed materials — a dependence that might be exploited by supplier states.

14. Thus, one would deduce from the propensity of governments to seek and experience superior power, domestically as well as internationally, that donors of aid could not resist the temptation to use leverage over recipients. They would do so either for extracting a benefit or for imposing ideas on how the recipients should use the funds.

15. See, for example, Rosenau (1974: 32-49).

16. How much such normative dispositions, and the positive inter-active identification on which they rest, will prevail is, of course, extremely doubtful. These tendencies are more pronounced within societies (where interdependence, incidentally, surpasses anything that has occurred internationally). But they do not seem to discourage strongly the attempts of groups, advantaged in terms of influence, to gain economic benefits at the expense of other groups.

REFERENCES

HOFFMANN, S. (1973) 'Choices', *Foreign Policy* (Fall): 3-25.
KNORR, K. (1966) *On the Uses of Military Power in the Nuclear Age*. Princeton: Princeton University Press.
—— (1975) *The Power of Nations*. New York: Basic Books.
—— (1977) 'On the International Uses of Military Force in the Contemporary World', *Orbis*, 21 (Spring): 5-27.
ROSENAU, J. N. (1974) 'Capabilities and Control in an Interdependent World', *International Security* 1 (Fall): 32-49.

8 Autonomy: What Do We Mean, and What Do We Know?

Bertil Dunér
The Swedish Institute of International Affairs

THE RELEVANCE OF THE CONCEPT

There seems to be a widely shared conviction that difficulties in the international arena have burgeoned so fast over the last decades that the system is now more than ripe for profound rearrangements. There is a quest for an international monetary system, for a new economic world order, and for new organizations and regimes in a number of fields.

In some nations this may be the outlook on the world that captures the prime interest of statesmen as well as social scientists: management of the international *system*. In other countries, on the other hand, there may be just as firm a belief that there are also other issues at stake: the freedom of action of the *individual nation*. We would guess that worries about the state of autonomy are more widespread among the smaller and weaker members of the international family. It also seems reasonable that, ipso facto, the latter aspects get far less coverage than the urge for system management in the on-going debates at international fora. This chapter focuses upon the international problems precisely from the point of view of the single nation.

In traditional thinking about international politics there seems to be a postulate that all states aim to shape their own destiny. Indeed, this striving may be conceived of as part and parcel of the existence of states as such. However, if all nations are thus autonomous to at least some extent, it seems on the other hand to be implied that not all of them can be equally successful in pursuing a policy of autonomy.[1]

Questions about the degree and distribution of autonomy in the world have been raised since the end of the Second World War, but mostly perhaps with reference to specific contexts or groups of countries, for example in relation to the process of decolonization or the Third World countries.

In the present decade the scope of scholarly as well as political interest has been broadened. There is an emerging preoccupation with the situation of the industrialized states as well and strong doubts have been voiced concerning their degree of autonomy. The background of such ominous points of view is of course to be found in the structural transformations that have taken place at the global level since the late 1940s. Analysts of international relations have been observing these processes for a long time. Various aspects have been pointed at, all representing strands in a net which have tied the international congregation of nations more and more closely together: a strong and steady growth of international exchange, of interaction which not only involves governments proper but also other entities, of so-called transnational actors, of interdependence and interpenetration, etc.

Observations of these tendencies logically may lead to queries about the area of manoeuvre of the individual state. Will it not be shrinking concomitantly with structural changes, bringing all countries more closely together? However, in case observed long-term developments have not been reasons enough for raising such questions, more turbulent experiences of recent years — the Arabs wielding the oil weapon, terrorism on an international scale, etc — have of course speeded up the questioning and perhaps also made the answers go in a more gloomy direction.

Some scholars, and particularly economists it seems, have lately put forward rather radical and sweeping assertions regarding the increasing degree to which the freedom of action of the individual state has been circumscribed.[2] One student of international relations has put it in a succinct way: 'The economic systems of the world have during recent decades increasingly expanded over the borders of the national states, at the same time as the political systems have continued to be mainly national in character...(This)...tends to make the national states less and less efficient decision-making units...' (Lindbeck, 1975: 45).

One of the protagonists in the international debate over structural transformations of the international system has expressed a similar idea thus: '... the actual ability to control events either internal or external to modernized socieites — even those that are Great Powers — has decreased with the growth of interdependence, and is likely to decrease further' (Morse, 1970: 372).

Whether one is to put confidence in such hypotheses or not is of course a matter of the quantity and quality of empirical evidence that may be marshalled to their support. However, it goes without saying that the tenability of propositions about the real world also hinges upon basic positions that are taken at a theoretical level. In this chapter we are concerned with the latter aspects only.

The main purpose of this chapter is to discuss ways of conceptualizing autonomy. We are concerned with the usefulness and implications of various theoretical approaches. We will try to show that several perspectives might be conceivable. Some of them, however, do not match reasonable requirements. However, an approach which does is deployed. Our thesis is that given this approach we have good grounds to question the validity of the kind of propositions that were cited above.

Before coming to grips with this endeavour let us just mention some points of departure for our reasoning. Autonomy is a concept that may apply to various kinds of social entities. However, in so far as we would like to denote some kind of freedom of action we must for logical reasons restrict ourselves to actors only. Hence, we may not think of a country as such for instance as being autonomous. In the present case it seems convenient to substitute for the country its state apparatus or government. For simplicity's sake the latter is understood as a unitary actor.

Moreover, we will only take into account external aspects of autonomy, i.e. a country's relations with its international environment. We are of course aware that problems of autonomy may also be conceived of in terms of relationships within a social system itself where the outside world is more or less abstracted away. An example of this would be the difficulties that a government of an underdeveloped country has in making its rule legitimate and enforced in all parts of the country or among all segments of the population. However, such aspects will play no part in our reasoning.

SOVEREIGNTY

A traditional way of looking upon a state's freedom of action has to do with the formal or juridical competence of making rules, being legitimate in a certain geographical or functional area. This is the aspect of sovereignty.[3] It seems almost trivial to state that this conception after all does not match too well with the problems of freedom of action that are discussed in current literature. On the contrary, the shortcomings of the concept of sovereignty have frequently been stressed.

The problems relevant to autonomy seem to go far beyond the legal aspects. In current discussions various circumstances are emphasized. It is said, for example, that states may have contradictory socio-economic goals (in terms of employment and the like). Increasing interchange may aggravate these more or less latent conflicts making individual policies more risky. Such contradictions may spring from the fact that policies pursued in one country may have unintentional repercussions in others, thereby damaging or obstructing national policies in the latter. Increased interaction, however, is also supposed to open up new possibilities for deliberate interference in other states' business by manipulating transactional flows. Moreover, transnational interaction would presumably give rise to new institutions — like the Euro-dollar market — lying outside the reach of the political authorities of individual states.

If factors of this and a similar nature are supposed to render management of government affairs more problematical than earlier, common efforts may be called for. Entering international cooperation, then, would probably solve some complications but would on the other hand easily spill over to new problems of autonomy. In so far as joint action implies give and take, liberty of action on the part of the single unit would necessarily be circumscribed.

In leaving this sketchy description of autonomy issues we are by no means intimating that aspects of sovereignty would be uninteresting in this context.[4] Some problems have apparent juridical contours. This is the case for example concerning the control of subsidiaries of transnational coporations, adherence to international conventions, and membership in international organizations.

It seems evident, however, that an empirical theory of autonomy which would be couched in terms of sovereignty most certainly would be able to cover only part of the problematique that one comes across in current literature. A more useful theory thus should grow out of a quite different theoretical substratum.

FREEDOM OF CHOICE

An idea of freedom of action which is quite dissimilar to the one of sovereignty refers to decision-making in social planning. It pinpoints freedom of choice in such situations and the interesting thing then is the historical perspective. Alternatives of action which may be available at one moment might get lost as time goes by since small-scale decisions are continuously taken which may steer the development in such paths that at some point there are for all practical purposes not the same alternatives available. Freedom of choice therefore is synonymous with the feasibility of switching over development into new directions.

Such a perspective is vital to defence planning. Any state must necessarily be ready at fairly short notice to restructure its military apparatus in response to new developments — political, technological, etc. — in the surrounding world. For example, there must be a very high degree of flexibility to be able to introduce new weapons systems and phase out old ones. But also in civic planning such a perspective might be of the utmost relevance. Many states find themselves confronted with commitment problems since the beginning of the 1970s with regard to energy politics. Efficiency requires that a more definite policy for the future be decided upon but on the other hand there is a need not to get to strongly bound to any particular form of energy supply until energy reserves and safety issues have been thoroughly investigated.

What consequences would ensue from applying this perspective? It appears that we would be led astray in the search for a useful approach. Social planning in general requires a certain amount of commitment for the future which may make the preparedness for drastic structural change a less interesting thing in most cases. At any rate such an approach would not correspond well to questions of the kind that were delineated in the previous section. These problems bear only partly on how alternatives of action get lost as a cumulative effect of one's own decisions in the past. They have very much to do with the actions and decisions of others and even with such behaviour which is not at all to be adequately captured in terms of decision-making, like the dynamics of a market.

Thus, we would tend toward thinking that we have not got a solid basis here for formulating an empirical theory of autonomy. To put it crudely, either wrong things would be pinpointed or right things would be dealt with in an inadequate way. But there is also another aspect to it. Unless a theory can be tested, it is of no use to us. However, we would assume that the issues of freedom of choice concern social planning in general and not an external side of it in particular. On the other hand, internal and external aspects seem to be inextricably intertwined which would make an approach in these terms not very susceptible to operationalization either.

In sum, therefore, an autonomy theory revolving around the concept of freedom of choice would probably be neither sufficiently relevant, nor sufficiently empirical.

GOAL-ACHIEVING CAPACITY

A third perspective seems far more fruitful than the ones mentioned so far. Autonomy may refer to the ability to frame and carry out societal goals (cf. Cooper, 1968 and 1972; Lindbeck, 1973 and 1975; Morse, 1970). Let us call this the goal-achieving capacity. This kind of approach evidently assumes some kind of isomorphism between a mechanical system amenable to manipulation and a social one. Certainly the relevant problem-setting could with advantage be perceived from such a point of view. The external environment might spread sand in the social machinery impeding the government's manipulations, the disturbance being an encroachment upon autonomy.

However, there are some severe complications here that have to be spelled out. Essentially they deal with the issue of operationalizing or testing. The ideal way of assessing goal-achieving capacity would be by directly measuring the extent to which a government has actually been able to implement its aims. The degree of fulfilment would thus be the appropriate indicator of autonomy. But, as is easily understood, this tends both theoretically and practically to be a cumbersome and fragile method.

Be that as it may, an alternative and indirect method is, de facto, more or less explicitly proposed in relevant literature. It starts out from the premise that if some political instruments lose their vigour, the capacity to attain set goals would be diminished. This appears to be a somewhat questionable assumption, however. It seems warranted only in the case when the set of available means is well-defined and fixed; otherwise it would be impossible to uphold a comparative perspective when testing hypotheses to the effect that autonomy has increased or decreased. Now, the goal-achieving capacity might remain unabated since new tools may be set in action if old ones fail. Incidentally, this autonomy approach has been proposed above all by economists and it is precisely in their field that new tools have constantly been introduced (to the extent that there has even been mention of a new mercantilism).

But still more important, however, than the existence of new means (which may be hard to define exactly, by the way) is the fact that there may be a whole range of potential means. These may never have been applied and will only be used as a last resort to ensure that the state's objectives are fulfilled. If, for example, the balance of payments cannot be stabilized by traditional or newer means, a government can turn to rationing or other similar stern measures.

Thus, a loss of goal-achieving capacity could, strictly speaking, only be confirmed if the reduced force of the means analyzed is not compensated either by new or potential instruments. It seems therefore that this kind of test would be complicated, if not impossible, to perform.

Hence, this approach would hardly be the appropriate base on which to build up an empirical theory. In practice it would never be capable of answering the most obtrusive questions about autonomy in today's world — whether it is being encroached upon or the governments are still holding their ground.

PROPERTIES OF INSTRUMENTS

To overcome the methodological complications that we have just touched upon we would suggest a reformulated or modified outlook which, for all practical purposes, leaves us with a new approach. The possibility of attaining the conditions desired is not considered. Instead, stress is laid upon individual political instruments or, more generally, upon properties of alternatives of action which are available to the state. This opens up a perspective which fits well into the problematique in focus and is sufficiently amenable to empirical testing. It therefore merits some elaboration.

The kind of properties of alternatives of action that we would have reason to consider would be stable rather than volatile and it would be natural to conceive of them as varying between certain limits. Since it may be fairly difficult to define such extremes, the most convenient thing to do would be to focalize relative changes. Thus, we would propose that autonomy be couched in processterms such as those changes of relevant properties that are attributed to international dependence. It may seem superfluous to add that not all changes of autonomy appear to be pertinent to the case but primarily those of a more enduring character or constituting some sort of stable pattern (which need not be specified here).

Since international dependence is what links a government's freedom of action to the external environment we should make it plain exactly what dependence means in this context. In current literature it may among other things refer to some relation of influence. This is also a convenient perspective here. In order not to exclude by definition possible changes of autonomy, we would advocate that a rather broad definition be adopted. More precisely dependence means that conditions or processes in one country influence or have a bearing upon what is happening in another country.

This kind of relationship may refer to a connection of the kind that events in one country trigger or change developments in other countries, as when an economic upsurge or a political uprising has international repercussions. In such cases the 'source' of dependence is characterized by a process or change, i.e. the perspective is dynamic. However, we could also conceive of relations referring to more stable situations in the external environment, as when the outcome of a political election in one state to some extent is a question of the nature of the regime of a neighbouring state, for example whether the latter is ruled by conservatives or radicals.

Incidentally, these two illustrations indicate that dependence may refer to all kinds of social entities, not only to relations of influence between governments proper. Also, relations between societies in a broader sense or between societies and governments are included. This seems to be in agreement with current terminological usage.

Thus far we have only made some preliminary remarks to clarify the core of our approach. Now, as for the properties of alternatives of action available to the state, what would be relevant to consider? In other words, along what dimensions would it be reasonable to talk about change in autonomy of the state? We will try to identify some aspects which intuitively may come to mind.

First, the size of the set of alternatives for political action that are at all available should be looked into. This may be called the dimension of *range*. For various reasons a political means may not be available to the state — either wholly or in part. A commonplace illustration of such a limitation taking root in relations with the external environment would be the signing of and compliance with some international agreement ruling out certain forms of behaviour — for example a code on international trade forbidding protection of national industry through tariffs.

Whereas range might in one sense be understood as a quantitative property, more qualitative dimensions must not be overlooked. Thus, *effectiveness* may be identified. By this we refer to a single political means and the degree to which it may serve the purpose of approaching a specific goal, i.e. the transition from one social situation to another in some well-defined respect. Some specifications could be made here. Effectiveness of an instrument is not only a question of how 'powerful' it is but also how long its potency lasts. These two aspects do not have to be correlated.

A second qualitative dimension relates to the drawbacks attached to the use of a certain means in relation to a given goal-variable. Monetary expenses or other negative consequences directly related to the use of the alternative of action may be involved and indirect consequences, such as difficulty in using other political instruments, may ensue. Let us simply call this the *cost*-dimension. What changes take place in this respect are determined by the criteria of evaluation that may be ascribed to the state.

As a short illustration of effectiveness and cost let us consider the following situation. A tax bill is enacted to produce resources for a government project. However, it does not produce the expected income for the treasury because of tax-dodging. The effectiveness of this action is thus affected. Moreover, some of the evasive capital is transferred abroad and permanently invested there, something which represents a certain cost. In order to be relevant to autonomy this change has to be related to dependence on the external environment. Let us say that the primary reason for tax-dodging was the existence of much more advantageous tax rules abroad at the time the bill was passed.

Whereas in this hypothetical example the two dimensions may not be too difficult to separate from each other, they might become closely intertwined in other situations. We could even imagine cases where a process may be exhaustively analyzed in terms of either one. However, since they are not logically identical, both dimensions may be used for analytical purposes.

When analyzing changes in autonomy it seems necessary to require that the political goals are the same over the whole period of analysis. Otherwise there would be no stable point of reference when studying the properties of various alternatives of action. A modification of political ambitions thus impinges upon the frame of analysis (which has to be modified) but in general it has in itself no particular bearing upon autonomy. However, under *one* condition it may be an interesting thing as such, namely to the extent that it does not stem from a shift in ideology or similar circumstances but rather takes place out of necessity: if state authorities have found that the cost or effectiveness of political instruments have changed — or if they anticipate their doing so — they might be willing or forced to adjust their ambitions accordingly. If for example national defence has diminished in effectiveness there may be a *goal-adjustment* such that goals are no longer as far-reaching as before; for example, the ambition to counter all external threats may be reduced to stopping a more restricted set of possible attacks from the outside, such as those excluding the use of nuclear weapons.

This aspect could perhaps also be looked upon as a dimension of change although it prima facie refers to a change of goal rather than of political means and although it properly is to be seen as a function of other dimensions. It appears as if goal-adjustment would be much more difficult to study than the other three dimensions. Certainly, to establish with accuracy the motives behind a change of political ambitions and sort out the ones relevant here is a most delicate matter.

We would not maintain that the aspects mentioned so far are necessarily the only conceivable dimensions. But intuitively they seem to refer to the properties most essential to autonomy. We would furthermore contend that of at least the first three dimensions none seems to be more important than the others from a theoretical point of view. However, even if we at this stage do not feel the need to specify how many dimensions to identify or how to define them, we would like to emphasize that our delineation at any rate points to the fact that change in autonomy should be understood as a complex phenomenon involving several aspects or dimensions.

We have already tried to illustrate the usefulness of this kind of approach in a study of a small industrial country, Sweden (cf. Dunér, 1977). A set of hypotheses and guidelines for operationalization have been elaborated, referring to change in the above-mentioned dimensions. For example, in the field of economic policy it has been assumed that because of increasing fluctuations in economic parameters in the international system (i.e. the dynamic aspect of dependence that we talked of above) the effectiveness and cost of planning is adversely affected. Hypotheses concerning for example tax policy and industrial policy may likewise be formulated. The idea is that the use of these means is combined with lowered effectiveness and increased cost to the same extent that the national policies deviate from conditions in other countries (which is a situation referring to the static aspect of dependence).

In the field of security, for example, policy hypotheses could be suggested in terms of military strength and economic defence. Because of Sweden's dependence on the outside world, military operational strength as a political means continuously increases in cost or decreases in effectiveness and there is a simultaneous and constant pressure towards goal-adjustment. Assumption-wise the same development goes for economic defence concerning pre-emptive storing for example. In that respect a goal adjustment has probably already taken place such that the lapse of time that Sweden is prepared to endure a complete cut off in supplies from abroad in time of war has been shortened.

In the study cited above (Dunér, 1977) we have also discussed changes in autonomy in the context of international cooperation. Policies of cooperation between states may involve a narrowed range of alternatives of action. On the one hand certain policies may be excluded, while on the other certain policies may be prescribed concomitantly with a de facto exclusion of other alternatives of action. This in turn may have a differential bearing upon effectiveness and cost dimensions.

CONCLUSION

We have commented on different ways of conceptualizing autonomy — in the sense of freedom of action in relation to issues discussed in current literature — and the implications of theoretical foci chosen. Several perspectives were identified. Three of them were found not to be useful for empirical theory formation. However, we were able to formulate a fourth approach matching legitimate requirements, i.e. autonomy regarded in terms of properties — quantitative as well as qualitative — of alternatives of action available to the state. This view depicts autonomy as a phenomenon with many facets. We suggested some dimensions along which change might appear. However, our proposal by no means claimed to be a fully-fledged one.

The reason for discussing how to theoretically round up the problems of autonomy has been — as we pointed out in the introduction — that the stand taken at a theoretical level will have a definite bearing upon propositions about the real world. This is of course particularly true for the question of whether autonomy is presently in the process of withering away or not. Let us therefore, for the sake of argument, assume that the approach that we have suggested and elaborated above is accepted. Given this point of departure, would it be possible to draw at least some conclusion about the status of autonomy in the world today?

We would maintain that an important, albeit tentative, conclusion might be formulated. Hypotheses of the kind to which we alluded in the introduction of this chapter — i.e. concerning the dwindling freedom of action of industrialized states — must be called into question, at least at the present stage of research. In our conceptualization autonomy is a multidimensional phenomenon. This would imply that very thorough-going and extensive empirical studies necessarily have to be carried out in order to confirm such general and definite theses. To our knowledge such research has not yet been carried out.

However, disregarding the matter of empirical knowledge at hand it is also doubtful whether a strong theoretical argument can be raised in favour of this kind of thesis. Let us discuss this point in a little more detail. A most important foundation of the kind of propositions that we object to seems to be an assumption that interdependence is rapidly increasing in the international system. Prima facie it might perhaps be tempting to interpret this alleged development as a cause of decreasing freedom of action. However, while we would contend that one might perhaps assume that a growing interdependence can be used as an indicator of autonomy change in some instances, there is no reason to suppose this to be the case generally. One may well conceive of growing dependence without this in any way affecting the status of autonomy.

Moreover, it even seems plausible that such an increase might be combined with an augmentation in or restoration of freedom of action. A good case in point is the coordination of national policies on an international scale. Such an enterprise represents a form of dependence from the point of view of the individual state in the sense that its behaviour is influenced by others' anticipated or actually performed actions. Now in a situation of environmental crisis, for example, it may turn out that some political instruments aimed at coping with the situation (like dumping of waste products in the sea) may lose their effectiveness or become too costly — for example because of similar or compensatory measures taken by others who may be affected or inspired by one's own actions. Increasing coordination would then mean that individual policies become more effective.

At this point it is not out of place to repeat that our comments start from autonomy and dependence being conceptualized as above. However, in current writings one may come across examples of definitional diffuseness such that the interrelationship between the two concepts becomes blurred at the theoretical level, a fortiori at the empirical level. For example, it may be that on the one hand an author would like clearly to point out a distinction between interdependence and autonomy — in the sense of capacity to achieve goals — but that he on the other hand defines interdependence precisely in the latter terms.[5] This may naturally cause some confusion and render it difficult to assess the question we are dealing with here, i.e. whether increasing interdependence may be taken a priori as an indicator of loss of autonomy. Let us also add that at times the two notions may become closely intertwined, not as a result of theoretical obscureness, but as a simple reflection of convention of language. Some authors explicitly use the first word to denote nothing but the very opposite of the second. This of course is a completely different matter and is in no way confusing to our discussion.

To return to our main thread of discussion, not only are convincing arguments lacking in support of the far-reaching theses that we are objecting to but, moreover, theoretical reasons might be adduced to the effect that these hypotheses probably never will match reality, simply because they are too general. Three points may illustrate this. First, it may well be that some international conditions will have to be interpreted as a diminishing autonomy along one dimension of change but that change goes in the opposite direction along another dimension. This case, by the way, is also illustrated by the example just given. Coordination of policies may represent a decrease of the range of alternatives of actions but, as was pointed out, also an increase of effectiveness. Secondly, autonomy change may occur in relation to various instruments which implies multidimensionality in a new, second sense. However, these partial changes may not necessarily be parallel. Thirdly, changes in the properties of one means bear on several political goals with opposite effects. For example, it turns out that to the extent that interest-rate policy becomes less effective as a regulator of domestic economic life (with respect to inflation and unemployment) this instrument becomes increasingly effective as a mechanism to affect the balance-of-payments position (cf. Cooper, 1972: 165).

These points indicate that change may manifest itself in a very complex fashion. If so, assessments in general terms will be practicable only to the extent that changes in relation to different goals, political instruments and change-dimensions are comparable so that they might be weighted together. Is it very likely that such conditions obtain? This is hard to say a priori but the most probable thing seems to be that we will have to go along with highly diversified hypotheses on autonomy at fairly low levels of generality.

NOTES

1. In Goldmann (1978) the author has synthethized traditional conceptions of international politics; cf. section 3.3.1.2.

2. This is of course not to say that only in the field of economics have such notions been put forward. In the realm of security policy there has been a questioning of the viability of the traditional state and this by the way already quite some time ago. In 1957, for example, a very thought-provoking article was published entitled 'The Rise and Demise of the Territorial State' by John H. Herz (1957: 473-493).

In the wake of this article many others proposed similar concepts about the obsolescence of the territorial state. Herz himself, however, later revised his view. See Herz (1968: 11-34).

3. This term may be somewhat inappropriate if the distinction is made between a functional and a geographical legitimacy, since sovereignty mostly refers to territory. However, this distinction is interesting: think of the policy of apartheid in the Republic of South Africa, for example. There, the 'autonomy' bestowed on black people is far more attached to territory than that bestowed on Indians.

4. The relevance of the concept is illuminated for example in *Government and Opposition* which devotes its number 1, Winter 1974, to the theme of 'Between Sovereignty and Integration'. See particularly Goodwin (1974: 61-78). The author argues for a redefinition and for modifying the concept of state sovereignty in response to the requirements of the modern international system.
5. This is what E. L. Morse does in a couple of articles when proposing hypotheses and otherwise. See Morse (1971: 373-398) and (1972: 123-150).

REFERENCES

COOPER, R. N. (1968) *The Economics of Interdependence: Economic Policy in the Atlantic Community*. New York: McGraw-Hill.
—— (1972) 'Economic Interdependence and Foreign Policy in the Seventies', *World Politics*, 24: 159-181.
DUNÉR, B. (1977) *Autonomi: Skiss till teoretisk referensram och illustration av dess tillämpning*. Stockholm: The Swedish Institute of International Affairs, Research Report UI-77-3.
GOLDMANN, K. (1978) *Det internationella systemet. En teori och dess begränsningar*. Stockholm: Aldus/Bonniers.
GOODWIN, G. L. (1974) 'The Erosion of External Sovereignty?' *Government and Opposition*, no. 1 (Winter): 61-78.
HERZ, J. H. (1957) 'The Rise and Demise of the Territorial State', *World Politics*, 9: 473-493.
—— (1968) 'Territorial State Revisited', *Polity*, 1: 11-34.
LINDBECK, A. (1973) *The National State in an Internationalized World Economy*. Stockholm: Institute for International Economic Studies, University of Stockholm, Seminar paper no. 26.
—— (1975) 'The Changing Role of the National State', *Kyklos*, 28: 23-46.
MORSE, E. L. (1970) 'The Transformation of Foreign Policies: Modernization, Interdependence, and Externalization', *World Politics*, 22: 371-392.
—— (1971) 'Transnational Economic Processes', *International Organization*, 25: 373-398.
—— (1972) 'Crisis Diplomacy', *World Politics*, 24: 123-150.

9 Multinational Corporations and the Small Industrialized State: Some Aspects of Dependency and Potential Power

Olav Knudsen
University of Oslo

INTRODUCTION

The questions to be dealt with in this chapter concern the measurement — or, perhaps better, the assessment — of power. Moreover, the power to be assessed is of a specific kind, namely that of multinational corporations (MNCs) over governments, and vice versa.

It is rather typical of the actors concerned — MNCs and governments — that neither likes to publicize how it gains and administers power. To study the power relations of MNCs and governments it may therefore be necessary to rely on a combination of public information and theoretical models.

At this point I shall stop short of actually defining 'power',[1] and will only make clear that as the term is used here it involves the conceptual linkage of two elements: *intention* and *ability*. The problems of measuring power are in large part reducible to the more specific problems of assessing intentions and abilities, to be further discussed below.

The following question will serve as my point of departure: What can public information on multinational corporations' activities in a country tell us about their power?

Author's note: A special thanks for useful comments to Per Heum.

In the Nordic countries, as in most other OECD countries, statistics on foreign-owned companies are annually collected and (to some extent) published. These statistics can roughly be said to cover three kinds of information: production statistics, accounts statistics, and financial statistics. In addition, the national banks annually publish some of their data on direct investment flows.[2]

This is a large body of information which seems to have been little used by political scientists interested in multinational corporations (MNCs), except for the occasional figure borrowed to serve as 'background information'.[3]

The aim of this chapter, then, is to examine to what extent and on what conditions the power of MNCs[4] in industrialized countries lends itself to assessment on the basis of such data. As a preliminary to this it will be necessary to discuss some definitional problems both in regard to 'multinational corporations' and in regard to 'power'.

ON DEFINING A MULTINATIONAL CORPORATION

The long professional debate over this issue has not really brought much clarification, whether on terminology or conceptual content.[5] Moreover, the definitions which have so far come out of the OECD and United Nations bodies concerned show clearly that no important problems have been solved in these fora. Both organizations have adopted (at least temporarily) the idea that an MNC is a corporation which owns or controls enterprises in more than one country.[6] By this standard, an MNC (or a 'transnational corporation' in the language of the UN) can be anything from a border-straddling bakery firm (e.g. one bakery on either side of the Belgian-French border) to the 'empires' of General Motors, Shell and ITT.

I would like to make some kind of distinction which separates the large international companies from the rest. This has been done, for instance, by the Harvard Multinational Enterprise Project.[7]

Following this tradition, I shall go by the following definition: A multinational corporation is a corporation with majority ownership of manufacturing subsidiaries in at least six 'foreign' countries — or, for non-manufacturing companies — majority-owned subsidiaries in at least ten foreign countries.[8]

The requirement of majority ownership may be debatable in that actual control is often achieved even with minority ownership, provided the remaining shares are sufficiently dispersed.[9] But data on this are frequently missing. Swedish official statistics, for instance, regularly report the number of minority-owned foreign companies in Sweden (foreign ownership of 20-50 percent of the stock).[10] Other sources, however, show that many of these are in fact *majority owned* by a *Swedish* shareholder.[11] Hence, by requiring majority ownership one avoids a cumbersome data problem, but may also 'lose' an unknown number of subsidiaries.

Indications exist that this number may be fairly small, however. Corporations active in several countries tend to prefer wholly owned (100 per cent) subsidiaries,[12] and studies made by the Bank of Norway and by a Swedish public inquiry likewise indicate a clear preference for majority ownership.[13]

Finally, a comment on MNCs as actors. For an MNC to be meaningfully attributed with power outside its home country, it must be assumed — or shown — to be a fairly unitary actor, in the sense that most of the important decisions are made by the parent company.[14] This appears to be true of many types of MNCs, but by no means all.[15] The discussion which follows rests on the assumption of a fairly high degree of centralization in MNC decision-making processes.

But can we attribute power to MNCs collectively? To what extent may the MNCs operating in a particular host country be analyzed as one coalition, or perhaps as several smaller coalitions? There is no obvious answer to this, because while large corporations are not adverse to *cooperation*, the idea of *solidarity* seems remote from the world of business. The question really requires a theory of its own, which is beyond the limits of this chapter. Hence, the following discussion will partly consider the MNCs in a host country as one coalition, and partly consider the situation of the individual company.

ON DEMONSTRATED VERSUS POTENTIAL POWER

I pointed out at the beginning that under the heading of *power* we shall be concerned with the elements *intention* and *ability*, and that the problems of measuring power in large part may be traced to difficulties in assessing these two elements. Where intention is concerned we shall return to the problem whenever appropriate during the remainder of the chapter. As for ability, however, I should like to add a few words at this point.

Measuring power involves the choice of suitable and valid indicators. There is, however, an underlying consideration here which needs to be spelled out. Power may be conceived alternatively as 'proven ability' or as 'potential ability'. The former conception rests squarely on empirical demonstration, for example, to the effect that actor A on specific occasions actually *did have power over actor B*, or *was more powerful than actor C*, or *had the power to do X*, etc. For the narrower purposes of studying proven ability, then, indicators serve strictly the function of measuring the dependent variable: A's degree of success. The explanatory element in a study of proven ability consists of showing why A succeeded or failed to the extent he did; in other words, showing what were *the sources of his power*. Studies of this kind form the empirical basis of theories of the sources of power (see for example, Salamon and Siegfried, 1977).

A study of power conceived as potential ability is of a markedly different kind, because obviously the question of A's degree of success cannot be empirically assessed at all. The purpose of studying power as potential ability is prediction, i.e. forecasting actor A's degree of success in future power contests. This can be done in several ways, all of which involve either or both of the following (in various combinations): (a) generalization of proven ability (of particular actors or types of actors), and (b) deductive theory (see, for example, Morgenstern et al., 1973). When a study of this kind fits empirical data into theories, the results can only tell us something about the *particular actors* covered by the study, and only to the extent that the theories are tenable. A study of potential power therefore cannot tell us more about *power as a general phenomenon* than we already know — it is simply a matter of applying the knowledge we have.[16] (Any attempt to *test* the underlying theories empirically would be a study of proven ability.)[17]

In what follows we consider the possibility of using statistics on MNCs both in order to study power as a proven ability, and in order to study potential power.

ON DEFINING 'POWER' AND 'INFLUENCE'

I shall not venture much further into the jungle of conceptual problems here, since I consider that kind of effort to be largely counterproductive. The essential task after twenty years of intense theoretical debate would seem to be to concentrate on the empirical application of available definitions and power theories, and to forget the imperfections involved until we can observe what they mean in actual research.

In defining 'power' I consider Russell's forty-year-old formulation — 'power is the production of intended effects' (Russell, 1946: 35) — to encapsulate the essential theoretical ingredients. Unfortunately it does not lend itself easily to empirical application. Recently, however, Jack Nagel has presented a related definition especially tailored for empirical use, which by his own claim could represent a major step forward. Nagel gives the following definition: 'A power relation, actual or potential, is an actual or potential causal relation between the preferences of an actor regarding an outcome and the outcome itself' (1975:29). Power, in other words, is viewed as a causal relationship, which is a useful restatement of Russell's idea.[18] Nagel's work deserves further comment.

In the quotation, an '*actor* refers...to an individual, group, organization, or other collectivity. In social power relations, the *outcome* must be a variable indicating the state of another social entity — the behavior, beliefs, attitudes, or policies of a second actor' (1975:29). Nagel makes the caveat that one must specify precisely both the time period, the domain (i.e. the 'second actor' referred to: power over *whom*?), and the scope (i.e. the particular type of event constituting the outcome: power with regard to *what*?).[19]

The approach proposed by Nagel is designed for empirical application in causal analysis, and the book sets out in a fairly detailed manner how this can be done. The essential variables for which data must be found are preferences and outcomes.

However, the crucial point is the linkage of the two. Nagel is not concerned with simple correlational analysis, but bases his entire approach on Herbert Simon's model of causality (Nagel, 1975: 35ff) and the statistical technique of path analysis. The use of his power definition thus requires an explicit theory linking preferences causally to outcomes:.

> *Any power attribution presupposes a theory of the outcome over which power is presumed to be exercised.* Any empirical power study must make its theory explicit (Nagel, 1975:40).

In other words, Nagel has demonstrated what looks like an ingenious solution to most of the conceptual problems involved in power studies, while at the same time pointing out that this is no philosopher's stone: each researcher must work out a theory, consistent with Simon's requirements, to suit his or her particular power problem. (Still, Nagel shows by an empirical example[20] that his approach actually 'works'.)

The causal approach linking outcomes to preferences is an elegant solution, but one wonders, as even the author does himself, whether a statistically satisfactory model always will provide insights worth the modelling efforts. One should keep in mind that where evaluation of an explanation's 'goodness' is concerned, the causal approach in large part substitutes statistical criteria for old-fashioned intellectual judgement:

> The explanation such a theory affords is minimal. If the causal specification is justifiable and coefficient estimates are significant, one can infer that events occurred as they did because various actors had certain preferences — an 'explanation' unlikely to satisfy anyone with normal curiosity (Nagel, 1975: 170).

This, in my view is a somewhat overstated self-critique, because such studies would form an important part of the work needed to establish empirically founded theories of the sources of power. But causal modelling is not the only available method for studying causal relationships, and it is not unlikely that methods without the heavy statistical emphasis could bring equally good or even better results.

Finally, using 'preferences' instead of 'goals', 'intentions', etc. may be an improvement in some respects, but it places greater demands on the researcher in other respects — notably when there is no conflict between the preferences of the parties involved. Only as pretty complex theory would enable us to apportion power between them in such cases. Indeed, I find the application of power theory to situations with common or compatible preferences to be problematic in itself. Moreover, a concept of potential power based on proven ability in no-conflict situations can hardly be a reliable predictor of power when the same parties clash in conflict.

POWER AND THE MULTINATIONAL CORPORATION

A few points will have to be clarified before we can move on. We shall be concerned with the power of MNCs. A full treatment of the topic would minimally have to consider their power vis-à-vis public authorities (national and local), employees and their organizations, consumers, and competitors (implicitly covering also relations with 'upstream' and 'downstream' independent companies — suppliers and customers). In the present paper I cannot possibly cover this vast area and will have to limit myself to power vis-à-vis public authorities.

A second point concerns the type of outcome (in Nagel's terminology) we are looking for ('power to do what?'). It would be fruitful when we speak of the power of MNCs to refer to their ability to cause a preferred state of affairs in the host country. But this can be achieved in two ways: by *affecting the policies of the government*, or by *affecting economic and social conditions in the country directly*. The power of MNCs vis-à-vis a host country may accordingly be described by two alternative models which specify how the effects intended are produced.

Let us first consider the possibility of using our data to study MNC power as *proven ability* to achieve both kinds of outcomes. It seems obvious that the task will be utterly unmanageable unless we specify that only *some* policies, or economic and social conditions, for instance those which *pertain directly to MNCs and their activities*, will be regarded as relevant outcomes. Furthermore, one should realistically expect that a causal approach, while not unworkable, would involve a massive research effort in establishing and testing the appropriate models for policies defined as outcomes.[21]

Moreover, by using either Nagel's approach or another of similar structure, one runs into the problem of common or compatible preferences just referred to: on the whole multinational corporations have encountered little opposition to their activities in industrialized countries. OECD member governments have in large part welcomed foreign investment.[22] It would hardly be possible, in my view, to show that these policies are products of the preferences of MNCs. This problem also applies to economic and social conditions considered as outcomes.

If economic and social conditions related to MNC activities are defined as outcomes, economists have developed relevant analytical methods to study the effects of foreign investment (see, for example, Stonehill, 1965; Knudsen, 1974; Koncentrationsutredningen, 1975; Statens Industriverk, 1977). But to show that such effects were intended, or preferred, by the companies would be very close to impossible.

So much for power as proven ability.

Hence, the obvious alternative is to ask whether our data can be used to estimate potential power on the basis of a general theory (deductive approach). The point of this would be to draw a picture of what the power constellation could be like *if* serious conflicts were to arise between OECD host governments and MNCs.

A promising deductive conceptualization of potential power is Emerson's work on power and dependence (Emerson, 1962: 31-41). By its nature, however, this approach can only be used to study potential effects on governmental policies — not on economic and social conditions. Nevertheless, its advantages are many, and I shall therefore use it for the remainder of this chapter.

Emerson's point of departure is a relationship of dependence: 'A *depends* upon B if he aspires to goals or gratifications whose achievement is facilitated by appropriate actions on B's part' (1962: 32). More formally, Emerson presents the following definition:

> *Dependence (Dab)*. The dependence of actor A upon actor B is (1) directly proportional to A's *motivational investment* in goals mediated by B, and (2) inversely proportional to the *availability* of those goals to A outside of the A-B relation (1962:32).

'Thus,' he says, 'it would appear that the power to control or influence the other resides in control over the things he values, which may range all the way from oil-resources to ego-support, depending upon the relation in question. In short, *power resides implicitly in the other's dependency* (1962:32). Emerson also points out that

> if the dependence of one party provides the basis for the power of the other, that power must be defined as a potential influence:
> *Power (Pab)*. The power of actor A over actor B is the amount of resistance on the part of B which can be potentially overcome by A (1962: 32).

Note that Emerson's definition of dependence contains a rudimentary proposition which could easily be converted into a theory of dependence.[23] As it stands, however, the propositional element serves as an amplified definition. It is also a guide to measurement.

The fact that Emerson does present a *theory* of power (rather than a power definition in terms of dependence) is easily seen. His definition of power contains no reference to terms involved in his definition of dependence, and he specifies the nature of the relationship between the two variables. According to the theory, then, the power of an MNC over a host government will be greater the greater the dependence of the government on the MNC. Conversely, the power of the host government is contingent on the dependence of the MNC. Thus, if our data can be used to measure dependence, we shall be able to predict the power of one over the other in the event of a conflict. Of course, this still leaves open the question of the tenability and accuracy of the prediction, but that is the essence of the very concept 'potential power'.

More problematic is the question of aggregated power. If the MNCs which have subsidiaries in a given country cannot be expected to act in concert, or to have the same preferences, their potential power must be assessed on an individual basis.

Although, as mentioned, we shall not introduce the theory of concerted MNC action which the problem actually demands, a rule of thumb might be suggested: when a policy or action of the host government directly affects only a single company, and without clearly setting precedence for subsequent cases involving other companies, the likelihood of concerted action is small. (This assumes the lack of solidarity referred to earlier.) When a government policy or action directly affects MNCs or foreign-owned companies *generally*, the likelihood of concerted action is great. Hence, the subsequent analysis is made with the qualification always in mind that the smaller the likelihood of concerted action, the smaller the potential power of the MNCs. (According to Emerson's theory the joint potential power of all MNCs in a host country would obviously be a function of the dependence of the government on all of them together.)

Even though we shall be discussing potential power in the following, it is still necessary to specify the kind of outcome we have in mind. The potential power of MNCs here refers specifically to the potential ability of MNCs to *prevent* the host government from adopting policies *inimical* to MNC interests in the country. Furthermore, we also include under the potential power of MNCs their potential ability to *induce* the host government to adopt policies *favourable* to MNC interests (to the extent that this is not logically implied by the absence of 'inimical policies' in the former case). The potential power of the host government may simply be defined as the obverse of the potential power of the MNCs. These formulations are consistent with Emerson's more generally stated definition of power: the amount of resistance on the part of the other which the actor is potentially able to overcome.

I consider the familiar problems of *anticipated reaction* and *compatible preferences* to be irrelevant to the following analysis, because the aim here is to assess *potential* ability, not proven ability. The problems referred to become relevant only when one seeks to verify the implicit hypotheses, which are involved in statements on potential power, by empirical testing.

FACTORS DETERMINING THE DEPENDENCE OF MNCs ON HOST GOVERNMENTS

We shall discuss these factors initially as they might appear to the *individual* company. In doing so it is important to remember that a given MNC often has several subsidiaries in the same country, and that these may even be under the direction of different parts of the concern abroad.[24]

By an 'individual company' is meant an *enterprise* in the standard statistical usage recommended by the UN: 'the smallest unit for which joint financial accounts and joint balance sheets are available'.[25] An enterprise may comprise several *establishments* (factories, offices), and may in turn be owned by a larger corporation, such as an MNC.

The factors to be discussed will be organized under two headings: motivational investment, and available alternatives.

Motivational investment

The more important it is to an MNC to continue its activities in a given country, the greater (by definition) its dependence on that country. In Emerson's conception, we are ultimately concerned with the *intensity* of the MNC's commitment to the goals fulfilled by its operations in the country. Put differently, we might ask: How hard would it be to the MNC to just pack up and leave?

The distinction between motivational investment and availability of alternatives needs clarification. Clearly, when we are concerned with business operations the *cost* of alternative solutions will be a crucial factor in determining motivational investment. This is fully integrated in economic analysis via the familiar concept of opportunity cost. Thus, we shall have to distinguish between (1) the cost (and benefits) of alternatives *known* to be available, and (2) the question of whether alternatives exist at all. Only the second of these will be discussed under the heading 'available alternatives'.

In assessing the corporation's motivational investment, a general point is that under normal circumstances it would probably prefer to keep its operations intact. Leaving a country is after all a more drastic change than most others on the company's decisional horizon. Part of the company's motivational investment is usually buried here.

Another general point is this: the greater the cost of available alternatives, the greater the motivational investment in the existing operations. A number of specific questions are involved.

First, there are the short-term considerations. Would it be difficult to *sell* the operations so that the investment could be adequately recovered? Are there potential buyers? How big is the market actually served by these operations — and what are the chances of loss of market share due to transition problems? Indeed, what are the transitional costs likely to be, all told?

Secondly, in long-term perspective a key question would be the expected future profits if the company stays. This consideration would be tied closely to the time required to build up a similar operation elsewhere. How long would it take to train a new labor force in the skills required? How large and costly are the physical facilities required for the company's operations?

These considerations assume a fairly high level of conflict in the MNC-host country relationship. But not all disputes escalate to top intensity — such cases may even be exceptional in industrialized countries. Thus, if the parent company can disregard the possibility of a threat to the subsidiary's very existence, its motivational dependence becomes substantially smaller. Instead, the question in such cases will be what unexpected changes might appear in the company's operational environment, and how significant they will be.

Available alternatives

As the preceding section suggests, multinational corporations may not always have the international mobility which has often been attributed to them. The main condition for mobility is that there exist attractive alternatives abroad to production in any particular country. In the following we shall consider some factors of potential relevance to this question.

A first consideration is whether the subsidiary concerned performs a unique function in the activities of the concern as a whole or at least in its regional (European, Asian, Western Hemisphere) operations. This is a typical feature of those MNCs that have split up the production process for their main product in several stages, and located each stage in a different country according to comparative national advantage (Stopford and Wells, 1972:58). Two main varieties of this strategy may be distinguished: one is found in vertically integrated industries like petroleum, aluminum, steel, paper, and glass.[26] The other is common in certain industries closer to the consumer side, in which vertical integration is less important, but where *components* for the final product are produced in different countries and brought together for assembly in a few strategically located plants (Levinson and Sandén, 1972: 55-56). In this way each subsidiary is assigned a specific function within the total multinational operation.

It seems reasonable to argue that in industries where such 'production rationalization' is common, it will be difficult for an MNC to rid itself of a particular subsidiary, if the latter is the only part of the concern (in this part of the world) in charge of the production stage in question.[27]

The most familiar manifestation of this problem is of course the extraction stage in industries like petroleum, where the raw material source is in itself the focal point. But other requisite input factors, such as large amounts of electric energy in aluminum production, have the same effect: moving to a different country is not always the easiest thing to do.

A second general reason why an MNC might have no alternatives is the case of 'closed' markets. The normal situation in manufacturing is probably that each manufacturing subsidiary produces for more than the local (national) market. In some cases, however, tariff barriers, or other obstacles, may be important enough to make it a question of either covering the local market by local production, or not covering it at all. Then moving out would mean a lost national market.

This problem may be still more acute in non-manufacturing activities, such as sales companies with specialized service facilities, hotels, advertising bureaus, car rental, airlines, and insurance,[28] where a close contact with the market is essential.

However, a different dimension of mobility should also be considered. Mobility does not necessarily mean to 'pack up and leave'. An element of mobility may often be implicit in alternative ways of utilizing the company's plants in a particular country. A factory which turns out cars could be converted to the production of buses, trucks, or tractors. An oil refinery or a petrochemical plant, however, is probably bound to its original purpose. The convertibility of plants is therefore likely to have an effect on the company's freedom of action. In general, the facilities of light industry ('consumer industry') are probably more convertible than those of heavy industry.

Thus, many MNCs should be considered mobile in the sense that they can reorganize their activities by changing the functions of their subsidiaries. This may also involve reducing production in some locations and expanding it in others. The outer limits of such flexibility must nevertheless be found in considerations of long-term profitability, which is always finite.

Summary of MNC dependence on host governments

We can tentatively make the observation that the following types of MNCs are likely to be less dependent than their colleagues on most host governments:

> MNCs in consumer industries/light industry, which control many producing subsidiaries performing the same functions in many different countries (e.g. automobile tires, canned food). (See also Levinson and Sandén, 1972: 97.)

> Non-manufacturing MNCs with small physical facilities and no special need for close contact with the market. (Sales companies in wholesaling *without* service facilities would be the most numerous category.)

The companies with the greatest potential dependence on host governments would be:

MNCs whose subsidiaries perform a 'unique' function, especially relevant in vertically integrated industries.

MNCs in heavy industry, such as steel, aluminum, but also machinery, transport equipment, and large-scale chemical industry.

Empirical study would require careful classification of industries, but most of the data needed would at least in principle be available. A problem with regard to a study of individual companies is that the official statistics of interest in this study cannot be broken down to that level. There are several other sources, however, which can supply such data.[29]

One type of required information is (to my knowledge) not covered systematically by any source, and that is the question of 'unique' functions. In some industries, the degree of specialization in production is a well-known fact (e.g., Norwegian aluminum industry), while in other cases one will have to search through a variety of sources.

FACTORS DETERMINING THE DEPENDENCE OF HOST GOVERNMENTS ON MNCs

Motivational investment

Whereas the motivational investment of MNCs can be determined largely on the basis of objective factors (money), a government's commitments to its policies derive from a complex combination of objective factors and a consciously chosen political strategy. Thus, a government's policy vis-à-vis MNCs cannot simply be explained by reference to the intrinsic characteristics of the MNCs and their local subsidiaries.[30] An important additional consideration is likely to be the indirect role that MNCs are playing in the economy at large, through which their activities may affect the overriding political strategy of the government. I shall try to take such indirect links in to account below. (Note that in this section a government's dependence on the foreign-owned sector will be considered in the *aggregate*.)

A key underlying element in a government's calculations is likely to be the role of the industrial sector in the national economy as a whole, and the importance of the foreign-owned sector in that context. Since this chapter deals specifically with industrialized countries, it is clear that the industrial sector would be highly important in most of them (we should include service industries — not just manufacturing — under this heading).

Within this general policy context, *the importance attributed to MNCs — as well as the policy conclusions drawn — by the host government are likely to vary with the amount and character of the MNC presence within the country.* In the following sections we shall elaborate on this general observation, which in my view is quite important. Note that we are concerned partly with *factual information* about foreign-owned companies (normally available in the public statistics of OECD countries)[31] and partly with the host government's *evaluation* of such information.

The extent of the existing MNC activities in a country is in itself likely to be a considerable motivational factor to the government, provided it exceeds a certain lower limit for the economy as a whole or within particular industries. When MNC activities are below this limit the question tends to be regarded as uninteresting. (The 'location' of this limit in particular cases is immaterial to the present general analysis.)

When the limit is exceeded, however, the aggregate activity of the companies is likely to be considered both important and valuable, and becomes something one would rather not lose or disturb. This in turn is likely to affect the government's attitudes in case of a conflict. The greater the aggregate volume of the foreign-owned sector, the stronger the commitment of the government to a 'good' relationship — up to some upper limit (apparently felt to have been exceeded by for example the Canadian government as early as the middle 1960s), beyond which the volume is seen as unacceptably large. The same relationship may be hypothesized for particular industries, but in this case the government's dependency would have a narrower scope and hence presumably be smaller.[32]

In the evaluation of specific industries the question of indirect effects also acquires concrete relevance. Closing down, scaling down, or reorganizing foreign-owned enterprises may affect other parts of the economy. The extent to which foreign-owned companies are integrated in the local economy is especially important in this connection. Some foreign subsidiaries, particularly of the large multinationals, tend to function as enclaves in the national economy; they are often strongly functionally integrated into the parent company while only to a small extent buying from — or selling to — locally owned companies. Operational changes in such companies may therefore be less important to the host country than corresponding changes in a foreign-owned firm which has extensive contacts with the local economy.

These factual conditions are important for the understanding of the government's relations with the MNCs. At the same time they provide only half the total picture, the other half being the government's evaluation of these facts. It is to guide the analysis of the latter that I have introduced the aforementioned limits: on the 'lower' side a limit to what is considered politically interesting; on the 'upper' side a limit to what is considered politically acceptable. As long as the volume of MNC activity, by individual industry or for the economy as a whole, lies *between* these limits, the motivational investment of the government in preserving good relations with the MNCs is considerable. If a conflict arises, the government is in other words likely to avoid pressing its views too far. Beyond the upper limit such reservations on the part of the government are likely to disappear, and the issue tends to be seen increasingly as a matter of national sovereignty. In this case the companies will also have high stakes to defend, and so the situation may easily turn into a sharp confrontation. Such prospects may have induced the efforts of many governments, among them those of Finland, Norway and Sweden, to keep the level of direct investments within certain limits (see, for example, Getz Wold, 1971: 182-184).

Below the lower limit, where the political significance of foreign ownership fades out, the government's preoccupation with the issue will disappear — but so will perhaps also its reluctance to take decisive action (unless it is campaigning abroad for more investments, of course). Should the companies raise a conflict under such conditions, they may find themselves in a weak position.

The motivation of the government thus seems to take shape in a complex interaction of factors. Further complexity enters if public opinion in the country is roused over the issue of foreign influence in the economy. If important organizations and groups in the electorate consider foreign ownership to have become too extensive, this may in itself be a political factor of considerable weight. As viewed by the government, this may serve to 'pull down' both the threshold of political significance and that of political acceptability. In other words, the government may be impelled to adopt a stricter policy vis-à-vis MNCs than they would otherwise have done. On the other hand, a situation like this may also be tactically exploited by the government in bargaining with foreign-owned companies.

Thus, the excitability of public opinion over the issue of foreign influence in the economy is clearly relevant to the overall analysis. The other side of the coin is the sensitivity of the government to such pressures. Whereas the former is likely to be more of a stable ingredient in a national political culture, the latter may change more abruptly with changes of government, parliamentary situations, current preoccupations in foreign policy, etc and will therefore be more difficult to take systematically into account in the analysis. It is worth noting that variation in the importance of these particular factors appears to exist even among the Nordic countries. National stereotyping is dangerous, but sometimes tempting: Danes seem to be less concerned about such matters than their Nordic neighbours. And among the latter three, Norwegians and Finns may tend to be more emotionally engaged while the Swedes are more pragmatically oriented in the question of foreign economic influence.

We may summarize the government's motivational investment as a partial function of three variables: (a) the actual statistical indicator; (b) public concern about foreign influence in the economy; and (c) the government's attitude on foreign influence in the economy (see Figure 1).

The figure shows only one independent variable, the statistical indicator of foreign control. The lower half illustrates what may happen as public opinion becomes engaged over the issue of foreign control.

In short, while most OECD-governments seem to regard foreign investment as desirable, the *strength* of this desire can often be a valuable thing, easily weakened by 'other considerations'. Only some of the latter have been mentioned here.

Available alternatives

To what extent is foreign direct investment indispensable in the economy of a small industrialized country? What alternatives exist?[33] For the sake of simplicity I shall group the attractions of MNCs, as viewed by the host countries, into three categories: (1) the generally stimulating effect on the economy which direct investment *may* have (under certain conditions); (2) the supply of capital — in particular for very large projects or for distressed sectors or areas; and (3) the transfer of technology in general, but particularly for specific projects of high priority to the government's industrial policy. The strongest element of indispensability may perhaps be found in the third category.

As for categories (1) and (2) one should first of all keep in mind that substantial portions of direct investment flows between industrialized countries are financed in the host country (Getz Wold, 1971: 175-176). Moreover, it is obvious that capital may alternatively be raised via private or public borrowing abroad. (In this connection it is worth remembering that foreign influence is not necessarily eliminated by substituting long-term loans for direct investment.) On the other hand, direct investment has an advantage over local/national projects in that the risk associated with the investment to some extent is moved out of the country. A locally initiated private project which fails may also jeopardize the investor's other local operations. Such repercussions may be less likely if the government is responsible for the failure, but the political effects may be equally unpleasant. The risk factor may thus reduce the attractiveness of alternatives to direct investment.

Joint ventures can be seen as a possible compromise, but like government-initiated projects they could hardly provide a *general* strategy for the import of capital since they are strongly project oriented. Furthermore, joint ventures seem to be less in favor with MNCs lately.

A quite different aspect of the question of alternatives is the military: MNCs play an important role world-wide in the develop-

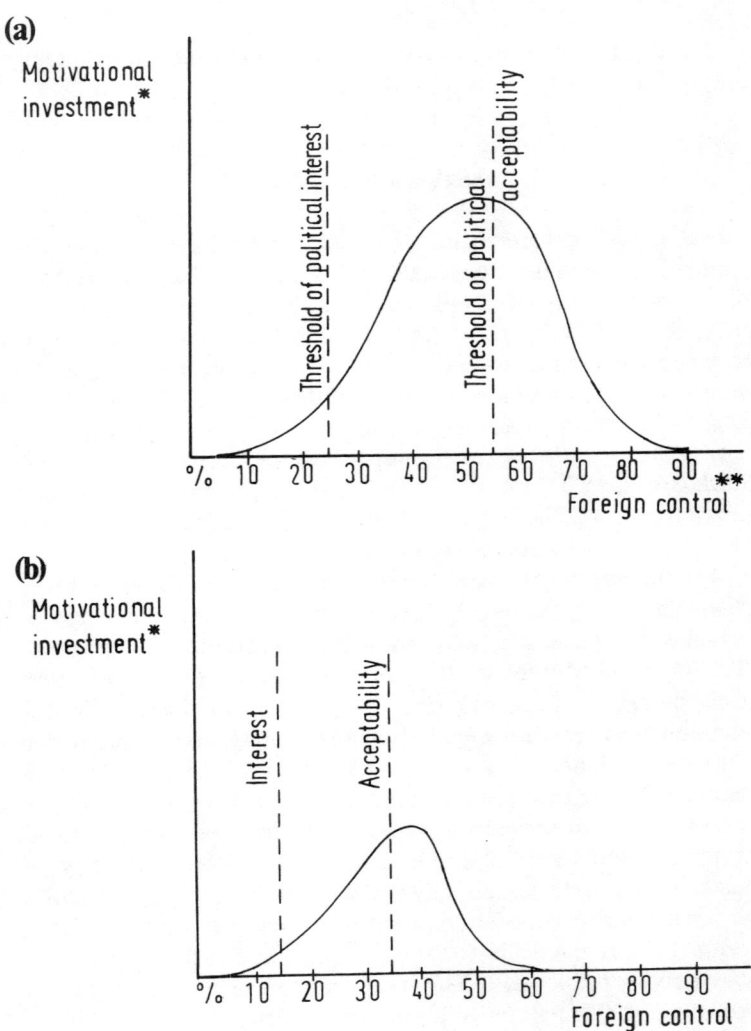

Figure 1.
Host government's dependence on foreign-owned sector (hypothesized relationships). (a) Normal situation; (b) effect of public opinion.

*Strength of the government's desire to keep good relations with foreign-owned sector.
**Statistical indicator of foreign-owned share of (a given sector of) the national

ment and production of equipment for military use. Beyond this direct link, many ostensibly civilian products and services of MNCs have great strategic significance, oil being the most obvious example. In this area we have to do with an aspect of dependence which is difficult to survey properly and the actual extent and implications of which at best are known only to the individual governments involved. Nevertheless, a country which has based its military defence on weapons, warning systems, and general equipment produced by MNCs would appear somehow to have committed itself to maintaining reasonably good relations with such companies. Military hardware, after all, is not replaced overnight.

Summary of the host government's dependence on MNCs

If the volume of MNC activities in a country is located between the limits of what the government regards as politically interesting and politically acceptable, dependence on the companies may be rather substantial. Within this range dependence will presumably increase proportionately with the volume of foreign-owned operations, and may be reinforced to the extent these activities are integrated in the local economy.

Under other conditions the government's dependence would probably be considerably smaller. Acute crises involving an exceptionally high level of dependence may occur in connection with the need for highly specified technology or capital to serve large investment projects. The Norwegian petroleum sector is a case in point. Similar crises may occur in connection with military requirements. The experience of such crises, however, tends to be seen as indicative of the general, long-run level of national dependence. Although such lessons may often be overdrawn, they may also inspire new efforts to find appropriate strategies for dependence reduction.

CONCLUDING REMARKS

The foregoing analysis has probably served more to clarify underlying issues — or demonstrate their complexity — than to answer questions about the power of multinational corporations. The lack of an overall summary of 'net dependence' may seem like a serious defect, but it follows naturally from my decision not to search for standard variables (common to both MNCs and governments) to express the theoretical elements of *motivation* and *alternatives*. Indeed, I would regard that kind of procedure as strongly misleading in a relationship of *multidimensional* dependence like the present one.

The essence of a complex relationship such as this is certainly not that complexity makes for symmetrical dependence, but rather that the direction of asymmetry can only be properly established after *careful* analysis. Remember, our objective here is not to provide a theory of power, but to measure the power of particular actors. Whereas a theory is improved by simplicity and inattention to details, measurement for predictive purposes is improved by precision. Hence, measurement in the present context is a messy task — it requires work.

For this reason I consider the more useful statements one can make on this topic to be those which set out the various conditions to be met before one can (or as one does) utilize aggregate data on MNCs and direct investment in studying power. To political scientists the temptation of official statistics on foreign business ownership is their availability — and the corresponding sin is to use them without fitting them into a carefully thought-out framework of measurement.

NOTES

1. A full definition of the term 'power' is given below.
2. Where no other source is given, information about statistics in Nordic national banks and statistical bureaus is based on extensive discussions between the author and officials of these institutions in the period August 1976 to March 1978.
3. A major exception is The Study of the Distribution of Power in Norway, a large-scale research project at the University of Bergen (Institute of Sociology)

which was initiated by the Norwegian government. Part of the project concerns the power of MNCs; see Knudsen (1974: 25-26).

4. The general question involved here is the subject of a rather large body of literature, only a small part of which has been utilized for this chapter.

5. On the question of definitions, see e.g. Vahlne (1974), who shows by empirical application what are the main consequences of different kinds of definitions.

6. See United Nations (1973); OECD (1976).

7. The Harvard Project employs the following criteria: at least 25 per cent of each subsidiary's equity, manufacturing subsidiaries in at least six countries, and consolidated world sales in 1967 of at least $400 million. See Vaupel and Curhan (1974:3, 16).

8. Non-manufacturing MNCs frequently have rather small subsidiaries in terms of persons employed and capital invested. The stricter requirement where number of countries is concerned is a way of making up for a (presumably) easier process of international expansion.

9. Informal control, of course, may well be attained via the financial structure, but data are hard to come by.

10. See, for instance, Statistiska Centralbyrån (1976).

11. Koncentrationsutredningen (1975: 58-59).

12. See, for instance, the column labelled 'number of share-owners' in the standardized series of reference works, '1000 largest companies', published in various European countries, e.g. *Norway's 1000 Largest Companies 1976*, Oslo: Økonomisk Litteratur, 1976. The general point is also made inter alia by Brooke (1972).

13. Mjelve (1970). The Swedish report has not yet been officially released, but the data in question were supplied by the Swedish Central Bureau of Statistics.

14. There may be an exception to this. If the subsidiary has a free rein, it may still be able to call on its parent company for support in the event of a conflict with the host country.

15. A good introductory treatment of this question is found in Wells (1971: 447-464). See also Stopford and Wells (1972), and Brooke (1972).

16. Nevertheless, it is for this kind of study that we use those familiar 'power indicators' to 'measure power'. In the normal usage, at least in international politics, an 'indicator of power' is not a measure of the actor's degree of success, but a measure of those of his characteristics which we assume will *cause* his degree of success in hypothetical situations (see, e.g., Petrén, 1976; Morgenstern et al., 1973).

17. Nagel discusses the question (1975: 171ff). He rejects the position that proven ability is the only grounds for attributing power. On potential power he says: 'Any use of "power" or "influence" to indicate a potential or capacity must therefore be an empirical hypothesis, derived from an implicit or explicit theory of power, one that may be strongly or weakly supported by past experience' (1975: 172).

18. The causal interpretation of power is nothing new in itself (see Goldmann, 1974 and Chapter 1 of this volume).

19. An excellent overview over the power literature is found in Nagel's book. For a good article-length discussion of key conceptual problems, see Goldmann

(1974). Questions of power in international politics are extensively discussed in Knorr (1975).

20. Nagel (1975: ch. 8, esp. 125ff).

21. Salamon and Siegfried (1977) show that such analysis is possible, although they make certain simplifying assumptions concerning the relationship of goals to outcomes which ideally (in Nagel's terms) should have been measured empirically.

22. The OECD Code of Liberalisation of Capital Movements is the most obvious evidence of this. Some member countries, including Sweden and Norway, have ratified with reservations. See OECD (1973; 1974; 1976).

23. On the use of propositions in definitions, see Chapter 4 in this volume.

24. Stopford and Wells (1972) cover this question in the first part of their book.

25. This particular formulation appears in Statistisk Sentralbyrå (1975: 14).

26. The Nordic glass industry is a current example. A major structural change will soon take place among the three Scandinavian subsidiaries of St Gobain, the large French MNC, so that the Swedish and Norwegian glass works will stop their production of the 'raw material' and confine themselves to the later stages of production. The Danish subsidiary will concentrate on supplying 'crude glass' to the two others. See *Veckans affärer*, 17 February 1977.

27. An important exception from this is found in some industries. An MNC moves in from abroad by buying up an existing establishment/company in the host country, the real motive not being to expand its own productive capacity, but to eliminate a smaller competitor. At the first suitable opportunity the MNC then closes down its newly acquired subsidiary and proceeds to supply the market from its factories abroad. The practice is known, inter alia, in Sweden and has been reason for strong concern in the Swedish labor movement. (Source: Miscellaneous working papers of the Swedish Federation of Labor (Utredningsavdelningen), 1976, mimeo.) The implication for the present analysis is that I am exaggerating the dependence of MNCs.

28. One of the few restrictions on foreign economic activity in Denmark is that an insurance company without a Danish subsidiary cannot legally sell insurance via home calls ('canvassing') (according to the Danish Ministry of Trade).

29. See, for example, those mentioned in note 12. General coverage of European companies is found in *Europe's 5000 Largest Companies 1976*, Oslo: Økonomisk Litteratur, 1976; *Jane's Major Companies of Europe 1976*, London: Macdonald & Jane's Publishers Ltd., 1976; and in *Fortune*'s annual register of the world's largest companies. Information on ownership is found in *Who Owns Whom*, four regional editions annually (London: O. W. Roskill & Co. (Reports Ltd). None of these sources is entirely reliable, but the problem is probably more one of omissions than of faulty information.

30. An obviously relevant factor which is not further discussed here is the structure of the national political system, with particular reference to the channeling of influence. See Salamon and Siegfried (1977: 1028-1030) and also Egeberg et al (1975).

31. However, no official OECD statistics exist on the subsidiaries of MNCs, as distinct from other foreign-owned firms. The OECD statistics on foreign-owned

companies still tend to be interpreted as if they referred to the global corporations alone, a tendency reinforced by the OECD definition of MNCs mentioned above.
32. Similar arguments are presented by Knut Getz Wold, director of the Bank of Norway, in a discussion of foreign investments in Norway (see Getz Wold, 1971: 182ff).
33. For a good article-length discussion, see Getz Wold (1971).

REFERENCES

BROOKE, M. Z. (1972) 'Problems in the Decision-Making process', in: M. Z. Brooke and H. L. Remmers (eds.) *The Multinational Company in Europe*. London: Longmans.
EGEBERG, M. et al. (1975) 'Organisasjonssamfunnet og den segmenterte stat', *Kirke og kultur*, 257-272, 368-378.
EMERSON, R. M. (1962) 'Power-Dependence Relations', *American Sociological Review*, 27:31-41.
GETZ WOLD, K. (1971) 'Utenlandsk kapital i norsk nringsliv', pp. 173-188 in: *Økonomi og Politikk. 15 Artikler*. Oslo: Aschenhoug.
GOLDMANN, K. (1974) 'Vem har internationell makt?' *UI Research Reports UI-74-3*. Stockholm: Utrikespolitiska Institutet.
KNORR, K. (1975) *The Power of Nations*. New York: Basic Books.
KNUDSEN, H. (1974) 'Flernasjonale selskaper i Norge. Noen samfunnsøkonomiske konsekvenser', *Statsøkonomisk Tidsskrift:* 25-56.
KONCENTRATIONSUTREDNINGEN (1975) *Internationella koncerner i industriländer*. Stockholm: Industridepartementet.
LEVINSON, K. and P. SANDÉN (1972) *Kapitalets international*. Stockholm: Prisma.
MJELVE, S. (1970) 'Utenlandske eierinteresser i norske bedrifter'. Working paper. Oslo: Bank of Norway.
MORGENSTERN, O. et al. (1973) *Long Term Projections of Power. Political, Economic, and Military Forecasting*. Cambridge, Mass.: Ballinger.
NAGEL, J. (1975) *The Descriptive Analysis of Power*. New Haven: Yale University Press.
OECD (1976) *International Investment and Multinational Enterprises*. Paris: OECD.
OECD (1973, 1974, 1976) *Code of Liberalisation of Capital Movements*, with Supplements nos. 1 and 2. Paris: OECD.
PETRÉN, K. (1976) 'Maktstrukturens huvuddrag. En kvantitativ analys av 20 maktindikatorer'. *UI Research Report*. Stockholm: Utrikespolitiska Institutet.
RUSSELL, B. (1946) *Power. A New Social Analysis*. 5th impr. London: Allen & Unwin.

SALAMON, L. M. and J. J. SIEGFRIED (1977) 'Economic Power and Political Influence: The Impact of Industry Structure on Public Policy', *Amerian Political Science Review*, 71: 1026-1043.

STATENS INDUSTRIVERK (1977) *Multinationella företag i svensk livsmedelsindustri*. Stockholm, Liber Förlag.

STATISTISKA CENTRALBYRÅN (1976) *Statistiska meddelanden*. Stockholm: SCB.

STATISTISK SENTRALBYRÅ (1975) *Kredittmarkedstatistikk 1972-1974*. Oslo: Statistisk Sentralbyrå.

STONEHILL, A. (1965) *Foreign Ownership in Norwegian Enterprises*. Oslo: Statistisk Sentralbyrå.

STOPFORD, J. M. and L. T. WELLS, Jr (1972) *Managing the Multinational Enterprise: Organization of the Firm and Ownership of the Subsidiaries*. New York: Basic Books.

UNITED NATIONS (1973) 'Multinational Corporations in World Development'. Department of Economic and Social Affairs. New York: United Nations.

VAHLNE, J.-E. (1974) 'Svenska multinationella företag: Prövning av ett par definitioner', in: J.-E. Vahlne (ed.) *Internationellt företagande*. Stockholm: Norstedts.

VAUPEL, J. W. and J. P. CURHAN (1974) *The World's Multinational Enterprises*. Geneva: Centre d'Etudes Industrielles.

WELLS, Jr, L. T. (1971) 'The Multinational Business Enterprise: What Kind of International Organization?' *International Organization*, 25: 447-464.

10 International Power and Foreign Policy Behavior: The Formulation of Danish Security Policy in the 1870-1914 Period

Nikolaj Petersen
University of Aarhus

The perspective of this chapter differs somewhat from most of the preceding analyses in discussing power as a predictor of foreign policy behavior. In the literature on international power this is a rather neglected perspective; very few attempts have been made to formulate general and comprehensive theories of how international power relates to foreign policy behavior. This essay should be seen as a small step in that direction. It will first present and discuss a framework for foreign policy analysis, developed on the basis of Rosenau's adaptation model (Rosenau, 1970), and then go on testing the framework in a case study of aspects of Danish security policy-making.

THE DIMENSIONALITY OF POWER

It is a main premise of this analysis, that in many cases 'power' is too general a concept by which to summarize the basic condition of the nation-state in international politics. Taxonomic parsimony is usually to be commended, but if carried too far it can also become an impediment to analysis. In the literature on international power there seems to be emerging some — though still not very explicit — recognition of the need to differentiate the power concept. For instance, Goldmann makes a distinction between 'offensive power'

('If *A* wants *B* to do *x*, *B* will do *x*') and 'defensive power' ('the kind of power *B* would possess, if *B* would do *x* regardless of *A*'s preferences') (see Chapter 1), noting that the two need not even covary . But since he regards offensive and defensive power as by definition the same phenomenon seen from two different perspectives, he does not apply the distinction systematically, but usually restricts himself to referring to the 'power' of a nation.

Klaus Knorr notes that there are two sides to national (economic) power, the *active* and the *passive* side.

> From the first point of view, national economic power is the ability of the state to benefit itself, using economic or financial policy, by hurting or threatening to hurt, benefiting or promising to benefit, economically weakening or strengthening another state. From the second viewpoint, national economic power is a state's ability to limit such use of economic power by other states against itself. Overall, a country's power is a *net* sum (Knorr, 1975: 79-80, italics in original).

However, in his concrete analyses, Knorr restricts himself to discussing the active side of economic power arguing that in this way passive economic power will be discussed, too, 'because one state's low passive power is the condition of another state's active power' (p. 80).

It is a central thesis of the burgeoning literature on interdependence that the modern nation-state is increasingly unable to function as the framework for the authoritative self-contained distribution of values among its members; this phenomenon is usually explained by reference to the growing sensitivity or vulnerability of the modern state to external influences over which it has only limited control. It is characteristic, however, that these concepts are more often than not left undefined, or if defined, at least unoperationalized.

To take an example, Keohane and Nye in their latest book on *Power and Interdependence* (1977) start out with a conceptual analysis of international power, in which they point to the necessity of distinguishing between two dimensions, *sensitivity* and *vulnerability* (pp. 11-19). The discussion does not, however, lead to any operationalization of these or the power concepts; nor are they used more than sporadically in the empirical sections of the book. Sensitivity in Keohane and Nye's terminology involves 'degrees of responsiveness [to external variables] within a policy framework', assuming that this framework remains unchanged (p. 12), while the vulnerability dimension 'rests on the relative availability and costliness of the alternatives' (ibid.); in this case the assumption is that the policy framework can be changed. Or put differently: 'sensitivity means liability to costly effects imposed from outside before policies are altered to try to change the situation. Vulnerability can be defined as 'an actor's liability to suffer costs imposed by external events even after policies have been altered' (p. 13). Keohane and Nye, furthermore, think of asymmetrical interdependencies, i.e. interdependencies defined by different actor position in the sensitivity and/or vulnerability dimensions, as important sources of power among actors (p. 18).

We may conclude this brief overview with the observation that there is some tendency to see 'power' as a two-dimensional phenomenon, with one dimension being represented by concepts such as 'offensive power', 'active power' or just 'power', and the other one by notions like 'defensive power', 'passive power' or 'sensitivity'/'vulnerability'. In this article we shall use the terms *influence capability* and *stress sensitivity*, respectively, as defined by Hansen (1974: 150), where influence capability denotes a country's ability to control and manipulate its external environment and to structure it according to its own values, while stress sensitivity represents the degree to which societal structures and the distribution of societal values are affected by changes in and demands emanating from the external environment.

We also noted that the authors we have discussed tend to look upon these dimensions as different *aspects* of the same phenomenon. This is of course basically correct; in a dyadic relationship one country's stress sensitivity (or whatever term is used) determines the other power's influence capability (and vice versa). From a systemic point of view the distinction between the two aspects may therefore not be crucially important. When it comes to analysis at the state level, the perspective becomes different, however. The 'cancelling effect' which in systemic analyses allows one to concentrate on one aspect of power, does not apply when explaining the behavior of a single international actor. To state that a nation is powerful in the sense that its behavior has some impact upon its environment does not necessarily mean that it is insensitive to influences from this environment. Indeed, one of the hallmarks of a state of high interdependence among a group of nations is that they mutually influence each other, i.e. that they combine a high influence capability vis-à-vis each other with a high degree of stress sensitivity. Nor is a weak nation in terms of international influence necessarily highly sensitive to its environment. We can illustrate this point by hypothetically filling a space determined by the two dimensions, presupposing that they are orthogonal, i.e. independent of each other. For the sake of illustration, Figure 1 refers to the distribution of influence capability and stress sensitivity in the internationial economic system. The figure illustrates that there is no fixed relationship between the two dimensions (or if there is some relationship it is of a probabilistic rather than a deterministic nature). To take some cases:

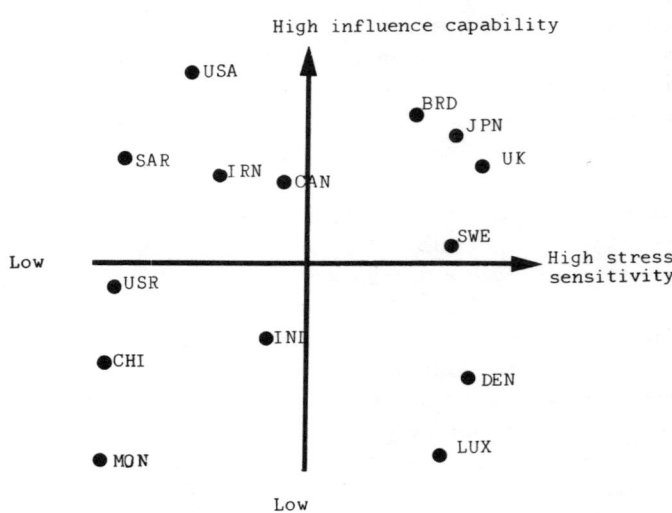

Figure 1.
Hypothetical distribution of influence capability and stress sensitivity in the international economic system.

Luxembourg combines a minimal influence capability with a high degree of stress sensitivity; the same basic configuration describes the international position of Denmark and presumably most small, modernized countries. Mongolia is even less influential than Luxembourg with respect to the international economic (capitalist) system, but is also virtually insensitive to its fluctuations. Other socialist countries like China and the Soviet Union show the same pattern of low stress sensitivity and rather low (though higher than Mongolia's) influence capability. Most developing countries, with the exception of the most highly integrated (or dependent) ones, would presumably also fall in this quadrant of the figure.

Saudi Arabia combines a rather low stress sensitivity (its oil revenues will be more than sufficient for current use no matter how the oil market and the international economy develops) with a fairly high degree of influence capability (by virtue of its control over the oil market and its dollar surpluses). Iran shows a similar pattern, but is more dependent upon oil prices and consumption and has less resources with which to gain influence upon the system. In this quadrant we also have the United States, the 'topdog' of the international economic system. The US is unquestionably the most potent power in the system, and at the same time relatively insensitive to its fluctuation; among other things this is due to its low trade/GNP ratio compared to other modernized countries.

The larger modernized countries like West Germany, Japan and Great Britain represent the nearest fit to our description of the highly interdependent state. They are relatively influential in international economics, Germany and Japan being normally considered together with the US as the 'locomotives' which may pull the Western world out of its present economic predicament, but at the same time they are highly sensitive to the business cycle.

The fact that there is no fixed relationship between a nation's position on the two dimension suggests that we have to do with separate and distinct dimensions which, furthermore, are very likely to be the basic dimensions that determine a nation's position in the system.

A MODEL OF FOREIGN POLICY BEHAVIOR

It is a logical next step to hypothesize that a nation's position in the influence capability/stress sensitivity space is an important determinant of its foreign policy behavior, as this position determines to what degree it can further its interests in the international system and to what degree it has to accept external influences on the functioning of its essential structures, i.e. the physical, political, economic or social structures of society (cf. Rosenau, 1970). Hansen (1974) has produced such a model by linking the two dimensions with a typology of foreign policy behavior which Rosenau developed in his work on national adaptation. Rosenau (1970) posits four basic patterns of foreign policy behavior on the basis of decision-makers' degree of responsiveness to external and internal demands and changes: namely 'preservative', 'acquiescent', 'promotive' and 'intransigent' policies. Rosenau's adaptation model and also Hansen's revision of it may be criticized in several respects (cf. Petersen, 1977), but — and this is the important thing — they can also be further revised. Figure 2 represents such a revision.

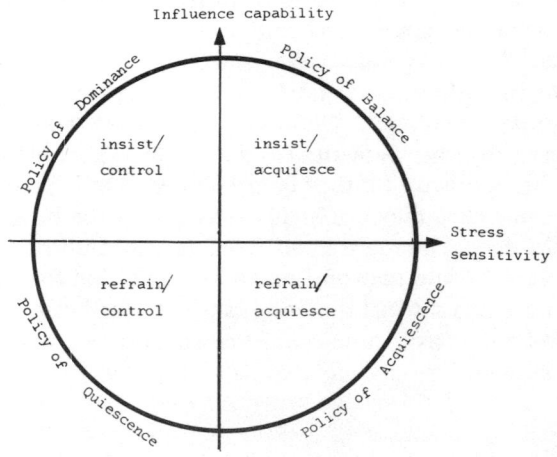

Figure 2.
A Model of foreign policy behavior.

Figure 2 specifies four patterns of overall foreign policy behavior: the patterns of *dominance, balance, acquiescence,* and *quiescence*, which are determined by two underlying variable clusters influence capability and stress sensitivity.

In each of the quadrants of the model the typical overall foreign policy reaction to external demands and changes (control/acquiesce) and to internal demands and changes (insist/refrain) are hypothesized. The politics of dominance and balance are characterized by *insist*-behavior in cases where changes occur or demands are formulated in the essential structures which call for some kind of readjustment of the balance between society and its environment or between the structures of society themselves. Generally, it can be postulated that statesmen will be tempted to externalize the need for readjustment which arises when societal structures decline in performance. Economic difficulties generated by endogenic imbalances, e.g. between production output and wage demands, very often lead to external measures such as tariffs and import quotas which can be seen as attempts to shift part of the burden of readjustment to the international society.

Such behavior, whereby a country *insists* that the international society must to some extent adapt to the demands of her internal structures, is not open to all countries, however, since it presupposes at least some ability to make demands felt internationally, i.e. some *influence capability*. Countries with little influence capability cannot externalize their domestic problems; they have largely to *refrain* from doing so, and instead try to solve the problems of balance by internal readjustment. In the economic sphere uninfluential countries have to refrain from attempts at 'exporting' their problems, be they unemployment, balance of payments deficits, etc. and try to solve them as best they can by readjusting the balance between and within her societal structures. A nation without monetary credibility must solve her balance of payments problem through a policy of unemployment rather than by floating loans in the international money market. This way of handling internal demands and the effects of internal changes is characteristic of acquiescent and quiescent policy postures.

Control and *acquiesce* behavior denote basic reactions to external demands. The 'natural' reaction to external demands and changes is to try to control their impact on societal structures. If such changes are seen to result in a state of disequilibrium among its internal structures their impact will be actively resisted. Examples of such behavior are the refusal of South Africa to accept other nations' rights to interfere in her racial policies or the Soviet Union's rejection of 'ideological co-existence'. To be able to do so requires a low degree of *stress sensitivity*. Until recently, South Africa has been only slighty stress sensitive due to her isolated position behind the *glacis* of Angola, Rhodesia, and Mozambique, the cohesiveness of the white community and the unwillingness of the major Western countries to side effectively with the anti-apartheid lobby. These factors are clearly changing with the likely result that South Africa may have to change her adamant posture. In the case of the Soviet Union low stress sensitivity has been a function of the ideological and political monopoly of the reigning CPSU and the fact that the Western nations have not until recently rated ideological influence highly in relation to military détente. If, on the other hand, external influences are considered beneficial in their effects upon society, efforts will aim at optimizing such effects and steering them so as to avoid negative side-effects. This kind of international behavior is of course typical of dominant nations, but also of nations pursuing a low-profile, non-involvement policy of quiescence.

Nations with a high degree of stress sensitivity are less able to follow such a course. Willy-nilly they have to *acquiesce* more or less to external demands; the rate of acquiescence may vary, but they always have to take account of the external factor. In 1914 Danish decision-makers had to acquiesce in (what they interpreted as) a German ultimatum to close the Danish Straits on the basis of their perception of extreme military stress sensitivity; in recent years the United States has had to acquiesce in the Soviet Union's claim to be a global superpower because of the stress sensitivity engendered by the strategic balance. As indicated, acquiescent behavior is a stance characteristic of balance policy as well as acquiescence policy proper.

As presented above, the model is a pure state-as-actor model. But of course, states are not international actors as such; the actors are those persons who have been authorized to act on behalf of the state, i.e. the decision-makers. The foreign policy behavior of a nation-state is therefore not directly determined by its position in the influence capability/stress sensitivity space, but rather on the decision-makers' *perceptions* of this position and the degree to which they can get these perceptions accepted in society at large. As history has repeatedly shown, unrealistic perceptions will result in a sub-optimal performance of essential structures. The 'corrective' influence of the 'real world' indicates that in the long term there will be a tendency towards congruity between actual and perceived influence capability/stress sensitivity. An over-optimistic foreign policy will quickly be put right by the external environment, while an over-cautious policy may come under attack from competing domestic elites for not safeguarding the national interest. On the other hand, as a nation's position in the influence capability/stress sensitivity space will tend to change with the passage of time, the problem of correct perception is likely to remain a crucial one.

OPERATIONALIZATION OF THE INDEPENDENT VARIABLES

To become empirically relevant and not just true by definition the model must be subjected to more determined operationalization efforts than have been attempted up to now; both independent and dependent variables have to be specified in a way which permits empirical hypotheses to be formulated and tested. In this and the following section such an attempt will be made and illustrated with aspects of the formulation of Danish security policy during the 1870-1914 period. However, to the extent Keohane and Nye's issue structure model (1977) is a relevant one, it is only partially possible to arrive at a generally usable operationalization of the model. If resources are not freely transferable from one issue-area to another, e.g. from the realm of international power politics to the arena of economic politics or to still more specific issue-areas (fisheries, education, etc.) and vice versa, then each issue and issue-area requires a separate operationalization of the variables which make up the model. The following discussion is therefore especially relevant to the national security field.

Influence capability — some general remarks

Influence capability can be defined as a function of all those negative *and* positive sanctions which nation *A* can use to influence nation *B*. Sanctions presupposes resources or 'power base elements' (Chapter 1) of some kind. Such PBEs can be either tangible or intangible, tangible PBEs being those physical and human resources which are commonly understood as the constitutents of military and economic capability. Petrén (1976, cf. Goldmann, 1977) reports a cluster analysis of twenty power indicators with a view towards analysing the dimensionality of power, one salient finding of which was the appearance of a strong and tightly related cluster of ten 'conventional' power indicators, i.e. GDP, investments, energy production and consumption, defence expenditures, economic aid given, steel and cement production, combat aircraft and international trade. The mean intercorrelation between these variables was 0.83 in 1971 (in 1957: 0.90). Other indicators — mostly relative ones like the international trade/GDP — were less, in some cases even negatively, correlated with these measures.

While this study indicates that we may be able to create quite good indicators of tangible power base elements, we should not for this reason ignore the importance of intangible, 'diplomatic' PBEs. First, the application of tangible PBEs presupposes will as well as skill on the part of decision-makers. During the inter-war period the actual international influence of the United States was considerably lower than her possession of tangible PBEs would lead one to expect, simply because its leaders lacked the will and urge to make use of them. Conversely, North Vietnam has recently compensated for her relative lack of tangible PBEs by an extraordinary exertion of will-power and an equally extraordinary, clever husbanding of her meagre power base.

Secondly, intangible resources include such elements as *prestige* and *reputation* which may apply to a long range of attributes. In the world of power politics, a reputation for toughness may be especially relevant; many consider the Finnish *sisu* as a special asset in her relationship with the Soviet Union. Another resource is *ideological power*, i.e. the 'possession' of an ideological message which, by appealing to values which are accepted generally or by sizable groups in other nations, may serve to further the interests of the 'keeper of the faith'. Both the Soviet Union, the United States and the Chinese People's Republic have consistently tried to shore up their tangible influence capabilities with an ideological message. A sub-category of this kind of influence capability might be termed 'normative power' in which the appeal is to international norms. Small nations often try to make the best out of this diplomatic PBE.

The foregoing propositions should be modified in certain important respects, since the influence capability of an actor should be seen as determined not solely by 'national attributes', but also by the nature of concrete bi- and multilateral relationships as well as by the general characteristics of the environing international system. First, at least certain PBEs can be 'borrowed'. A country with a weak economic base can borrow or be given funds from other countries which make it more able to affect its environment, just as powers with a weak military base can 'borrow' military PBEs by entering an alliance with other and stronger powers.

Secondly, what constitutes international power and influence is largely determined by the characteristics of the international system. The international system which is emerging tends to give less general influence capability to military PBEs and more to economic PBEs than the international system of the fifties and the sixties, for instance (Keohane and Nye, 1973: 119-120). The best illustration of this change is the dramatic rise in the international influence of the oil-producing countries in the seventies. Without any significant rise in their output of oil the OPEC countries have acquired a large say over a wide range of international issues, simply because the possession of energy resources is suddenly at a premium. The balance between the influence potential of tangible and intangible PBEs may also vary considerably between systems. International politics is not exclusively determined by the balance of power, but to a certain extent also by the existence of international norms like those recently codified in the final documents of the European security conference in Helsinki. 'Territorial integrity', 'the sovereign equality of nations', 'peaceful conflict resolution', and now also 'human rights' are such norms which — to the extent they are respected, of course — may affect the relative importance of tangible and intangible power base elements.

The *state* of the system is another modifying factor. For instance, international tension may be expected to upgrade military variables at the expense of normative or ideological variables.

Thirdly, and as previously suggested, what constitutes influence is also determined by the character of the values at stake. Where 'status values' (Rosenau, 1966) like security or national independence are at stake, what constitutes influence capability is clearly different from situations where economic welfare and other tangible values are central. While abundant military and economic resources may give its possessor influence capability over a broad range of international issues, the degree to which PBEs can be translated into actual influence capability varies between issue-areas.

Influence capability — Denmark in the 1870-1914 period

Robert L. Rothstein who has written one of the few books on the interaction between small powers and their systemic environments (Rothstein, 1968) notes that small nations are dominated by the system 'in the sense that the opportunities they have are dependent on the kind of system that exists. They can rarely create their own opportunites...' (p. 182). Rothstein's basic thesis is that the influence of the small state as well as its security primarily depends on the *balance of power* between the dominant powers of the system and the *level of conflict* among them (p. 187). According to his view, the influence of small powers is only small (negligible) in an unbalanced system; its limited resources cannot significantly affect the central balance and hence will have little 'market value'.

In a more balanced system the basic condition of the small power is different. If the dominant powers in the system are status quo oriented (and international tension is low), the resources of the small states are again more or less redundant and their influence is consequently low; this may be the reasoning behind the fears of some smaller countries that the present state of détente between the superpowers may negatively affect their own international influence. If, however, the dominant powers or some of them are revisionist (and tension is high), the situation is different. In this case, the PBEs of the dominant powers will quickly be mobilized to a point where the opportunity costs of engaging even the small lumps of power which the smaller states can supply, becomes less than those involved in increasing internal mobilization. In the most extreme case, when a single conflict dimension dominates the system, the influence of the small state is at its peak. This increased influence capability has its price, however: 'the belief that the increased influence of various Small Powers means increased security is essentially illusory and ephemeral... since it reflects the development of a situation which may be disastrous: an imminent general war' (p. 190); a bipolar balance of power system may therefore increase the influence capability of smaller states, but often at the expense of their security (i.e. stress sensitivity).

The main determinants of Denmark's influence capabilities in the 1870-1914 period should therefore primarily be found in the character and state of the European system and only secondarily in her own national attributes. After the defeat in the 1864 Schleswig War, which led to the curtailment of the monarchy by about one-third, and after the loss of her former naval supremacy in the Western Baltic in the 1870s Denmark was unquestionably a weak military power, especially vis-à-vis Imperial Germany which was the target of her main interests in the diplomatic-military security field, namely the 'reunion' of the Danish-speaking parts of Schleswig and the wish to avoid another German aggression. Diplomatically, Denmark also lost status (as measured by the rank and number of accredited diplomatic missions) during the rest of the century (Singer and Small, 1966).

During the period in question the European system underwent a significant change from a multipolar system dominated and moderated by Germany in the Bismarck period (1870-1890) to an increasingly bipolar configuration in the following Wilheminian period with the Triple Alliance (Germany, Austria-Hungary and Italy) pitted against the Triple Entente between Britain, France and Russia. In retrospect this development seems both uninterrupted and logical, but in fact the polarization process was uneven and perhaps at no point irreversible. This meant that after the turn of the century it became increasingly difficult for decision-makers, especially from the smaller countries, to make correct evaluations of the international situation.

The Bismarck system whose principal method of conflict resolution was great power diplomacy (in some cases the convocation of the European 'concert'), gave the smaller powers little influence.

Tension among the powers was usually held at a low degree of intensity and as their mobilization potential was only partially tapped, the small amounts of power which the smaller countries could throw into the balance had little impact. Alliances were therefore usually unavailable to the smaller powers; the larger powers had little incentive to rock the boat by furthering their specific interests against another great power, and an international organizational system through which small power interests could be channelled did not exist at the time.

On the other hand, because of its relative stability the system did not in general endanger the survival and integrity of the smaller powers. If a small power was 'satisfied' it might therefore be relatively content with its position; if it were revisionist, it could do nothing much but to 'await the dawn of Great Power conflict' (Rothstein, 1968: 210).

The few and half-hearted attempts by Russia (1871) and Sweden-Norway (1875) to intervene on Denmark's behalf in Berlin clearly showed the limited diplomatic possibilities of Denmark. Still more significant was the Danish failure to capitalize on the specific 'normative resource' she acquired in article 5 of the Prague Peace of 1866 between Prussia and Austria, according to which the 'northern districts' of Schleswig should be allowed to decide in a referendum whether they wanted to return to Denmark. Negotiations followed between Denmark and Prussia, but quickly showed that Prussia's terms were totally unacceptable to Denmark. In 1878 Germany persuaded Austria-Hungary to abolish the article without Denmark being able to do much about it.

With regard to the Schleswig question, the Danish influence potential was therefore insignificant. And so was her influence capability via-à-vis a German attack, if no external assistance was available. During the half-century after 1870, where Denmark narrowly escaped the conclusion of a military alliance with France, no clear alliance possibility against Germany came in sight. In the 1880s Russia came to some extent to be considered a protector of Denmark in European diplomacy. The factual background of these perceptions is still very much in the dark. The Danish Foreign Ministry actively discouraged such notions (Sjöqvist, 1962: 196) which, whether they had any substance or not, were based on the personal relationship between Czar Alexander III (1881-1894) and his father-in-law, King Christian IX (1863-1906). Sjöqvist notes that these notions may have been the reason why Germany made a few overtures to Denmark in the late 1880s; nothing significant came out of these, however. On the whole, though, Denmark's influence capability remained slight.

Several authors (Rothstein, 1968; Branner, 1972) argue that by and large the evolving bipolar system of the early twentieth century gave the smaller powers a great influence than the old one. With the gradual hardening of the great power system and the increasing mobilization of their internal resources, as witnessed by rapidly growing defense budgets, even small amounts of power became of importance to the balance of power, at least locally. The great powers therefore became interested in acquiring the assets (military or territorial) which the small powers could supply — or at least in denying them to their adversaries. Diplomatically the smaller powers also came to have more influence, at least formally, as their participation in the Hague conferences of 1899 and 1908 indicates.

Various German contacts with Denmark in the 1905-1914 period suggests a genuine though deftly camouflaged anxiety for Denmark's orientation in a European war which might possibly have been translated into a greater Danish influence vis-à-vis Germany. The effectiveness of this potential — which was constrained by a clearly stated British refusal to commit herself on Denmark's behalf — hinged, however, on the extent to which Danish decision-makers became aware of the possibilities and their eventual willingness to use them.

Stress sensitivity — some general remarks

Stress sensitivity as a concept is more difficult to pin down than the concept of influence capability. Like the latter it is a very complex cluster of variables pertaining to the nation as well as to its environment. In his study of Danish market policy Hansen (1974) equates the concept with the dependence on foreign markets by an economy with an exceptionally high trade/GDP ratio. McGowan and Gottwald (1976: 475) state that societal modernization may be the basic empirical referent of the concept and refer to the fact that one of its characteristics is the increased sensitivity of domestic structures to international events, but like Hansen they do not try to speculate on a more general description of the variable.

The concept corresponds to Goldmann's concept of 'defensive power' and Knorr's 'passive power'. As noted earlier, Keohane and Nye introduce a distinction between sensitivity, meaning exposure to external influences within a given policy context, and vulnerability, meaning exposure in a wider setting which includes the possibility of rule-changing. As Denmark has never had any perceptible rule-changing capabilities, sensitivity and vulnerability for her part tend to be indentical, which means that the distinction, which can be seen as the short-term and long-term aspects of the same phenomenon, loses most of its importance in the present context.

To begin with, we may distinguish between internal and external aspects of stress sensitivity. For each of the four essential structures of society it is possible to point to traits which enhance their propensity to become affected by changes in the environment. In the *economic* sphere modernization is usually seen as increasing the vulnerability to international business cycles (and of course also the ability to profit from them). Several of Petrén's 'unconventional' variables can probably be interpreted as more or less suitable indicators of stress sensitivity; this applies to the so-called development cluster (made up by GDP/per capita and the contribution of agriculture to GDP) and still more clearly to her foreign trade/GDP variable. Many concomitants to modernization, such as urbanization and the build-up of complicated infrastructures, may also increase the stress sensitivity of the *physical structures*; the less urbanized Soviet Union is generally considered less vulnerable to nuclear attack than the United States. In this sphere, stress sensitivity may also depend on topographical variables. Denmark's long and readily accessible coastline and the gentleness of her terrain has always been a negative factor in her security policy calculus. The *social* structure of society may, together with the *political* structure, generally prove to be the least prone to stress sensitivity of the four societal structures (which is just another way of saying that global interdependence may be higher in the physical and economic spheres than in the social and political ones). Constituting the basic fabric of society the social structure will normally not be directly susceptible to external impacts; influences will rather be indirect through the economic, political and physical structures. The central variable seems to be the degree of national integration achieved. Alienation of sizable groups — be it for ethnic, racial, religious or political reasons — reduces the performance of the social structure as an underpinning of the remaining societal structures.

Finally, the performance of the *political* structure is also directly dependent on the degree of national integration. If political life is marred by polarization and strife then the quality of decision-making will tend to go down, while the potential for external factors to influence political decisions goes up.

Other indicators of stress sensitivity are determined by the interplay between internal, structural traits and characteristics of the international system. The degree of integration of the nation-state in the international system appears to be the central variable. The more a nation participates in international politics and economics, the more stress sensitive it will be to the fluctuations in the performance of the international system. Integration and participation may be more or less voluntary. Nations may opt to take part in some international undertaking, an economic organization or a military alliance, which will make them more stress sensitive to developments both within the organization and in its functional surroundings. In joining NATO Denmark increased her military capability by 'borrowing' part of the American deterrence, but she may very well also have become more stress sensitive to developments in the Cold War. If there is any doubt whether Denmark's stress sensitivity did in fact increase by joining NATO (a proposition many would probably deny), it is because of the geographic factor. Stated generally, stress sensitivity decreases with distance to the potentially influencing factor. It has always been easier for geographically remote nations to keep away from involvement in and so avoid the stresses of global politics than for nations with a more central position.

As with influence capability the above-mentioned elements of stress sensitivity depend on the nature of the relevant international system. Monetary stability and international tension are types of system-states which vitally affect the stress sensitivity of nations.

Stress sensitivity — Denmark in the 1870-1914 period

In the specific arena of Danish security policy in the 1870-1914 period, stress sensitivity can be seen as depending upon the structural vulnerability of Danish society to external attack or threats thereof, and upon the specific and general risks inherent in the international system of the day.

Structural vulnerability hinges, inter alia, on topography, which in the case of Denmark involves two problems: the hardly defensible land frontier in Jutland with its lack of natural defenses to invasion from the south, and the less accessible island archipelago of which Zealand is the absolutely most important part. A related variable is infrastructure which involves among other things, the possibilities of increasing inaccessibility through fortifications — a much discussed theme those days. In a technical sense much of the Danish defense debate in this period centered round the possibilities (and consequences) of reducing stress-sensitivity through a land and sea fortification of Copenhagen. As a third variable in this cluster could be mentioned national cohesion; on one side the period was characterized by a strong all-pervasive anti-German nationalism, and on the other side by bitter and alienating debates on national defense.

The more important variables should be found in the systemic sphere, however, and especially in Denmark's degree of involvement in the European power system. Denmark did not participate in international alliances in this period, but this did not mean that she was outside the scope of European power politics. Rothstein notes that the survival of small powers may among other things depend on the attention which great powers pay to them (Rothstein, 1968: 212), and in the same vein Branner (1972:55) points out the difference between being placed centrally or peripherally in the war planning of the great powers. In a conflict great power interests may focus upon the possible use of the territorial and other assets of the small country and/or their denial to the adversary. In the case of Denmark the principal coveted asset is probably territory. The sensitivity engendered by the strategic position across the entry to (or exit from) the Baltic has always been a major parameter in the formulation of Danish security policies. (After 1864 — and the loss of Schleswig-Holstein — Danish territory ceased to be coveted for other than strategic reasons). During the period under consideration the most salient relationship involved Germany and the other powers, i.e. her relations with Russia, France, and especially with Britain, the most stress-producing situation being a British-German antagonism. However, relations between Russia and Britain were also of great concern to Denmark.

Another important variable is represented by the conflict-proneness of the system; the more conflictual the system the more stress sensitive Danish society was likely to be. If Denmark's influence capability was low during the Bismarck period, her stress sensitivity, as measured by the magnitude of the external 'threat', was not particularly high, either. Germany was 'satisfied' and had no further demands on Denmark except than she accepted the status quo.

The most threatening and stress-producing situations during the period therefore arose out of the Russian-British rivalry. On two occasions (1878 and 1885) war seemed imminent which actualized the strategic importance of the Danish straits, and led to intensive deliberations over how best to avoid being entangled. (In this connection it might be added that Denmark's military possibilities of guarding her neutrality against Britain or Russia were normally considered somewhat better than her possibilities against Germany; neither Russia nor Britain would be able to land as many troops on Danish soil as Germany.)

As hypothesized by Rothstein, potential small power influence in the following period was very often coupled with increasing stress sensitivity. The level of international tension was rising, and so was the danger of being involved in war. A country's actual degree of sensitivity seems to have depended very much on its position in the increasingly elaborate and rigid war plans of the great powers (Branner, 1972: 55), cf. the different fates of Belgium and Holland in the First World War.

From the Danish point of view the most salient and potentially dangerous feature of the evolving system was the growing rivalry between Britain and Germany which automatically served to enhance the strategic importance of the Danish Straits and of Denmark proper. Until 1905 the most likely conflict to involve Denmark was still one between Russia (in combination with Germany) on one side and Britain on the other. Both the Czar and the Kaiser were at least tempted by such a combination which, however, in the end was deemed too provocative by responsible German decision-makers. After 1905 (with the Russian Baltic navy lying on the bottom of the Strait of Tsushima) the most likely scenario became a German-British conflict.

Until about 1905 the combination of a potential Russian-German alignment against Britain *and* the specific main tenets of German naval planning which foresaw a partial occupation of Denmark in order to block the Baltic to the British navy (Branner, 1972: 66) gave Denmark a highly exposed position.

Around 1905 a shift in German war planning occurred. The general staff, preoccupied with the difficult problem of planning a two-front war against France and Russia, had been opposed to opening a third front against Denmark, however weak, from the beginning, and in 1905 it succeeded in having its view accepted at the highest decision-making level. From then on the German navy had to base its war planning on respect for Danish neutrality, and gradually its planning came to focus more on the North Sea than on the Baltic. In Britain, a somewhat similar development took place. The so-called Baltic Project by Lord Fisher, First Lord of the Admiralty, according to which Britain should land an expeditionary force on Germany's 'soft' Baltic coast in case of a war together with France and Russia, had to be given up around 1910 when it was decided that any British intervention should be on the Western Front. By and large, we can say then that Denmark's stress sensitivity while still pronounced was on the decline in the last decade before the War; the clearest indication of this is of course that Denmark actually managed to keep her neutrality in 1914. But, again, the policy consequences of this change would depend upon decision-makers' perceptions and not upon the objective condition which our post facto analysis may reveal.

OPERATIONALIZATION OF THE
DEPENDENT VARIABLES

A typology of security policy postures

Security policy has been defined as 'those political activities which a primary actor in the international system initiates in order to attain its goals in situations where it is confronted with threats from other actors in the system' (Andrén, 1972: 32). In what follows a crude — and very preliminary — typology of such activities is discussed and hypotheses are formulated which link it to the independent variables of our model.

Basic military posture

Military capabilities may be the most direct means of influencing and controlling the security policy behavior of others. The external functions of military establishments are at least fourfold. It may be compellence, i.e. using military means to force an opponent to do something he would not otherwise do. The interventions of the United States in Vietnam and of the Soviet Union in Czechoslovakia illustrate this mode of behavior. Successful intervention presupposes supreme influence capability and low stress sensitivity; it may thus be argued that the American failure in Vietnam was at least partially due to the high degree of sensitivity of American society to the personal and moral strains of the war. Compellence and intervention are typical aspects of a dominance policy.

Another function is deterrence, i.e. influencing a potential aggressor's risk calculus by raising the opportunity costs of an attack. Again, deterrence requires sufficient capabilities in order that deterrence may be credible, and as the need to deter only arises when stress sensitivity has reached a certain level, deterrence can be seen as the typical security posture of balance-oriented powers.

Defense in the traditional sense, i.e. forcing an aggressor to abandon an initiated military attack by raising its costs, to be a viable proposition presupposes adequate influence capability and is thus typically linked with a balance posture, the need to defend in itself signifying a high degree of stress sensitivity. Countries with a low stress sensitivity are, eo ipso, rather unsusceptible to the eventuality of military attack, while states with a low influence capability may only court disaster if they were to go in for a defense posture as described.

For states with a low influence capability and a high stress sensitivity a posture, which in the Danish security policy tradition is termed neutrality defense, may be more relevant. Neutrality defense has as its primary aim to make credible a policy of neutrality in great power conflict by giving the powers some reassurance that its territory cannot be occupied by others in a coup de main, but is not designed to meet a full scale premeditated attack of overwhelming force. This posture can be seen as an aspect of an acquiescent policy.

It follows from the above analysis that if both influence capability and stress sensitivity are low, the need for military resources is also low — at least in the short run; in this case a very low posture which is consonant with a general policy of quiescence will be possible, though — as experience shows — not given.

External security policy relationships

As mentioned, military capabilities can be 'borrowed' abroad, so to speak, to compensate for the lack of own power resources. This presupposes some kind of a formal arrangement with other powers either through a collective defense arrangement, i.e. a military alliance, or through a collective security scheme. The alternatives to these stances are 'going it alone' and non-alignment which both signify efforts not to be tied down by foreign entanglement, but which differ in most other respects.

'Going it alone' in 'splendid isolation' is only a viable option for nations with a high degree of control over their environment and a low degree of stress sensitivity; it is consequently a typical aspect of a dominance posture. Dominant countries *may* seek alliances, but then mainly either as an instrument for exerting dominance (the Warsaw Pact may play this role for the Soviet Union) or as a means for establishing dominance vis-à-vis an opponent (this was at least part of the American rationale for NATO).

However, the military alliance seems more typical as an ingredient in a balance posture. States with such an orientation will usually have both the incentive — a high stress sensitivity — to conclude an alliance as well as the assets which may make others interested in forming forces with her.

For stress sensitive states with little military power in the traditional sense the availability of the alliance depends on other assets, such as political allegiance or the possesson of coveted territorial assets. (The American interest in having Denmark as a member of NATO was primarily due to Denmark's possession of Greenland.) The weak power must, however weigh the increased influence capability which alliance membership gives, against a possible increase in stress sensitivity; and this calculation may very well result in a non-alignment or neutrality posture being adopted.

Non-alignment can be seen as a means of reducing external stresses by lessening involvement in the international power system. Non-alignment is the typical aspect of a quiescent foreign policy, but is also compatible with an acquiescent policy, namely in those cases where alliances are either unavailable or would result in an intolerable increase in the risk factor relative to the guarantee aspect.

As collective security schemes by definition are universal, membership in them is not related with any one adaptive mode. However, it may be hypothesized that collective security has a special attraction to smaller powers by offering a prospect of protection at a low cost. However, as the Danish reservations against the League of Nations show, even collective security may be seen as too entangling by weak states in a difficult security position.

Political-diplomatic postures

Defense and alliance/non-alignment policies are designed to directly affect a nation's security policy environment. In a broader, more indirect way nations try to manipulate their influence capability and stress sensitivity through a number of diplomatic behaviors ranging from the day-to-day management of external affairs to efforts to influence and change the functioning and in some cases even the structure of the international system.

In order to increase their influence capability, for instance, nations that are low on conventional military capabilities will often try to work for changes in the system which will upgrade the importance of non-military resources such as prestige and reputation or ideological/normative 'power'. Smaller European countries have been active in furthering international détente because a reduced level of tension is expected to increase their diplomatic influence and at the same time reduce the external stresses emanating from the great power conflict.

It should be stressed, however, that normally the lesser countries do not have the resources to change the functioning of the system on their own; they are therefore more or less dependent upon diplomatic coalitions, i.e. multilateral diplomacy, formal or informal, to acquire international influence. On the other hand, powers with a high degree of independent influence capability will usually rely more on bilateral relationships in which their capabilities can be more directly exploited, though without neglecting multilateral diplomacy. As a rule of thumb, but admittedly a very tentative one, one could perhaps say that multilateralization of diplomacy is primarily sought by states with a basic acquiescence posture while bilateral diplomacy is most typical as an aspect of dominance.

In order to reduce stress sensitivity several policy stances can be used. An active détente policy was already mentioned as a general means of reducing external stresses.

Non-provocative behavior is another related mode. It is motivated by the wish not to give other powers the incentive or excuse to demand changes in the essential structures of society. Put another way, this means refraining from activities which can be interpreted as threatening the security interests of others. This type of behavior is especially called for by countries in an exposed security position to whom any increase in external stress is intolerable; like détente policy it is therefore a typical aspect of balance and acquiescence postures.

'Stay put' (*ligge död*) behavior is really an extreme variant of non-provocative behavior. It denotes a policy which is based on the calculation that almost any activity in the security policy arena is to be discouraged because it will inevitably increase external interest and hence also external stresses. In the words of the young P. Munch who later (1929-1940) became foreign minister 'the first and last we should demand from Danish diplomacy is that it keeps quiet and does its utmost so that we may live as unnoticed as possible' (quoted in Pedersen, 1970: 417). Stay put behavior is typical of nations wanting to reduce external stresses as much as possible and which have little faith in their possibilities of influencing its environment. To be successful, it seems to require that stress sensitivity is not too high. This stance is the quintessence of international quietism, but it may also be attractive as an aspect of a mainly acquiescent foreign policy.

Active reassurance designates a policy which is designed to give some other power, in relation to whom stress sensitivity is considered intolerably high, maximum confidence in the political course of the state so as to take away the other power's incentive for making stress-provoking demands to it. Such reassurance may for instance be in the form of assurances that the state will never ally with enemies of the other power, or perhaps that in case of war it will actually side with this power. Such behavior which tends to establish a patron-client relationship between the two, will typically occur as a response to demands for engagement on the part of the stronger power or as an anticipated reaction to demands whose formulation would provoke still greater stress. This policy posture seems to be the quintessence of international acquiescence.

Hypotheses

To sum up this general discussion we may formulate the following hypotheses on the relationship between international power and foreign policy behavior:

H_1: High influence capability combined with low stress sensitivity makes a policy of dominance feasible. This is characterized by a defense posture with a comprehensive list of functions: compellence, deterrence and defense. A dominant power may beef up its position through an alliance, but has also the option of going it alone. Diplomatically it may use channels of multilateral diplomacy, but will usually prefer bilateral diplomacy. Its general diplomatic mode can probably best be described as assertive.

H_2: High scores on both influence capability and stress sensitivity indicates a balance policy which is characterized by a defense posture aiming at deterrence and defense; it relies heavily on alliances and diplomatic coalitions as well as bilateral diplomacy. Détente and non-provocation policies seem to be highly characteristic of a balance posture, which generally is characterized by a higher level of international activity.

H_3: High stress sensitivity in combination with low influence capability suggests an acquiescent policy posture. Acquiescence is typically linked with a 'neutrality defense posture' and a general non-alignment line. Diplomatically multilateral action is preferred. To reduce stress sensitivity a range of policy modes are adopted: détente policy, non-provocation and active reassurance; if conditions are right, a stay-put policy may be preferred.

H_4: Finally, a low score on both dimensions allows for a quiescent foreign policy. Quiescence by definition denotes a low-activity posture. Stay put behavior is the typical policy stance corresponding in the defense area to non-alignment. Quiescent states have no high immediate need nor adequate resources for defense and diplomacy. Defense forces will therefore have mainly internal functions, while diplomacy will tend to be conducted in a multilateral framework.

Analysis of Danish security policy behavior 1870-1914

In the following we shall analyze the security policies of two Danish cabinets, led by J.B.S. Estrup (1875-1894), and I. C. Christensen (1905-1908), respectively.

The Estrup cabinet (1875-1895) represented a coalition of landed and urban middle class interests, whose political power rested on a majority in the *Landsting* (i.e. the First Chamber). From 1872 when the Left Party (*Venstre*) which primarily represented farming interests, got a majority in the *Folketing* (i.e. the Second Chamber), a fierce constitutional battle on the issue of parliamentarism raged between the two parties which was not solved until the so-called 'change of system' 1901 which brought the Left into power.

On the basis of the preceding analysis which suggested a combination of a very low international influence capability and a relatively low stress sensitivity, we may hypothesize a largely quiescent foreign and defense policy posture, perhaps with an admixture of acquiescent policies in times of stress and crisis, as the most relevant mode of national adaptation in this period.

By and large the main aspects of Denmark's international positon *were* realistically evaluated by relevant decision-makers, particularly by P. Vedel who, as director of the Foreign Office for more than a generation (1858-1899), was the single most important decision-maker in his time. On the other hand varying evalutions of Denmark's influence capability and stress sensitivity and especially a lack of coordination between foreign and defense policy did lead to a total posture which was not always clear and consistent.

After Germany's victory over France in 1871 Vedel realized that Denmark's possibilities of engineering a revision of the 1864 settlement had almost vanished, and that the diplomatic value of Article 5 was now negligible. In 1876 after the unsuccessful Russian and Swedish interventions in the Schleswig issue he concluded in a memo that Denmark had hardly any means to influence the case and that any initiative in the matter might only result in the repeal of the Article (Sjöqvist, 1962: 106). As mentioned above, this happened a few years later, after which Denmark did not raise the question again until after the German defeat in 1918. It is also characteristic that he does not seem to have believed very much in Russia as a potential protector of Denmark against Germany in the 1880s.

While he thus had very little confidence in Denmark's ability to influence Germany's behavior against her, he did not view her stress sensitivity as especially high, either. In the gloom of 1871 there were — in Vedel's words — 'hopeless people' who advocated that Denmark seek security in a narrow alignment with Germany, i.e. in a policy of acquiescence. To Vedel such a course was unacceptable since it would open up wide possibilities for German interference in Danish politics, and furthermore it was not called for in view of Germany's limited interests in Denmark. Instead, he consistently tried to follow a quiescent strategy of non-provocation and detachment. In his view Denmark should be very careful not to engage in direct political contact with Germany so as to avoid that Germany put forward proposals which might compromise Denmark's independence (Sjöqvist, 1962: 98). The basic reasoning behind Vedel's policy line was not very much different from Munch's above-quoted dictum that Danish diplomacy 'should keep quiet and do its utmost to ensure that we may live as unnoticed as possible'. But, in contrast to Munch, the international context within which Vedel was working did make such a policy a viable option.

At least on one occasion a strategy of alignment with at least reassurance of Germany was given prominent expression. In the

1878 crisis, which was created by a threatening confrontation between Russia and Britain, the Danish government discussed how to meet the situation and specifically how to formulate official neutrality rules. In this situation Vedel, who was very much aware of Denmark's dependence on overseas trade and especially on British coal, argued for a pro-British neutrality posture. Prime Minister Estrup who believed in a possible German intervention on the side of Russia (which Vedel — probably correctly — did not) took the opposite side. In a famous memo he outlined his basic viewpoint:

(a) The foreign ministry fears every rapprochement with Germany which might result in our later having to follow Germany in battle and having to take the first thrust.
(b) I want such a rapprochement. The next battle in which Denmark came to stand (together with allies or alone against G.) would probably be Denmark's last battle, and I therefore deem it necessary that we approach G. so much *in time*, that she can not harbor any doubt whatever, that D. will stand at her side — in any case *never* against her...I consider England's friendship worthless, her enmity unimportant compared to that of Germany (Sjöqvist, 1962: 124).

The main difference between Vedel and Estrup lay in their differing perceptions of Denmark's stress sensitivity vis-à-vis Germany. Vedel's less pessimistic view led him to adopt a quiescent 'stay put' posture, which on one the hand did not permit any progress in the Schleswig issue, but which on the other hand might keep the level of external stress at a tolerable level through a kind of dissocation from great power politics. Vedel was also conscious of the fact that although Germany remained the main problem, some consideration of the interests of other countries was also called for. Estrup's policy line was based on a very pessimistic view of Denmark's sensitivity which led him to advocate a more active policy of reassurance and rapprochement, i.e. a typically acquiescent policy posture. This policy line was never translated into actual policy during this period, but Estrup's formulation foreshadowed the basic concept behind the formulation of Danish foreign policy in later situations of perceived high stress sensitivity.

When we take defense policy into account, a third main posture which is more associated with a *balance* posture seems to emerge in the 1880s. In the 1870s Danish defense thinking was dominated by the so-called 'sea strategy' school aiming at a perimeter (or coastal) defense of Zealand, where Copenhagen is situated, Jutland being considered completely indefensible. This defense posture was generally regarded as more effective against British and Russian expeditionary forces than against a German invasion force, and therefore to be compatible with a general posture of neutrality in European politics and with a stay put policy towards Germany; that is to say it would give Germany some assurance that other powers could not occupy Denmark by a coup de main. In the 1880s the 'land strategy' school became dominant. This strategy was mainly predicated on a possible German invasion, against which the only feasible — albeit temporary — defense was a fortification around the capital, the general idea being that the defense forces would be able to hold out there until some other power (presumably Britain or Russia) in its own interest came to the rescue. This strategy, which came to be implemented between 1886 and 1894 when the Copenhagen fortification was built, therefore rested on an alliance assumption. But as the Left party was quick to ask, which alliance? As mentioned, there may have been some more or less well-founded expectations of Russian intervention if Germany invaded Denmark, but these were certainly not firm enough upon which to base a totally new and very costly defense strategy. Another puzzling aspect is its anti-German bias. Some of Estrup's cabinet colleagues, most notably the Minister of War, Bahnson, who was the brain behind the fortification scheme, were more or less openly *revanchiste*, but as we have seen, Estrup himself was very much aware of the need not to antagonise Germany, and although he may have been influenced by the anti-German opinion wave after the repeal of Article 5 in 1878, he remained on a good personal footing with Bismarck.

Most analysts therefore tend to play down the external aspect of defense policy formulation in this period, and focus instead upon the internal side. In this view, Estrup consciously chose defense policy and the concept of the Copenhagen fortification (which the opposition was set against) as the main arena for the continuing constitutional battle with the Left party, in the hope that this would enhance the endemic cleavages in the opposition and retard the erosion of the government's voting strength. To some extent — but only some — this calculation held good.

We can therefore conclude that the external and internal aspects of Denmark's security policy in the 1880s were less than optimally coordinated. Vedel, who never seems to have been consulted on defense policy(!), was clearly against the fortification strategy because of its anti-German bias, and saw it as a potential threat to his own course by raising German suspicions against Denmark. In the short run this fear proved somewhat exaggerated; in the German view the Danish defense efforts did not perceptibly change the balance of power. It was not until the late 1880s when the balance began to turn against Germany that the potential dangers were perceived; and in a *Reichstag* speech in 1893 the Chancellor von Caprivi openly mentioned Denmark along with Russia and France as one of Germany's potential adversaries (Fink, 1958: 31).

The Christensen cabinet (1905-1908)

In 1901 the first Left government (Deuntzer 1901-1905) was formed after about thirty years in the political wilderness. In 1905 the party split with the leader of the moderate majority, I. C. Christensen, forming a new cabinet (1905-1908) while the anti-militaristic minority group formed a new political party, the Radical Left.

According to our analysis the two Left governments were placed in a rather difficult security policy situation. Especially the period until 1905 was characterized by a high degree of international stress sensitivity. After 1905 Denmark's stress sensitivity decreased somewhat, mainly due to Germany's emerging two-front problem, and with the stiffening bipolarity of the European system the smaller powers presumably increased their influence capability vis-à-vis the great powers. Decision-makers therefore had more alternatives than the previous cabinet. When evaluating the actual policies of the period, we must however remember that the fluidity of the European system and of great power interests in and around Denmark made it quite a difficult task for the decision-makers to realistically judge the possibilities and constraints which the external environment created. The information-gathering capacity of the small diplomatic service was limited, and the new political leadership was inexperienced in the foreign policy field as a result of having been kept out of all influence before 1901.

Christensen seems to have had a very pessimistic veiw of Denmark's position in European politics, which may have been strengthened by the fact that Germany's dominance in the Baltic seemed to be growing after the demise of the Russian navy in the Russo-Japanese War and as the German naval building program progressed. In this view (and in the consequences he drew from it) he was influenced by a certain Captain Lütken whom he made Head of Department in the War Ministry in 1905. During a stay in Berlin a few years earlier Lütken had established influential contacts who gave him the following general impression of German attitudes to Denmark: 'If we (the Germans) cannot trust you (the Danes) completely during a big war, then we shall have to paralyse Denmark right at its start' (Fink, 1959: 19). Lütken and Christensen maintained this view in the following years, not realizing that the risks of a German unpremeditated occupation actually diminished after 1905. The conclusion which both of them drew was that in order to keep neutral in a European war, this neutrality had to be made acceptable to Germany; if neutrality could not be kept, then Denmark had no choice but to align herself with Germany. This policy of reassuring Germany found expression in a number of contacts with Germany during 1906-1908, mostly between Lütken and General von Moltke, who had succeeded von Schlieffen as Chief of the General Staff in 1905. In these talks von Moltke seems to have had two aims in mind: first to get as precise an evaluation of Denmark's likely posture in a European war as possible, and secondly to influence Denmark to commit herself to a pro-German course; both these aims were reasonable enough in view of the fact that the guiding assumption now was to respect Danish neutrality in case of war. On the other hand, Germany did not want to provoke Britain unnecessarily by concluding a formal alignment with Denmark. The dominant theme in Molkte's message to Lütken was that Denmark had to choose between Germany and Britain, and to declare herself friend or foe — the sooner the better. If not, Denmark might be in for serious trouble. As we now know, there was little substance in these thinly veiled threats, but as they confirmed Danish expectations, no one thought of calling the bluff. To accommodate German suspicions the government primarily sought to convince Germany about its sincere will to keep neutral and never to go against Germany; and it also pointed out that it would be ready to shoulder the military implication of this, i.e. to give the defense sufficient strength to meet an English invasion (Germany feared not only for a British break-through into the Baltic, but also a landing in Jutland, which might threaten Schleswig-Holstein). So far, this was a reasonable policy in view of the evident distrust and nervousness in German government circles. The government, however, went further in its efforts to reassure Germany. On several occasions it was said that if neutrality became unfeasible, then Denmark could only side with Germany; it was even hinted that the two countries might conclude a formal alignment after a solution had been found to the Danish defense problem. The latter hint was conditioned upon the cession of Northern Schleswig. This was not on the cards, however. A convention of 1907 in which Germany gave some concessions on the treatment of the Danish-speaking majority in Northern Schleswig and which Denmark had to buy through an explicit recognition of the border and also of the repeal of Article 5, represented the limit of what Denmark could hope to get from Germany.

As mentioned, Germany did not want to antagonize Britain by a formal arrangement with Denmark, so Denmark escaped the client relationship which lay implicit in the Christensen government's overtures to Germany. But still the policy was potentially dangerous enough and, as far as we can judge, not really prescribed by objective conditions. Denmark was still stress sensitive enough vis-à-vis Germany to make a non-provocative policy posture more or less a necessity, but not the degree of positive reassurance and rapprochement contained in Lütken's messages to von Moltke.

Several of the formulations used by Lütken bear a striking resemblance to the expressions used by Estrup back in 1878. This is somewhat ironic insofar as Estrup and Christensen were leaders of fiercely warring parties, the Right and the Left. A further twist of irony is added by the fact that the same main policy line can be found in the policy formulated by the Radical Left government and its Foreign Minister, E. Scavenius, during the First World War, as at this time the old Left party and the Radical Left stood as main opponents in Danish politics.

The tradition of *acquiescent* foreign policy which we have just sketched was thus not party bound (as it became to some extent in the inter-war period), just as the *quiescent* tradition represented by Vedel was not. Both traditions should rather be seen as responses to foreign policy situations of low influence capability and varying degrees of stress sensitivity, in which the perceptions of decision-makers of these crucial variables seem to account for a great deal of the variance we have observed. Both traditions can be traced further on in Danish security policy in the inter-war period, too; it is only after the Second World War that a new policy posture more related to a policy of balance came to dominate Danish security policy. The single most important determinant of this change was that with NATO, the alliance option presented itself in a realistic form for the first time since 1870. But even in its new alliance setting, Danish security policy retained many of the traits which had characterized her traditional behavior in the security policy field, e.g. the non-provocative low-posture tradition.

CONCLUSION

This essay has aimed at developing and testing an analytic framework based on two propositions. The first is that the traditional one-dimensional notion of power may be less relevant in at least some research contexts and should be replaced by a power concept resting upon two dimensions: influence capability and stress sensitivity. The second proposition is that a nation's position on these dimensions — to the degree it is correctly perceived by the relevant policy-makers — is a main predictor of the general mode of its foreign policy behavior.

For reasons of space the empirical testing of the framework has been somewhat sketchy; however, the analysis suggests that the framework may be a useful tool in comparative analyses, both of the cross-national and the diachronic variety. In the concrete case, the framework proved useful in allowing the integration of theoretical assumptions and empirical findings in the existing, mainly historical, literature on the subject, and the identification and explanation of fundamental modes or 'traditions' of Danish security policy behavior. As it is presently formulated the framework refers — just like James Rosenau's adaptation model, from which it is developed — 'to the "eras" in a nation's foreign policy and not to the specific situations in which it becomes involved' (Rosenau 1970: 4). However, provided relevant operationalizations of its main variables can be arrived at, the framework may very well be useful in analyzing the latter problems, too.

REFERENCES

ANDRÉN, N. (1972) *Den totala säkerhetspolitiken*. Stockholm: Rabén & Sjögren.
BRANNER, H. (1972) *Smaastat mellem stormagter. Beslutningen om mineudlaegning 1914.* Copenhagen: Uúnksgaard.
FINK, T. (1958) *Fem foredrag om dansk udenrigspolitik efter 1864.* Aarhus: Universitetsforlaget.
—— (1959) *Spillet om dansk neutralitet 1905-09.* Aarhus: Universitetsforlaget.
GOLDMANN, K. (1977) 'Notes on the Power Structure of the International System', *Cooperation and Conflict*, 12: 1-20.
HANSEN, P. (1974) 'Adaptive Behavior of Small States: The Case of Denmark and the European Community', *The Sage International Yearbook of Foreign Policy Studies*, vol. II: 143-175.
KEOHANE, R. O. and J. S. NYE (1973) 'World Politics and the International Economic System', in C. F. Bergsten (ed.) *The Future of the International Economic Order: An Agenda for Research.* Lexington, Mass.: D. C. Heath.
—— (1977) *Power and Interdependence. World Politics in Transition.* Boston: Little, Brown & Co.
KNORR, K. (1975) *The Power of Nations. The Political Economy of International Relations.* New York: Basic Books.
McGOWAN, P. J. and K. P. GOTTWALD (1976) 'Underdog Foreign Policies: A Comparative Study of Small, Less Modern States of Black Africa', *International Studies Quarterly*, 20: 469-500.
PEDERSEN, O. K. (1970) *Udenrigsminister P. Munchs opfattelse af Danmarks stilling i international politik.* Copenhagen: Gad.
PETERSEN, N. (1977) 'Adaptation as a Framework for the Analysis of Foreign Policy Behavior', *Cooperation and Conflict,* 12: 221-250.
PETRÉN, K. (1976) *Maktstrukturens huvuddrag. En kvantitativ analys av 20 maktindikatorer.* Stockholm: Utrikespolitiska Institutet.

ROSENAU, J. N. (1966) 'Pre-theories and Theories of Foreign Policy', in: R. Barry Farrell (ed.) *Approaches to Comparative and International Politics.* Evanston, Ill.: Northwestern University Press.
—— (1970) *The Adaptation of National Societies: A Theory of Political System Behavior and Transformation.* New York: McCaleb-Seiler.
ROTHSTEIN, R. L. (1968) *Alliances and Small Powers.* New York: Columbia University Press.
SINGER, D. and M. SMALL (1966) 'The Composition and Status Ordering of International System: 1815-1940', *World Politics* 18: 236-282.
SJÖQVIST, V. (1962) *Peter Vedel. Udenrigsministeriets direktör,* vol. 2 Aarhus: Universitetsforlaget.

Concluding Remarks
Gunnar Sjöstedt
The Swedish Institute of International Affairs

1. SOME GENERAL GUIDE-LINES FOR FUTURE RESEARCH

In Chapter 1 Kjell Goldmann argued that it is a vital task to improve our knowledge about international power bases. Subsequent chapters have given support to that view. They have illustrated some of the many problems connected with the study of international power relations, particularly the need to clarify and elaborate central concepts like superpower, interdependence and autonomy. The theoretical speculation typical for most of the contributions to this volume gives witness to the urgent need for systematically gathered data about the conditions for international power.

The study of power is motivated not only because this is an area which in its own right deserves the attention of researchers. A better knowledge about international power bases would also help researchers gain a deeper understanding of other important issues in contemporary international relations. Changes in power configurations in the world can, for instance, be expected to have significant consequences for East-West or North-South interaction, the current transformation of the international economic system or the ability of international organizations such as UNCTAD and GATT to solve world problems.

There are alternative ways to elucidate the meaning of power base, which can be said to be the key concept in studies dealing with changes in the power relations of the world. The research strategy which I shall suggest here is the comparative study of different cases of the exercize of power. If it were possible systematically to build up knowledge of how power is exercized by various actors and under differing conditions this would imply a corresponding contribution to the theories of power bases.

When such comparative research is undertaken it should be taken into consideration that the circumstances contributing to making a nation influential in relation to other countries may vary considerably from one situation to another, as argued by Olav Knudsen in Chapter 4 of this volume. Systematic comparisons should be made of cases of the exertion of power controlling for issue area, arena for confrontation (e.g. different international organizations) and other situational features which can be expected to be of relevance.

The analysis of the exercize of power should particularly aim at answering the following questions:
1. What different strategies for the exercize of power can be discerned?
2. How are different strategies for the exercize of power related to different elements of the power base of nations?
3. How should the 'activation of the powerbase' be defined in theoretical terms? Is it, for instance, reasonable to conceive of this phenomenon as the manipulation of concrete resources? Or is the metaphor of a production function more appropriate?[1]

The exercize of power needs, no doubt, elucidation generally. Data and theories available are relatively scanty and not very systematized. But there are some aspects of the exercize of power which have been particularly neglected in the literature and which therefore deserve the most immediate attention of researchers, and accordingly also in the present discussion. For that reason a special interest will be devoted to two kinds of the exercize of power, *the use of non-coercive strategies* and the *exercize of power in a multilateral setting*. The third and implicit category, the non-coercive exercize of power in a multilateral frame-work, is especially important to concentrate efforts on. In this area the lack of verified data is striking. What is more, the theoretical and conceptual tools to be used in empirical research are also relatively underdeveloped.

It is not surprising to note that researchers traditionally have devoted most of their interest to the undisguised coercive forms of power exertion, such as military actions or various forms of economic sanctions. This focus is merely a reflection of the traditionalist paradigm of international relations with its conception of the international system as a jungle-like anarchy and its preoccupation with the 'supreme interests of the nation' and military security.²

Another typical property of the power literature is its almost exclusive preoccupation with 'dual-like' confrontations between two parties only. One reason for this 'bilateral bias' may be that dyadic power relations are easier to analyze in theoretical terms than a multilateral power game. A confrontation between two opposing actors or blocs further often becomes dramatic and thereby more easily attracts the attention than multilateral negotiations going on for longer periods of time concerning matters which are technically complex. Whatever the explanation, it is a fact that most definitions and models of the exercize of power schematically can be described as a relationship between the two parties which may be called *the actor* and *the target*.³ The behaviour of the target is to be thought of as the dependent variable of these models and the behaviour (or the intentions) of the actor is according to the same logic the independent variable. This may be described as in formula 1.

Actor  Target

Formula 1.

This sort of definition can be used also when more than two actors, say *A* and *B*, become involved. One possibility is that the actor, nation *A*, exercizes power in relation to several other nations at the same time as illustrated by formula 2.

Actor (A) 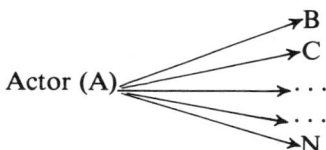 B
C
...
...
N

Formula 2.

Another possibility would be that the target nations, B, C, ..., ..., N, somehow are so closely interrelated that they can be said to constitute some sort of a system (S) so that this entity rather than the separate nations can be conceived of as the target. This is illustrated by formula 3.

$$\text{Actor (A)} \longrightarrow S$$

Formula 3.

It can convincingly be argued that all possible cases of the exercize of power in a multilateral context in principle should be captured by either formula 2 or formula 3. But these formulas may in some cases be extremely difficult to transform into operational terms. Take for example the powerplay between nations in international organizations like GATT. The number of participating nations is here considerable. Sometimes more than one hundred countries interact simultaneously. The problems involved are often of a complex nature requiring a long period of deliberations to be resolved on the part of the actors involved. Such a process is not easy to break up into a pattern of dyadic relations between actors and targets as is presupposed by formulas 1-3. It is true that in e.g. the MTN (multilateral trade negotiations) informal bilateral — as well as trilateral — bargaining and consultations between the great powers, notably the United States, the EC and Japan are of critical importance for the outcome, and that those patterns of interaction may in fact be described in terms of a dyadic model of power exertion. But it is also clear that other aspects of the MTN, the work in committees, the plenary meetings and their respective contributions to the outcome of the negotiations do not easily let themselves be analyzed by the bilateral model of the exercize of power.[4] Therefore, the question has to be raised if the three formulas of a dyadic form had not better be supplemented with still another formula for the exercize of power which is more suitable than formulas 2 and 3 for cases where, for various reasons, it is virtually impossible to discern the underlying pattern of dyadic interaction.

Nagel and others have argued that under some conditions systemic outcomes may be a better choice for a dependent variable in a model of the exercize of power than the behaviour of the target (Nagel, 1975, p. 13). This conception seems to be a good solution to the problem of finding an alternative to the bilateral models of power exertion represented by formulas 1-3. A fourth description of the exercize of power is thus as follows:

$$\text{Actor (A)} \longrightarrow \text{Outcome}$$

Outcome = the result of a process of interaction between A and a number of other actors.

Formula 4.

In Chapter 1 Kjell Goldmann argues against the use of outcomes as a dependent variable. The main reason for this stand is that he wants a clear-cut line of demarcation between social power, which is our concern here, and other forms of power, for instance power over nature. Because, Goldmann says, if outcomes are employed as a dependent variable '...the distinction between the exercize of power and goal-attainment seems difficult to maintain' (Chapter 1, p. 5).

Goldmann is no doubt in principle right in this assertion. But it should also be taken into consideration that the unambiguity of the dependent variable he prefers — the behaviour of the influencee — is the product of a trade off in which the costs are certain limits as to the range of application of the model of the exercize of power to which it belongs. As I see it a definition should not only clarify and specify the meaning of a phenomenon. It should also provide guide-lines for operationalization. If such guide-lines are lacking the definition can not function well as a theoretical basis for empirical research.

Now, there are seemingly important cases, notably concerning 'the powerplay' in multilateral contexts, in which it is not possible to find operational concepts which in a consistent way reflect one of the bilateral models of the exercize of power (formulas 1-3) and at the same time are useful for practical research. If only these three formulas are considered to be acceptable the logical consequence must be that those cases to which the dyadic models do not easily fit have to be left out when comparisons are made of the power of international actors. Considering that numerous important issues are dealt with in international organizations and at ad hoc conferences this may lead to serious distortions in the picture of the international power relations. Therefore, formula 4 represents a useful completion to the set of bilateral models illustrated by formulas 1-3. Although formula 4 implies difficulties of the kind pointed out by Goldmann it also offers a way of surmounting the operational problems of bilateral models when these are used in situations when dyadic relationships are not discernible.

So, in the discussion to follow below a model of the exercize of power is implied which is best represented by formula 4. Accordingly, the power base of a nation, A, is equal to those properties of A, of A's relations to its external environment or of that environment which determine how much A is able to shape the outcome of a process of interaction involving A and other actors.[5] It is, further, assumed that the model will only be applied to such processes of interaction in which other actors, whose interests are not identical to those of A, like A itself, try to determine the outcome of that process to the greatest extent possible.

2. THEORIES OF NEGOTIATION: AN AUXILIARY CONCEPTUAL FRAMEWORK

Existing theories of the exercize of power offer little help when it comes to find theoretical concepts pertaining to how the outcome of a process of multilateral interaction is influenced by various actors. Here large theoretical gaps exist which are urgent to bridge. Pending viable solutions to these problems provisional theoretical arrangements have to be made. One possibility is to use an auxiliary conceptual scheme as a departure for the search for concepts and 'models' directly pertaining to the exercize of power.

Such an auxiliary scheme must be relatively closely related to the problems of power and it must be of such a quality that it can be expected to serve as a source of ideas. One body of literature which seems to meet these requirements fairly well are the theories of negotiation, strategic interaction and bargaining.[6] These analytical models pertain to a kind of interaction which clearly has something to do with the exercize of power. The theories of negotiation are further generally speaking relatively highly developed and sometimes also formalized. Here belong, for instance, game-theoretic models (Nash 1950, 1953, Harsanyi 1956, 1965) economic models of bargaining (Zeuten 1930, Bishop 1964, Cross 1969). There also exist a number of books in which a penetrating although not so rigidly formal theoretical analysis of a process of negotiation is carried out (Iklé 1964).

But these theories, henceforth referred to as orthodox models of negotiation, also have clear limitations as far as the analysis of the exercize of power is concerned. In particular, problems can be expected to arise when the purpose is to analyze how power is exercized in a multilateral setting. The most important of these deficiencies will be briefly reviewed below.

The first observation to make is that theories of negotiation, like most models of the exercize of power, have a 'bilateral bias'. Theories of negotiation, bargaining and game-theory more often than not conceive of a situation with only two parties. It is true that, for instance, in game-theory N-person games have been developed, involving at least three parties. These models are, however, generally considerably more loosely structured than the two-person games. To the extent that N-person games claim to predict determinate outcomes they have usually been transformed into a two-person game. One mechanism by which such transformation can be brought about is coalition-building. Assumptions are made that players group themselves into coalitions until there are only two coalitions left, which then behave as in a normal two-person game. According to one scholar, who has undertaken a careful theoretical comparison between different theories of negotiation, the results of the N-person games are of a limited value. 'Many of the conclusions seem more applicable to prescriptive analysis than to the production of descriptive theory' (Young, 1975, p. 35).

The general state of affairs is, thus, that the bilateral models of negotiation predominate. Such models at least have to be modified before they are applied on a multilateral setting. In many cases it is questionable if such application is possible at all.

A second fundamental deficiency of orthodox theories of negotiation is that they generally presuppose a highly structured choice situation for the parties involved. These theories, and especially the more formalized ones, are based on a set of highly potent assumptions, such as the stipulation of a decision rule (e.g. rationality), clear and consistent utility functions and access to perfect information.

These, and other demanding assumptions evidently circumscribe the applicability of the theories of negotiation considerably. It is probably rare that all the assumptions are met to a sufficient degree at the same time. According to Oran Young the orthodox theories of negotiation thus 'are heavily restricted in terms of applicability, and they exhibit a mechanistic quality which stems from the fact that they abstract away all the manipulative activities commonly associated with bargaining. Moreover...(they)...have not yielded predictions about bargaining which correspond at all with the actual processes and outcomes in analogous real-world situations' (Young, 1975, p. 303).

This harsh judgement concerns the applicability of the theories of negotiation in general but is also valid for their usefulness for studies of power relations. But even if this opinion is accepted — and I tend to agree with it — this is no reason why the theories of negotiation should be rejected as an analytical framework for the study of the exercize of power. Only the relatively formalized models represent in fact a number of quite different approaches. There is no doubt but that in many situations in which power is exercized game theoretic or economic models can serve as instruments for analysis. There are probably at least some negotiations which are so highly structured from the beginning that orthodox theories can be directly applied. One example would be bilateral, recurrent negotiations about quotas for catches of fish. In such negotiations several of the conditions of orthodox models may very well hold. The value disputed is unidimensional and possible to express in quantitative terms. The actors can be expected to behave in line with a rational decision-rule, that is to maximize their quotas as much as the situation permits. As the negotiations occur at regular intervals 'rules of the game' which regulate the negotiations may have been established. There may, for instance, be an implicit understanding between the two parties that the quotas arrived at one year should not deviate too much from those agreed upon the year before and that due consideration should be taken to their interest of ensuring the sufficient reproduction of fish species.

But even if direct applications of the orthodox models are not possible, these can still be helpful in several ways in an analysis of the exercize of power. They can, for instance, provide concepts which facilitate the precise formulation of the problem of research. Or they can be used to define different types of situations in which the exercize of power occurs. It is also clear, however, that the models of negotiation are of a limited use for the study of many cases of power exertion due to their demanding assumptions which make them 'unrealistic'.

It therefore seems worthwhile to investigate if the orthodox theories cannot be made more realistic, that is applicable on a larger number of situations, if some of their assumptions are exchanged or dropped. Such an elaboration, particularly of the formalized models of bargaining, can be expected to lessen their consistency and 'logical beauty'. Sacrifices of this sort may, however, be acceptable if they contribute to increasing the instrumental value of theories of negotiation for power analysis.

3. MANIPULATIVE THEORIES OF BARGAINING: AN EXTENSION TOWARDS APPLICABILITY

Some of the 'strategists' themselves have reacted against the game-theoretic and economic models of negotiations. Their response has been to modify these theories so as to make them somewhat more realistic. A common name for these amended models is *manipulative theories of bargaining*. Their starting-point is a basic conception of negotiation as a process of interdependent decision-making.[7] The adherents to this school of thought have to some extent kept the general theoretical framework of game-theoretic and economic bargaining models, but they have made their version of a theory of negotiation less mechanistic by relaxing some of the assumptions of orthodox models. The manipulative models thus have the following notable properties, which all deviate from those pertaining to the game-theoretic and economic models.

A first observation to make is that manipulative models acknowledge that negotiations often have the form of strategic interaction. To explain why this can be said to represent a main difference in relation to orthodox models a brief exposition is necessary.

Strategic interaction will occur when two or more actors are involved in interdependent decision-making and they discover that the outcomes associated with their choices are partially controlled by each other. Assume the special case with only two actors, A and B. These two actors are engaged in strategic interaction when A finds his choices contingent upon his estimates of the actions of B, and B in the same way finds his choices contingent upon the actions of A (Young, 1975, p. 5-9).

It is easily seen that strategic interaction can be expected to occur in a large number of situations. It is in fact difficult to imagine cases of negotiation without at least an element of strategic interaction. Therefore, it is necessary for any theory of negotiation to take strategic interaction into account. This is in fact the raison d' être for manipulative models of negotiation as orthodox models have had serious difficulties to come to grips with strategic interaction. The reasons for this represent a complex theoretical problem which requires a lengthy discussion to be described in detail. Suffice it here to indicate the general nature of this problem.

Orthodox models of bargaining among other things manifest an ambition to define determinate solutions to various game situations. This is why the situation of negotiation has to be so strongly structured by means of assumptions. These assumptions, and notably that of perfect information, are not wholly compatible with strategic interaction. As Young puts it: 'Perfect information requires either that the individual's decision-making environment be fixed (at least in terms of probability distributions) or that he be able to make accurate predictions or develop confident expectations concerning the probable behaviour of any other purposive actor whose actions affect his own choice. But this is precisely what the presence of strategic interaction precludes. Strategic interaction means (by definition) that the choices of two or more individuals are reciprocally contingent and that leads inevitably to an "outguessing regress" ' (Young, 1975, p. 14).

There are different ways to go in order to reconcile this incompatibility. The orthodox theories choose to introduce restrictive assumptions which — to put it simply — 'define away' strategic interaction. Game-theoretic models, for instance, eliminate the dynamic aspect of the bargaining process — and with it strategic interaction — by stipulating that the initial phase of the game is a static situation. Economic models, although generally more dynamic than the game-theoretic ones, are also based upon assumptions which in effect preclude strategic interaction.

Manipulative models in contrast accept the existence of strategic interaction as an inevitable premise. They do not try to evade this phenomenon. Instead they seem to want to lay the theoretical foundation for analyses of how decision-makers in reality cope with strategic interaction. These models are therefore more process-oriented than the orthodox ones. But on the other hand they possess still less capacity to predict outcomes.[8]

Their respective responses to the problem of strategic interaction clearly reflect the fundamental difference in nature between manipulative and orthodox models of negotiation. This basic dissimilarity, however, also implies a number of other important assumptions on the part of the manipulative models which all represent a deliberate repudiation of the conditions of the orthodox models. Three such assumptions seem especially important to recall here (only two actors, A and B are supposed to be involved):

(1) They assume imperfect information on the part of A and B. It is also regarded as possible that one of the actors may have access to better information than the other (asymmetrical distribution of information).

(2) They assume fixed utility functions neither on the part of A nor of B. Nor is the pay-off matrix of the game assumed to be given. It is instead assumed that bargainers will try to manipulate the perception of the opponent of such factors as the strategies available, the preference-order of the opponent as to various possible outcomes of the game and also the risks involved in the game for the opponent.

(3) It is assumed that extensive communication can take place between A and B. Communication, in effect, occupies a central place in manipulative theories.

It is not necessary for the present purposes to describe the manipulative models in more detail. Suffice it to conclude that these theories are less rigorous than the game-theoretic and economic ones and that they have more modest aspirations as to predictive capacity. Neither can the manipulative theories generally be immediately applied on a concrete situation and employed for empirical research. Their importance is instead that they go beyond the orthodox models in the sense that they point out a greater number of factors which can be expected to determine the outcome of negotiations. In the present context it is especially interesting to note that the manipulative models help identify ways and means which actors can employ to influence the negotiation process.

For the current analytical purposes it seems useful to make a distinction between two different categories of measures which a party in a negotiation can rely on in order to influence the behaviour of the opponent. The first category of such devices can roughly be described as *pure bargaining tactics*. They typically pertain to a situation which among other things has the following two properties:

(1) Two opposing parties, A and B.

(2) A fixed payoff matrix, which is known at the outset by both A and B.

Assume that the situation is looked upon with the eyes of A and that A and B have to count with the 'given' payoff matrix in Figure 1.

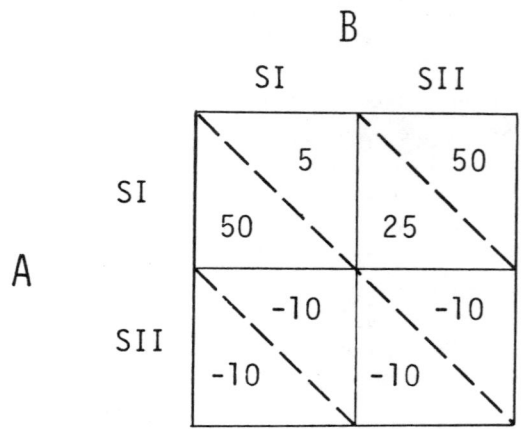

Figure 1. The 'pure bargaining game'

This thus implies a typical distributive game, where both A and B try to get the better part of a given value. Looking at the premises of the game A's first move is to decide his basic approach to it. Particularly he has to make up his mind whether B should be regarded as such a dangerous opponent that A should take on a cautious attitude and assume that the worst could happen within the constraints of the game.[9] If A is cautious and rational A has to accept an outcome making A the loser of the game. Because if B is assumed to behave in a reasonably rational way A can count that B will play his strategy II, giving A 25 units of utility but B twice as much.

But if A is willing to take a risk there is a possibility to get more out of the game than 25 units of utility. If A can make B choose SI this will give A 50 units of utility. One way for A to do that would be to threaten to play his strategy II if B plays his strategy II. According to 'orthodox rules of the game' this would be irrational because it would signify unnecessary sacrifices on the part of A. But if A could make his threat credible — and B did not try the same tactics successfully — B would probably let A have 50 units of utility and at least get five himself rather than suffer a loss of 10 units of utility.

There is thus good reason to believe that this game between A and B could result in an outright confrontation where the two parties resort to actions which could be described as pure bargaining tactics. This is the game of threats, promises and coercion which has been described so eloquently by authors like Thomas Schelling and Daniel Ellsberg. Here belong a host of tactical measures and considerations which have been carefully analyzed by such strategists.

The tactics of pure bargaining are clearly relevant for the study of the exercize of power. There is no doubt but that the means for the manipulation of a process of negotiation is of great importance for a theorist trying to construct a general model of power exertion.

It should be recalled, however, that the present discussion is meant to concentrate on the non-coercive exercize of power. So, after having acknowledged the significance of pure bargaining tactics we should look more closely at the other kind of measures pointed out or indicated by manipulative models of negotiation. Lacking a better term they may be called *measures for the structur-*

ing of a process of negotiation. The meaning of this expression will be explained shortly.

When the assumptions pertaining to the negotiation situation depicted in Figure 1 are slackened, or completely dropped, it becomes harder to describe 'the game' in a precise and formal way. There is, however, another consequence which deserves a greater attention in the present discussion about mechanisms of power exertion. The possibilities for an actor to influence the negotiation process seem to increase. New manipulative devices and measures have to be taken into consideration by actors as well as by analysts. Such measures of power exertion can be identified by the systematic withdrawal of underlying assumptions of the distributive game implied by Figure 1.

Assume, for example, that the assumption of a fixed payoff matrix is dropped. One possible interpretation of this contingency would be that the payoff matrix is variable. It is then still assumed that it is possible to structure the game in the form of a payoff matrix. But the contents of the cells of the matrix can be altered during the game by means of deliberate actions, such as negative or positive sanctions. Such a game would in all probability retain much of the character of the game with a fixed payoff matrix. Pure bargaining tactics can still be expected to play a central role. But new possibilities for manipulation have also been introduced into the game. Actors capable of changing the contents of the payoff matrix would have access to a larger number of means of influence than actors lacking these capabilities.

Assume now that *all* the specifying a priori conditions of the game in Figure 1 are eliminated. One effect will be that the number of potential measures available for the manipulation of the process of negotiation is still further increased.[10] Many of these are measures for the structuring of the situation of negotiation.

A process of negotiation often starts in a situation which is relatively unstructured. Imagine, for example, that an actor, *A*, becomes involved in discussions with a number of other actors about how to solve an international problem they share, without exactly knowing such things as:
(a) what other actors will participate actively in the future negotiations. (New actors may become engaged. Or some of those actors which helped initiate the process of negotiation may

become passive, perhaps because they lack resources — knowledge, negotiators, etc. — necessary for active participation.)
(b) how the problem should be defined, that is, what its basic elements are;
(c) what sort of solutions are available;
(d) what consequences various alternatives for action will have at large, or more specifically for A himself.

In such an unstructured situation it is virtually impossible for A to start bargaining with the other countries involved in the same way as if a fixed payoff matrix existed. A simply does not know what measures are favourable and what measures are unfavourable. Under these conditions the initial phase of the negotiation process probably consists in the structuring of the situation in order to make it negotiable. The actors involved undertake actions to identify actors, components of the problem etc, and to formulate possible alternatives for action. These activities represent the structuring stage of the negotiation process which in principle can be separated from the distributive stage. Expressed schematically the distributive stage — or game — logically presupposes the determination of a payoff matrix (something to bargain about) and this can be said to be equal to the structuring process.

The structuring process does, however, not necessarily have to result in a payoff matrix, or in a distributive game. Examples of rounds of negotiation in real life which contain very little of true distributive bargaining would be UNCTAD conferences, the Special Sessions of the UN General Assembly concerning a New Economic Order or the Paris Dialogue. These conferences did not lead to concrete results, if by that is meant actual transfers of resources between actors. Instead participating nations rather have used these discussions as means for the exchange of information in order to clarify their respective interests and their interpretations of the nature of the international economic problems.

The structuring process takes place on at least two different levels more or less simultaneously. First, each actor has to clarify the situation for himself in order to make it possible to consider different alternative solutions either in order to be able to take an initiative or to react on the proposals of others. Second, the situation has to be structured on a collective level. Some common understanding of the nature of the situation probably has to be arrived at in many cases if systematic distributive bargaining is to become possible. It should be recalled that a process of negotiation may contain considerable cooperative elements. This is particularly true when negotiations concern how to solve a common problem. Then the participants have strong motives to cooperate, because a viable solution may require the active and voluntary participation of all, or at least most, countries involved in the negotiation for its implementation. This need to cooperate does not preclude that considerable elements of conflict may be present at the same time, because individual countries may find that one particular solution is more favourable for them than others. So, in order to find the solution which all parties concerned desire it may be necessary to structure the situation collectively. At the same time some of the actors may find it useful as well as attainable to try to influence the structuring process as much as possible to their own advantage.

The significance of the structuring process for the powerplay in multilateral negotiations can not be said to be reflected in the literature. The main reason is that the distributive stage has been at the centre of the analysis when negotiatons have been analyzed. Accordingly it is not surprising that the theoretical instruments available for the analysis of the structuring phase are few. Therefore it is the more important to take advantage of the fact that manipulative models of bargaining are clearly relevant for the analysis of the structuring phase. Although the term 'structuring process' is not explicitly used in manipulative models these no doubt contribute to the elucidation of this phenomenon. What is particularly useful in the present context is that the manipulative models are so constructed that they open the way for an understanding of how the structuring process can be influenced by actors involved in a negotiation process.

Manipulative models, process-oriented as they are, identify various key stages and elements of the negotiation process, including the structuring stage. These elements of the negotiation process can be said to represent linkages between actors and the outcome of the negotiation process.

Young points out that on a fairly high level of generalization three aspects of the structuring process can be discerned:
1. The definition of the problem or issue concerned.

2. The identification of strategies available for each side.
3. The building up of a general preference structure for each side.

The meaning of these three aspects can be considerably specified with the help of a detailed discussion of the manipulative theories. But already Young's scheme of classification is sufficient to illustrate the usefulness of the manipulation models for the study of the exercize of power. The assistance manipulative models can give in this respect is in effect manifold. But first of all they provide concepts and guidelines for the organization of research.

However, Young also implies a number of ways a structuring process can be influenced. In particular Young points out that as far as the structuring process is concerned the exercize of power has much to do with the manipulation of the perception and expectations of other actors. The influencing strategies which belong here can in a more concrete way be described as the distortion or supply of information which other actors involved in the negotiation process rely upon. Such manipulation can be expected to vary depending on the current stage of the structuring process. An actor's instruments and methods to influence the formulation of the problem (issue) are probably different compared to the same actor's attempt to modify the preference structure of an opponent.

It is true that the manipulation of information has interested strategists like Schelling and Rapoport. But these authors have generally analyzed fairly structured games of a distributive nature. Systematic knowledge is therefore particularly scarce about manipulation of information in unstructured situations with relatively manifest cooperative elements. Massive empirical research in this area is thus clearly needed.[11]

4. COLLECTIVE DECISION-MAKING: AN APPROACH TO THE PROBLEM OF MULTILATERALISM

Although manipulative models of negotiation in several ways seem to be useful for the systematic study of the exercize of non-coercive power, they also have severe limitations in this respect. They are, after all, based on the game-theoretic and economic models of bargaining and they have retained many of the properties of these theoretical constructions. One weakness of manipulative models which is particularly important to take into consideration in the present discussion is that the elaboration of the 'orthodox' models into manipulative ones have not eliminated their 'bilateral bias'.

Also manipulative models are clearly much more difficult to apply on a multilateral than on a bilateral situation. Therefore, theories of negotiation have to be still more extended than what the manipulative theories permit in order to become useful for the study of the 'power game' presumably going on within the framework of multilateral processes of interaction in international organizations or at ad hoc conferences. I would argue that one way is to conceive of multilateral interaction of the kind discussed here as a process of collective decision-making. It should be recalled that this conception is closely related to that of the manipulative models of bargaining, which also are elaborated out from the basic assumption that negotiations represent one form of interdependent decision-making. It can be noted that the three aspects of a process of (manipulative) negotiation defined by Oran Young, and briefly referred to above, closely resemble the stages of a process of rational decision-making. 'Issue formulation' thus seems to correspond to 'the formulation of goals', 'identification of strategies' to 'the identification of alternatives for action', and 'the building up of a preference structure' is akin to the 'selection of the best alternative'.

This resemblance does not, however, conceal that manipulative models should be considered to be theories of bargaining rather than theories of decision-making. My belief is that if the focus is somewhat turned over from the bargaining aspect to that of decision-making in a more pronounced way, new insights can be gained as to how nations are able to influence the outcome of the interaction in organizations and at international conferences.

If it were possible to discern the elements and stages of an interaction process thought of as decision-making, these analytical categories would probably represent ways and means by which it could be possible to link the behaviour of actors, expressed in terms of influencing strategies, to the outcome of that process. The objective establishment of such linkages would, in turn, help the researcher identify instruments for the exercize of power employed by

Concluding Remarks

actors and ultimately also elements of the power base related to these instruments.

Systematic knowledge about international collective decision-making, relevant for the study of the exercize of power, is strangely enough relatively scarce. It is true that numerous studies have been undertaken to clarify how decisions are taken in international organizations. These works are, however, for the most part monographs of a descriptive character. They generally give a careful picture of how the decision-making machinery functions in one particular organization. The analyses made are also normally of an institutional or juridical nature and seldom describe the decision process in behavioural terms.

This sort of organization study, although it certainly helps build up our knowledge about international organizations in general, does not have any explicit contributions to offer in relation to a generalized behavioural theory of international collective decision-making. Properties of a process of decision-making in a more general meaning are hard to distinguish from idiosyncracies of the particular organization under study. My own impression is, further, that most monographs of international organizations tend to emphasize too much formal procedures, tasks and competences. One consequence of such an approach is that the significance of the more informal interaction between the member states of an organization, perhaps taking place outside the official agenda of meetings and sessions, may become underestimated. Thereby an important segment of the political interaction — 'the power game' — in an organization is downplayed so that the description of what happens when conflicts are solved and decisions are taken runs the risk of becoming distorted.

Another problem with monographs is in my view that they often tend to exaggerate the autonomous character of international organizations. It is, in fact, often extremely difficult to determine exactly to what degree such a body is a truly independent institution with an identity and an actor capability of its own. It is not certain that the most accurate conception of an organization is that of a set of organs. Organizations should perhaps rather be regarded as facilities and instruments for the exchange of information between members, or even as institutionalized communication. That kind of conception of an organization puts the emphasis not primarily on its formal structures but rather on another kind of component part, the member states.

Nations may very well choose to concentrate the interaction concerning a certain matter exclusively to one particular organization, but this is not the only possibility. The countries concerned may also, as happens frequently, deal with the same issue in several organizations more or less simultaneously. The individual organization then represents only one limited amount of all the instruments used by nations in that issue area or, in other words, only one aspect of the total cooperative machinery at their disposal.[12] The tools used for monetary cooperation and cordination between industrialized nations are a case in point. They consist of a considerable number of organizations, e.g. IMF, BIS (The Bank of International Settlements) the Group of Ten or even segments of organizations like Working Party no. 3 of the Monetary Committee of the OECD, but also of bilateral (or trilateral) communication between key countries, and ad hoc multilateral meetings like the one held in Bonn in July 1978.[13] That means that it is misleading, and probably outright faulty, to consider what happens in one particular organization, like the OECD, as an autonomous process of surveillance, planning or decision-making. The work done in each individual organization can only be understood if it is related to what happens in the other organizations involved in monetary cooperation. The situation is probably similar in other issue-areas.

These circumstances demonstrate the need for a theory of international collective decision-making, which in principle has general validity in the sense that it is valid for multilateral interaction regardless of in how many organizations it takes place and irrespective of the identity of these organizations. Some attempts to go in that direction have indeed been taken. Particularly worth mentioning are the contributions made in this respect by neo-functionalist integration theorists like Ernst Haas and Leon Lindberg during the 1960s. These scholars have tried to define the properties of the decision-process of the European Community in theoretical terms (Haas, 1958, Lindberg, 1970).

These models are of special interest here as they represent a behaviouristic approach permitting them to combine the problem-solving and the bargaining aspects of decision-making. The neo-functionalist models should therefore be useful to lean on at the study of quite a number of international organizations. At the same time it has to be admitted that those models are not easily directly applicable to organizations other than the EC itself. The neo-functionalist theoretical constructions are highly dependent of the special features of the Community system, such as the stipulations of the Treaty of Rome, the particular role played by the Commission etc. These theories are further — as they should be — constructed so as to take particularly into account the research aims of integration theorists, that is to reflect significant changes in the level of integration in the Community system. My own assessment is, however, that researchers trying to develop more universal models of international collective decision-making should be able to profit considerably from the results and experiences of neo-functionalists.

To my knowledge few attempts have been made to study particularly how nations, or other international actors, try to, and are able to, exert power within the framework of decision-processes going on in international organizations. The only more extensive study of this kind that I know of is *The Anatomy of Influence*, by Robert Cox and Harold Jacobson (1973). The conceptual framework these two authors use to capture the decision process consists of two central parts. The first is a taxonomy including seven kinds of decisions which presumably can be taken in international organizations. The seven categories are called 'representational', 'symbolic', 'boundary', 'programmatic', 'rule-creating', 'rule-supervisory' and 'operational' decisions. The second part of the scheme is another taxonomy describing the roles which, according to Cox/Jacobson, the actors operating within international organizations can play in order to influence decision-making. Actors can thus be 'initiators', 'vetoers', 'controllers' or 'brokers'.

There is no room for an extensive and fair evaluation of the Cox/Jacobson scheme here. The concepts and taxonomies used seem, however, to deserve some critique which also has to be indicated here. It may thus be argued that the definitions and concepts used are too vague. The different categories of decisions are hard to differentiate from one another. One could, for instance, imagine that a decision may be programmatic and role-creating at the same time and moreover have a symbolic meaning. The roles are no clear-cut categories either. Cox/Jacobson are in fact quite elusive when it comes to describe concretely what functions actors actually perform and what different instruments they dispose of when playing their respective roles. In spite of these critical observations it can be argued that the Cox/Jacobson scheme indicates a general direction to go in order to construct a model of international collective decision-making suitable for the analysis of power exertion.

The main problem to solve when the exercize of power in a multilateral setting is studied is to find operational representations for the dependent and independent variables. The Cox/Jacobson scheme presents an idea for a solution to this problem. The taxonomy of decisions can be said to be a substitute for the dependent variable. Each category of decisions is equal to one kind of organizational outcome, which according to *formula 4* (see p. 275, above) is the definition of the dependent variable employed here. The organizational roles in turn may be regarded as the independent variables of the model.

Unfortunately, this model is not directly usable for the actual analysis of the exercize of power in a multilateral setting. The validity of the categories of the two taxonomies is uncertain as these are justified neither theoretically not empirically. Further, even if the validity of the taxonomies is assumed their categories are very vague. In particular the meaning of the four roles constituting the independent variables of the would-be model are unclear as to their meaning. So, the importance of the Cox/Jacobson scheme for the study of the exercize of power is indirect. It indicates a theoretical approach which may become productive if it is developed.

An important implication of the Cox/Jacobson scheme is that it should be possible to get an idea of the relative power of individual actors in a process of collective decision-making by determining their roles therein. This puts the organizational roles at the centre of the analysis. A number of research problems emerge. Among other things the following questions become important:
1. How should the organizational roles indicated by Cox/Jacobson be specified?
2. What are the properties of the various roles?
3. What circumstances determine that an actor is able to play a certain role at all, and in particular with skill?

4. To what extent and under what conditions do different roles effectively help determine the outcome of the international decision process?

The answer to these questions should help elucidate the nature of the power game in a process of international decision-making. But in order to get these answers it would be necessary to have a more profound knowledge than the existing one about the general nature of international decision-making. This in turn indicates a need for systematic research aimed at finding regularities in such processes. Equivalent research has been carried out with great success on the intra-national organizational level. One well-known example of this kind of study is *A Behavioral Theory of the Firm* by Cyert and March (1963), in which the general structure of the decision process in a business organization has been identified, seemingly with a considerable degree of accuracy. The Cyert/March model can be employed to illustrate the usefulness of a comparable generalized model of decision-making valid for international organizations and conferences.

Assume, for instance, that a monetary crisis breaks out which needs to be controlled quickly if serious negative consequences are to be avoided. Assume further that 'simplistic and sequential search' is typical for international decision-making, as it is for the business firm, and that international decision-makers 'satisfy' rather than 'optimize' when they take decisions. These two characteristics of the decision process imply a substantial amount of influence on the part of those actors which are able to present viable solutions of the problem at hand quicker than other actors. Such actors can be expected to have a relatively superior analytical capability in the issue area concerned. They probably also have a capacity for effective direct informal communication with key decision-makers in the other countries concerned.

The more the general properties of decision-making in international forums can be discerned and defined in theoretical terms the better the conditions for an improved understanding of how such processes can be influenced. Different stages of the decision-process represent different possibilities for the manipulation of information in order to alter the expectations and perceptions of other actors. Knowledge about international collective decision-making does not in itself elucidate how power is exercised in a multilateral setting. But it opens the ways for a theoretically justified categorization of situations in which power can be exercised. Each type of situation would represent a defined set of conditions for the influencing of the collective decision process. With access to this typology the next step would be to identify strategies and mechanisms for the exercise of power which typically or exclusively belong to the various kinds of situations defined. Thereby hypotheses and empirical knowledge pertaining to theories and models not directly dealing with the analysis of power could be taken advantage of. It would for instance probably be productive to integrate elements of the manipulative theories of negotiation in such a typology.

5. A FINAL WORD

The discussion in this chapter started out from two propositions:
(1) The systematic study of the exercize of power is of crucial importance to increase our understanding not only of this very phenomenon but also of the nature of the power bases of nations.
(2) It is motivated to give priority to research about the noncoercive exercize of power in general, and in particular in a multilateral setting. In these areas knowledge is especially scarce and the research needs accordingly particularly great.

One possible strategy for the research about the exercize of power would be to carry out comparative case studies. The key problem is then the measurement of 'the dependent variable', conceived of as that behaviour of the target which is influenced by the nation exercising power.

The more situation-specific and circumscribed the individual case study is, the less difficult should it be to find ways to express the dependent variable in concrete operational terms. Assume for example a negotiation between two actors concerning the distribution of a certain good, such as the resources at the bottom of the sea or the profit of a joint venture between two countries for the production of an airplane. In this case the dependent variable can be approximated from a comparison between, on the one hand, the final distribution of the good between the two actors and, on the other hand, their initial aspirations. The search for the reasons why the most successful actor has been able to get the lion's share of the value disputed, is equal to an assessment of why this actor is the most powerful in this particular situation.

More complicated problems arise when the dependent variable has to be defined and operationalized in such a way that systematic comparison between a great number of cases is possible. How can, for instance, the behaviour of the target nation, conceived of as this actor's giving in because of the economic sanctions of another actor, be compared to the acceptance of a technically solid argument in a round of multilateral negotiation concerning the international monetary system? The difficulties involved here are so evident that they do not have to be spelled out. The introduction of the outcome of a process of interdependent decision-making as an alternative dependent variable offers some possibilities but does not solve the problems.

The lack of a generally valid conceptual framework for the exercise of power is the reason for the third initial assumption for the discussion of this chapter:

(3) One approach to the systematic and theory-oriented study of the exercise of power is to search for auxiliary theories, which in various indirect ways can facilitate research about this phenomenon.

One such auxiliary family of concepts and theoretical elements consists of models of negotiation and bargaining. These have been the topic of this chapter.

Exercise of power is not identical with negotiation: it seems reasonable to regard the latter as a special case of the former. But particularly the non-coercive exercise of power can probably often be defined as a form of negotiation. Theories of negotiation are therefore seemingly in a general sense relevant for the study of the exercise of power. The overview above further gives witness to the fact that the models of negotiation have contributions to make to the study of the non-coercive exercise of power. These contributions are of different sorts. The various models referred to above should not be regarded as a set of alternatives from which the best solution is to be chosen. The models should rather be considered to be a large and fairly loose conceptual framework whose components, the individual concept or model, each covers some limited aspects of the problem in a multilateral context. Under some conditions one branch of the theory, say manipulative models, is useful but under others it has no contribution to offer.

It has thus been argued above that only the most elaborate models, the 'orthodox' game-theoretic and economic ones, can possibly be directly applicable for empirical studies. But on the other hand the scope of applicability of these models is strongly circumscribed due to the potent assumptions upon which they are built. Therefore, the greatest use of the models of negotiation is to serve as a source of ideas concerning the formulation of concepts, theoretical propositions and empirical hypotheses. In this respect the manipulative models have most to offer. They contain or imply a large number of hypotheses concerning the exercise of non-coercive power, for example by means of the distortion or supply of information. However, like most theoretical discussion about the exercise of power the theories of negotiation, orthodox as well as manipulative ones, have a bilateral bias. In order to make them applicable to a multilateral context the theories of negotiation themselves have to be extended. One possible way of doing this is to integrate components of particularly the manipulative models into a generalized theory of collective decision-making in international forums.

The topic of this chapter has been how theories of negotiation may give insights into the exercize of power. It should not be forgotten, however, that cross-fertilization may also work in the opposite direction. A general weakness of the theories of negotiation is that they include rather unclear and unspecified notions of the power of nations. It is pointed out that the power of an actor in several different ways is a determinant of its negotiating behaviour. Therefore, it is a deficiency of these theories that they are vague or even completely tacit when it comes to describing what they mean by the power of a nation. It seems that a clarification of what the nature of the power base of nations is and of how nations exercize power can make possible a corresponding elucidation of the nature of negotiations, in particular manipulative bargaining.

NOTES

1. Traditionalists seem to conceive of 'activation of the power base' as something similar to the manipulation of resources. It is, however, hard to determine exactly what is meant by this formula as traditionalist authors generally are not very explicit or specific on this point.

The metaphor of 'the production function' has been elaborated by Harsanyi (1965) and Alker (1973).

2. See Chapter 1 for a more extensive description of the traditionalist paradigm of international power.

3. The discussion of this chapter concerns relations between nations. The terms actors and target therefore exclusively refer to nations. This does not preclude that some of the arguments or concepts may have a more general validity. The problem of the dependent variable which will be discussed below pertains to the study of power exertion on various levels of analysis. But here actor and target will be used interchangeably with nation.

It should further be noted that it has been considered motivated to disregard the problem of 'the unitary actor' here. It is not necessary to take this problem explicitly under consideration in the general discussion pursued in this chapter.

4. This argument does of course not imply that it is excluded that multilateral interaction can be analysed as direct interaction between actors. One example of such a study is Alger's analysis of the direct communication between delegates in one of the committees of the UN General Assembly (Alger, 1968).

5. This is a modification of Goldmann's definition of power base in Chapter 1. The fact that Formula 4 is preferred does not mean that this model of the exercize of power is to be regarded superior generally. The research problem in each particular case should be the ultimate criterion for the choice of a dependent variable, and with it the model of the exercize of power.

6. No exhaustive presentation is given here of this body of literature. The purpose is not to undertake a comprehensive survey but only to illustrate by means of concrete examples how theories of negotiation, directly or after modification, can be combined with models of the exercise of power.

7. Representatives of this school are Schelling (1960), Ellsberg (1975) and McKersie/Walton (1965).

8. In real life most models of negotiation have a poor capacity to predict outcomes. The difference between orthodox and manipulative models in this respect is that the latter have a lesser predictive capacity also in theory.

9. If A chooses this approach he would behave as it is assumed in most game-theoretic models, that is, follow minimax or maximin criteria of decision.

10. The new means of influence are potential because they are not necessarily put at the disposal of all actors. It has to be assumed that they have different capabilities to take advantage of these new instruments.

11. It may be argued that 'setting the agenda', which Keohane and Nye (1977) talk about is something similar to the structuring process. But Keohane/Nye are rather vague when they describe what 'setting agenda' means. The general meaning is that a certain issue is politicized. But Keohane/Nye do not specify how this effect is brought about or what countries can do in order to influence this process.

12. This can obviously differ from country to country. One nation, like for ex-

ample the United States, may have the option of using several organizations whereas other countries can participate only in one or a few organizations. Certain international institutions have a limited membership, as for example the Group of Ten or the summit meetings of the greatest industrialized countries. It can be expected to be an advantage to have access to a relatively great number of organizations.

13. This was one of the top meetings of the most influential industrialized countries which seem to have become a recurrent phenomenon after the oil crisis of 1973.

REFERENCES

ALGER, C. (1968) 'Interaction in a Committee of the United Nations General Assembly' pp. 51-84 in D. Singer (ed.) *Quantitative International Politics, Insights, and Evidence*. New York: The Free Press.

BISHOP, R. (1964) 'A Zeuten-Hicks Theory of Bargaining' pp. 410-417 in *Econometrica* XXXII.

COX, R. and H. JACOBSON (1973) *The Anatomy of Influence. Decision-Making in International Organisation*. New Haven: Yale University Press.

CYERT, R. and J. MARCH (1963) *A Behavioural Theory of the Firm*. Englewood Cliffs: Prentice-Hall.

ELLSBERG, D. (1975) 'The Theory and Practice of Blackmail', in O. Young (ed.) *Bargaining. Formal Theories of Nagotiation*. Chicago: University of Illinois Press.

HAAS, E. (1958) *The Uniting of Europe. Political, Social, and Economical Forces 1950-1957*. London: London Institute of World Affairs. Stevens & Sons Ltd.

HARSANYI, J. (1956) 'Approaches to the Bargaining Problem before and after the Theory of Games' pp. 144-157 in *Econometrica* XXIV.

—— (1965) 'Bargaining Conflict Situations in the Light of a New Approach to Game Theory' pp. 447-457 in *The American Economic Review*, LV.

IKLÉ, F. (1964) *How Nations Negotiate*. New York: Harper & Row Publications.

KEOHANE, R. O. and J. S. NYE (1977) *Power and Interdependence: World Politics in Transition*. Boston: Little, Brown.

LINDBERG, L. and S. SCHEINGOLD (1970) *Europe's Would be Polity. Patterns of Change in the European Community*. Englewood Cliffs: Prentice-Hall.

McKERSIE, R. B. and R. WALTON (1965) *A Behavioural Theory of Labour Negotiations*. New York: MacGraw-Hill.

SCHELLING, T. (1960) *The Strategy of Conflict*. Cambridge, Mass.: Harvard University Press.

YOUNG, O. (1975) *Bargaining. Formal Theories of Negotiation*. Chicago: University of Illinois Press.

ZEUTEN, F. (1930) *Problems of Monopoly and Economic Warfare*. London: G. Routledge & Sons.

Notes on Contributors

Berill Dunér is a Research Associate at the Swedish Institute of International Affairs.

Kjell Goldmann was formerly Research Director at the Swedish Institute of International Affairs and is now Professor of Political Science at the University of Stockholm since 1972. His publications include *Peace-Keeping and Self-Defence* (1968), *International Norms and War Between States* (1971), *Tension and Détente in Bipolar Europe* (1974), and *Det internationella systemet* (The International System, 1978).

Christer Jönsson is Assistant Professor in the Department of Political Science, Lund University. He is the editor of *Sovjets utrikespolitik* (Soviet Foreign Policy, 1972) and author of *The Soviet Union and the Test Ban* (1975).

Klaus Knorr is Professor of Public and International Affairs, Woodrow Wilson School, Princeton University. He is the editor of *World Politics*, and author of *Military Power and Potential* (1970) and *The Power of Nations* (1975).

Olav Knudsen has been at the Institute of Political Science, University of Oslo, since 1971. He is the author of *The Politics of International Shipping* (1973).

Robert D. McKinlay has been Lecturer in the Department of Politics at the University of Lancaster since 1971. He has published, mainly on the subjects of military regimes and the politics of foreign aid, in major journals, such as *World Politics*, *American Political Science Review*, *Comparative Politics* and *British Journal of Political Science*.